LIFE

WITH

UNIX

LIFE

WITH

UNIX®

A Guide For Everyone

Don Libes & Sandy Ressler

PRENTICE HALL, Englewood Cliffs, New Jersey 07632

Library of Congress Cataloging-in-Publication Data

Libes, Don
    Life with UNIX: a guide for everyone / Don Libes & Sanford Ressler
        p.   cm.
    Bibliography: p.
    Includes index.
    ISBN 0-13-536657-7
    1. UNIX (Computer operating system)   I. Ressler, Sanford.
II. Title.
QA76.76.063L52 1989
005.4,3--dc19

UNIX is a registered trademark of AT&T.

Production: Sophie Papanikolaou
Cover production: Eloise Starkweather
Cover design: Lundgren Graphics, Ltd.
Cover artwork: Sandy Ressler
Marketing: Mary Franz

Life With UNIX was edited and composed with Frame Maker on a Sun Microsystems workstation running UNIX. Camera-ready copy was prepared on a Linotronic 100P by Professional Fast-Print Corporation using PostScript files generated by Frame Maker.

©1989 by Prentice-Hall, Inc.
A division of Simon & Schuster
Englewood Cliffs, New Jersey 07632

Printed in the United States of America

10 9 8 7 6

ISBN 0-13-536657-7

Prentice-Hall International (UK) Limited, *London*
Prentice-Hall of Australia Pty. Limited, *Sydney*
Prentice-Hall Canada Inc., *Toronto*
Prentice-Hall Hispanoamericana, S.A., *Mexico*
Prentice-Hall of India Private Limited, *New Delhi*
Prentice-Hall of Japan, Inc., *Tokyo*
Simon & Schuster Asia Pte. Ltd., *Singapore*
Editora Prentice-Hall do Brasil, Ltda., *Rio de Janeiro*

To our loving families

Contents

Preface

This book is the "other" book about UNIX. It covers everything that the manual didn't, that your *Intro to UNIX* book didn't, and that your UNIX course didn't. This book is a study in reading between the lines – which is very much what learning UNIX is like.

However, you won't be reading between the lines of *Life With UNIX*. We spell it all out – what's missing between the lines of those other books, plus the history, present and future of UNIX, and everything else we could think of. Oh, and we also include all the important anecdotes and strange UNIX humor that we could dig up.

No matter what people have told you, you can't learn UNIX from the manuals, or even the sources. UNIX is so much more than that. To understand UNIX is to understand its users and its applications, as well as its failures and flaws. This is just some of what this book hopes to cover.

Make sure you realize what this book isn't. It isn't a textbook on C or UNIX programming. (There are already plenty of good ones.) You won't learn how to write shell scripts or what is in the kernel. Well, maybe a little. But you will learn plenty of useful things. Things that will fill in the gaps between the other useful and useless things you already know about UNIX.

We would like to think this book is a little like Ted Nelson's *Computer Lib* crossed with the *Whole Earth Catalog* but all focused on UNIX. You should find it informative whether you are a UNIX beginner or expert. If you program on mainframes using VM, micros using DOS, or any other proprietary operating system, you will learn what the vendors have tried to hide from you. And you will find out all the BS about UNIX as well. We pull no punches – UNIX has its shortcomings as well as its advantages, and we discuss both.

Disclaimers

This book is a synthesis of what we, the authors, know about UNIX. We have tried to present the truth as best we know it. It has been especially difficult tracking down certain historical information, which seems not to have been rigorously preserved except by oral passage from the mouth of one UNIX guru to another.

Mention of any specific companies, brands, or products does not imply endorsement by the authors.

Acknowledgments

Thanks to Sol and Lennie Libes for reading many drafts for technical accuracy and grammatical style. Thanks to Susan Libes, Stephen Clark, Dave Fiedler, Larry Welsch, Faye Taxman, Ken Manheimer, and Janet Shapiro for proofreading and helpful criticism. Thanks to Tony Shaw for digging through the patent office files for us.

Thanks to Marc Rochkind, Greg Chesson, Rick Rashid, Mel Ferentz, Dick Haight, Mike Accetta, Peter Langston, Ken Arnold, Ted Dolotta, Doug Gwyn, Ed Barkmeyer, Dave Yost, Guy Harris, Chris Torek, Tom Duff, Rob Rosenthal, Donn Seeley, and George Goble for some extremely pleasant and valuable conversations while digging up UNIX history. And thanks to the UNIX user community – especially through Usenet, which dredged up much of the hard-to-find and never-before-published material that appears here.

Thanks to our crew of UNIX experts who actually had the patience to read through our error-filled drafts. It is hard enough to find UNIX experts, no less ones that can consume 350 pages and comment intelligently while working under the deadlines that we gave them. Brian Kernighan helped us with the History chapter by reviewing it and checking the facts with people from `research`. Armando Stettner gave us a perspective of early years at Bell and DEC. Mike O'Dell made many suggestions about the book in general. John Quarterman corrected many inaccuracies in our section on standards. Finally, special thanks to Eric Allman who corrected many of our misstatements about Berkeley and the rest of the UNIX world, and who made this book **much** better than it could have been.

Our UNIX experts also included anonymous reviewers supplied by Prentice Hall who critiqued several drafts. In addition, David Greenstein told Prentice Hall to encourage us to write the rest of the book, after having only seen the outline, and a few sketchy chapters.

Finally, thanks to the Prentice Hall staff, whose professional work made the book look so good. In particular, we would like to mention the pleasure we had working with Sophie Papanikolaou, who was in charge of production. While working on 20 other books at the same time, she showed us it was possible to keep a sense of humor even while striving for perfection 24 hours a day. Thanks to her and everyone else who helped.

Don Libes

Sandy Ressler

How To Read This Book

This book wasn't written front-to-back – you don't have to read it front-to-back. If you already know some aspect of UNIX, read about the other parts. However, we hope that you will read the whole book at some point. You may find that there are things you never knew about the things you knew.

Every subject in UNIX is related to many other subjects. Thus, you will often see references to other parts of the book. In addition to those references, we suggest many other articles, books, magazines and companies. If you are interested in learning more about a particular subject, take the effort to get the reference we recommend. You will find it worth your while. Many references have associated addresses which can be found in Appendix A. We have chosen not to print addresses after each reference because some references appear several times in the book.

Life With UNIX is divided into four sections. Each section is broken into several chapters.

The first section describes UNIX in a historical sense. The first chapter covers UNIX history by setting the scene for the entrance of UNIX. The second chapter is a snapshot of UNIX as it is today. The last chapter in this section concludes with some predictions for the future of UNIX.

The second section covers information. The chapters in this section include discussions on information sources such as UNIX manuals, books, magazines, user groups and conferences. Of course, all the other parts of the book cover information as well, so don't fail to read the other sections, too.

The third section is a look inside UNIX. Each chapter in this section covers UNIX from a different perspective – the user, the programmer or the administrator. You may find yourselves using these chapters as reference material, since many UNIX concepts are mentioned but not explained in other chapters. You will find them explained here.

The fourth section is a look outside UNIX. This includes anything that is not part of UNIX proper. For example, many third-party applications and services are described here. The Underground chapter covers public-domain programs and many other things you will never see advertised. The last chapter is a set of short essays on the problems and solutions UNIX has met in the real world.

Many of the topics presented in the book easily fall into several areas. Naturally, we did not want to duplicate material unnecessarily; thus, we placed topics in the chapter that seemed most appropriate. For example, Usenet is covered in the Underground chapter although it could have as well been presented in one of the Information chapters.

We have also been fairly liberal with our groupings into chapters. Rather than artificially fragment a single discussion into several chapters, we have often placed the complete subject in the chapter which best describes the discussion. For example, you will find some predictions for the future in the History chapter, and some history in the Future chapter. Think of it as incentive to read the other parts of the book.

Dialects

We have tried to provide a reasonable number of concrete examples to motivate much of our discussions. You may find it educational, useful, or simply fun to try some of these things out on your system, and we encourage you to do so.

However, UNIX comes in many dialects, and some of the things that we say may not be exactly the same on your system. Of particular annoyance to new users is that UNIX is so easily modifiable, that it is possible to sit down at someone else's system for the first time and find many discrepancies between the manual and reality.

Rather than place lots of footnotes after every discussion (e.g., "as long as you are using `csh`" or "if you have virgin System V Release 4"), we have attempted to write about specifics as they apply to the majority of existing

UNIX systems. When we necessarily write about a particular implementation, we have qualified it as such.

Typographical Notes

Throughout the text, certain words will be emphasized by appearing in different fonts. Anything embedded in a paragraph that would appear on a terminal such as a filename or output will appear in computer font boldcased. For example, **/etc/passwd**. Extended terminal excerpts will simply appear in a computer font. For example:

```
% date
Fri Dec 25 22:52:43 EST 1987
%
```

Words or phrases that are being defined or otherwise definitively described will appear in italics. For example, "*Pacman* is an arcade video game."

Throughout this book you will see many *information boxes*. These boxes are not critical to the rest of the text but usually contain something of interest and related to it, such as a humorous anecdote. The four types of boxes are as follows:

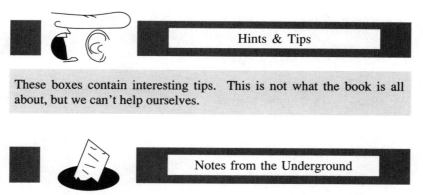

Hints & Tips

These boxes contain interesting tips. This is not what the book is all about, but we can't help ourselves.

Notes from the Underground

These boxes contain information from underground sources such as unofficial spokespersons or electronic (i.e., unpublished) network communiques.

From the Wizards

These boxes contain secret knowledge that for some reason is not allowed to be written down except in these silly boxes. Don't look for it in your manuals.

UNIX Funnies

These boxes contain humor or amusing anecdotes about UNIX. They will probably be the only thing that anyone reads in this book.

Section 1

Past

Present

Future

Chapter 1: UNIX History

"One half of the world must sweat and groan that the other half may dream."
– Henry Wadsworth Longfellow

This chapter discusses the history of UNIX as best we can rec'lect from the dim dark ages of the '60s and '70s. Several articles are suggested for further reading.

The history of UNIX explains many things about the UNIX philosophy, from why it is so omnipresent today, to why it has such strange licensing arrangements. We describe the steps taken along the path to UNIX maturity and elaborate on the subject of the UNIX philosophy and how it evolved.

1.1   Before the Beginning

It is worth discussing the eve of UNIX, to make the following two observations:

1) While much of UNIX and the execution of its implementation was innovative, several very important ideas are traceable back to earlier operating systems; and

2) UNIX might never have been written were it not for Ken Thompson, and how he reacted to the tools available to him at the time.

The year was 1968. Ken Thompson and neighboring staff, working in the Computer Research Group at Bell Labs, had made substantial contributions to the MULTICS project. MULTICS was a visionary computer environment that had taken the wrong evolutionary fork. While providing very sophisticated features, it required substantial computing resources. Production versions were too large and slow. The original design had to be scaled back during implementation.

Nonetheless, several working versions of MULTICS were completed, providing extremely pleasant computing environments. The alternative at Bell Labs was a GE 645 emulating a GE 635. While that system provided timesharing, it was primarily batch-oriented and made for a clumsy and unfriendly environment. Ken and friends (particularly Dennis Ritchie and Joseph Ossanna) did not want to lose the comfortable environment provided by MULTICS, so they began lobbying management for an interactive time-sharing machine, such as the DEC-10, on which they could then build their own operating system.

The DEC-10 was one of a series of machines that had just been introduced by DEC (Digital Equipment Corp). The machine came with a very slick interactive, time-sharing environment. Unfortunately, like all time-sharing machines of the time, the DEC-10 was very expensive.

Fortunately for us, Ken's request for a DEC-10 was turned down. Unfortunately for Ken, this occurred several times. Management was not impressed by the failure of the MULTICS research, and they were not interested in funding another attempt to design an operating system that clearly seemed like MULTICS, just on different hardware.

At this time, one of Ken's interests was in a program called Space Travel which simulated movement of the major bodies of the solar system, along with a spaceship that could be landed in different places. Ken installed it on the GE system but was disappointed by the jerky response from the time-sharing system. It was also extremely expensive to run – $75 a game according to Dennis. Finding the now famous "*little-used PDP-7 sitting in a corner*," Ken and Dennis used the GE to create a paper-tape executable image of Space Travel that would run on the bare machine.

1.2   In the Beginning...

With Space Travel, Ken now had a reason for implementing the theoretical file system that he had designed and simulated earlier during the MULTICS project. Naturally, the machine needed more than a file system to make it useful. Ken and friends wrote the first command interpreter (or *shell*) and some simple utilities to manipulate files. Initially the GE system was used to cross-compile for the PDP-7, but as soon as an assembler was written, the system became essentially self-supporting.

At this point the system already had UNIX-like features (such as `fork()` to support multiprocessing). The file system was very similar to the modern

UNIX file system. It used i-nodes. It also had special file types to support directories and devices. The PDP-7 supported two users at the same time.

The word "MULTICS" actually stood for MULTiplexed Information and Computing System. In 1970, Brian Kernighan jokingly referred to their two-user system as "UNICS," for the "UNiplexed Information and Computing System" since MULTICS seemed to be a vastly oversized operating system by comparison. (Some claim that MULTICS stands for "Many Unnecessarily Large Tables In Core Simultaneously" and that UNIX was a castrated version of MULTICS. (see §10.6.2)) Soon after, "UNICS" became "UNIX" and the name has stuck ever since.

The computer science research group was not entirely satisfied with the PDP-7. For one thing, it was a borrowed machine, but more importantly, it was simply underpowered and could not support the demand for computing service. Thus the group put forth another proposal, this time for a PDP-11/20 to research text processing. A distinguishing characteristic of this proposal and prior ones was that the price of a PDP-11 was a fraction of the price of a system like the DEC-10. With a more concrete proposal than before, specifically to create a text-processing system, management relented and bought the PDP-11.

UNIX was ported to the PDP-11/20 in 1970. This was a not inconsiderable task since the entire system was written in assembler! The group ported **roff** (also known as **runoff**, a predecessor to **troff**) written in assembler, from the PDP-7 to the 11/20. This, plus an editor, was apparently enough to be called a text-processing system.

At the same time, the Bell Labs patent office was looking for a text-processing system. It selected the group's PDP-11/20 based UNIX system over a commercial system. The Lab's patent office became the first official users of UNIX.

It is interesting to note some of the characteristics of this first production system. This PDP-11/20 ran UNIX with no memory protection. It had a 0.5Mb disk. It supported three concurrent users editing and formatting, plus the original group doing further UNIX development. The documentation for this system was labeled "First Edition" and dated November 1971.

It is now tradition to name releases of UNIX after the edition of the manual. While this seems clear, *editions* are also called *versions*, but they mean the same thing. For example, Version 7 is the same thing as the 7th Edition.

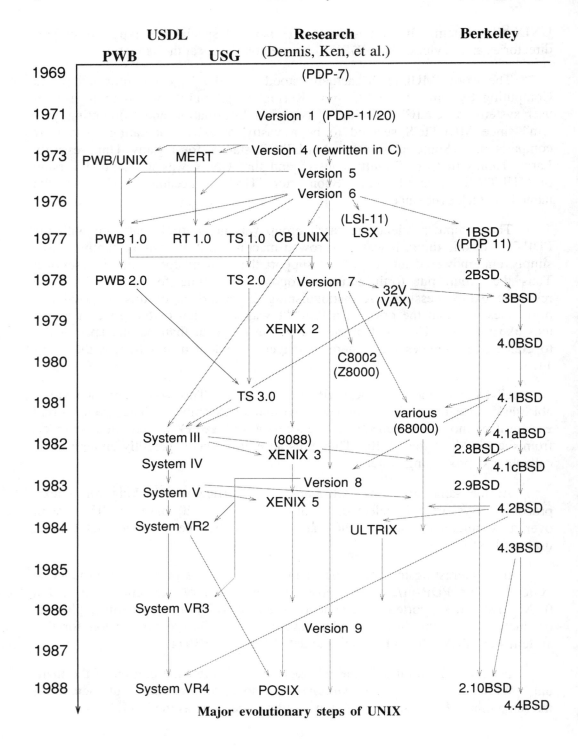

Major evolutionary steps of UNIX

The Second Edition was released in 1972 and featured the addition of pipes. This edition also incorporated work on supporting and using languages other than assembler. In particular, Ken had attempted to rewrite the kernel in the NB language.

1972 Population Explosion

"The number of UNIX installations has grown to 10, with more expected." — *The UNIX Programmer's Manual*, Second Edition, June, 1972.

NB was a locally modified version of the B language (designed by Ken and Dennis), which was a descendant of BCPL. BCPL (Basic CPL) was designed by Martin Richards at Cambridge in 1967. CPL (Combined Programming Language) was a joint project of Cambridge and the University of London in 1963. CPL drew heavily from the ideas of Algol60 (designed in 1960).

All of these languages share a resemblance to C in control structure, however B and BCPL are "typeless" languages (although that is a misnomer), since they only support access to memory by "words." NB evolved into C, which quickly became the language of choice for new utilities and applications.

Experience with MULTICS (which had been written in PL/I) taught Ken and Dennis that writing a system in a high-level language is worthwhile. Hence, they kept trying to do this. In 1973, C was enhanced to support structures and global variables. At this point, Ken and Dennis successfully rewrote the UNIX kernel in C. The shell was also rewritten (from assembler) into C. This improved the robustness of the system and made programming and debugging much easier.

At this point, there were approximately 25 UNIX systems. A UNIX Systems Group was created at the Labs for internal support. Several universities contacted Bell Labs and received copies of the Fourth Edition. Agreements were signed not to disclose the source code, but no licenses were in use at this point. Ken made the tapes himself and didn't charge anything. The first tapes went to Columbia University in New York.

In 1974, Ken and Dennis published a paper in *Communications of the ACM*, describing the UNIX system. At that time, *Communications* was the premier journal for computer science research, and the article raised interest in UNIX considerably throughout academia. The Fifth Edition was officially made

available to universities "*for educational purposes.*"   The price was nominal –
enough to cover the cost of reproducing a set of tapes and manuals.   The Fifth
Edition was used as a teaching aid at many universities.

Ken and Dennis were still actively involved in UNIX research at this
point; however, they continued to avoid any explicit promise of support.   Their
group became known as "Research" (or "1127," inside of the Labs).   Their
machine was named `research`.   You could send them bug reports over `uucp`,
call them on the phone, or even drop into their office and discuss UNIX problems with them personally.   Generally, they would fix bugs by the following day.

Unrelated to `research` was another group at Bell Labs that became
known as PWB, or Programmer's Workbench.   Led by Rudd Canaday, the
PWB group supported a version of UNIX for large software development
projects.   The PWB system tried to provide UNIX services as if it was a utility
for users who were not necessarily interested in UNIX research.   A lot of
effort went into vulcanizing the UNIX kernel, as well as supporting large numbers of users.   Two particularly useful projects that came out of PWB were a
source code control system (SCCS) and a system (RJE) for using UNIX as a
uniform front-end to other mainframes around the Labs.   PWB was eventually
licensed outside the Labs as PWB/UNIX 1.0.

UNIX displaced more and more of DEC's own operating systems on
PDP-11s.   While UNIX was still unsupported, it had attractive strengths over
other systems that outweighed its problems.   In addition to the features of the
system itself, the source was available, and UNIX was comprehensible in its
entirety.   Modifications and extensions were easy.   These attributes made
UNIX unlike any other operating system in its class.

In 1975, the Sixth Edition UNIX system was released.   This was the first
UNIX that became widely used outside the Labs.   AT&T (through Western
Electric Co.) began offering licenses to commercial and government users.

Mike Lesk released his Portable C Library.   The library was a set of I/O
routines that could be implemented on any machine supporting a C compiler.
This was an essential step in making C capable of producing portable code.
Dennis later rewrote this and called it the Standard I/O Library (now commonly
called "stdio").

The first UNIX users meeting was held in New York City, hosted by Mel
Ferentz at City University of NY.   Forty people attended.   Held twice yearly
after that, meetings were extremely informal.   If you wanted to make a presen-

tation, you would raise your hand, and then do so. These meetings were the best way to swap bug reports, fixes, and software. Everyone brought two tapes with them – one with things to give, one blank to get new things.

Ferentz began a newsletter called *UNIX News* that he sent to UNIX users free of charge. When a representative from Bell showed up and told him that he could not use "UNIX" in the name, it was changed to *;login:*. As more and more people wanted the newsletter, Ferentz couldn't afford to keep sending it out for free. An organization was created to handle the dues. It was called USENIX. USENIX quickly took on other roles, including responsibility of the user meetings and software distributions.

At the University of New South Wales in Australia, John Lions prepared a set of course notes for an operating systems class. The subject of the class was a case study of UNIX, and the class notes were published as *A Commentary on the UNIX Operating System*. The notes included the entire V6 UNIX kernel accompanied by Lions' running commentary. Almost every line was explained (including the one you were "*not expected to understand*").

Permission for its publication was eventually withdrawn, due to the large amount of source material involved. But while the book was in print, it made UNIX far more accessible than before.

In 1977, Interactive Systems Corporation became the first company to resell UNIX systems to end users. UNIX was finally a supported product.

During that same year, three groups ported UNIX to different machines. Steve Johnson and Dennis Ritchie ported UNIX to an Interdata 8/32. Richard Miller and others at the University of Wollongong in Australia ported UNIX to an Interdata 7/32. And Tom Lyon and associates at Princeton ported UNIX to the VM/370 environment.

Each of these ports was considered quite a feat.† Internally, all three machines differed significantly from the PDP-11. Indeed, that was the whole point. Operating systems are not designed to run on more than one computer. Similarly, computers are almost always designed with a particular operating system in mind. For example, if the computer supports protection between multiple processes, it makes sense to have an operating system use the hardware feature in just the way it was designed to be used.

---

† The Australian port was particularly challenging – the PDP-11 in Sydney was separated from the Interdata in Wollongong by 100 kilometers!

As each vendor supplied hardware with nifty options, specific operating systems were written and optimized to understand the hardware. They were almost always written in assembler for access to the unusual hardware and for optimal speed.

Dennis and Ken's greatest breakthrough arose from the realization that there was a trade-off between efficiency and utility. If they could port the operating system to another computer without the cost of starting over from scratch, it would be worth it if they didn't sacrifice too much speed. It wasn't hard to make this decision – they had already succeeded using a similar philosophy when they rewrote the kernel in C. That is, UNIX would have been faster and smaller if it were written in assembler, but the operating system was so much easier to modify, understand and port, that it was worth the sacrifice in speed and memory.

UNIX was soon ported to many other types of PDP-11s. Each one had interesting features that gradually added to the complexity of hardware that UNIX could support (i.e. floating point processors, writable microcode, memory management and protection, split instruction and data regions).

However, the PDP-11 line was clearly based around a 16-bit address space. Because of this, all of the programs were limited to 64Kb. Ironically, this emphasized the building of small programs. With the advent of pipes to support cooperating processes, and **exec()**, which supported program chaining, it was possible to build large systems by linking together several smaller utilities. This is a hallmark of UNIX programming, and it is possible that we have the restricted address space of the PDP-11 to thank for it.

UNIX was ported to the IBM Series 1 minicomputer (although some thought this analogous to the bringing together of matter and antimatter). The Series 1 had the same size words (two bytes) as the PDP-11, but the bytes were swapped. Hence, when the machine started up for the first time, it printed out "NUXI" instead of "UNIX." Ever since then, the "NUXI problem" has referred to byte ordering problems.

In 1977, the University of California, Berkeley, Computer Science Department began to distribute their Pascal interpreter. Also included on their distribution tape were some new drivers, fixes to the kernel, the **ex** editor, and a new shell (the "Pascal shell") that was easier to program then the V6 shell. This distribution was called 1BSD (1st Berkeley Software Distribution).

1.3   Philosophy

By this time, UNIX had most of the features that we associate with it today. We have already mentioned its portability. Other features that were touted were: 1) the unification of file, device and interprocess I/O, 2) the ability to initiate asynchronous processes, 3) the ability to replace the default shell with another, and 4) a hierarchical file system.

There were other attributes that made UNIX great, but the preceding attributes were considered absolutely inarguable. What is amazing is not that most systems in the '70s did not have these attributes, but that many recent systems in the '80s do not (e.g., the flat file systems of IBM's CMS).

Some other noteworthy attributes were:

1) The consistency of the commands and libraries. This allowed the building-block approach, as already noted, to work easily. Since programmers had to assume the output of their program might be used as input to another, they did not throw in excess verbiage such as pockmarks the landscape of other operating system's utilities. Most programs used standard input and output.

Libraries and system calls provided one way of doing things, typically the simplest that would solve most of the problems. This carries over from the kernel, which was so small that it could be read and understood in its entirety by a single programmer.

2) The dominant file type was text. For example, **/etc/passwd** could be modified with a text editor. On most other systems, you had to use a special program to read and write the data files required for each part of the operating system. With UNIX, however, once you know an editor, you can edit and control everything.

3) The shell could be used for programming, since it had rudimentary control structures and parameter passing. Many people never bothered to learn C because the shell and existing programs could be combined so easily. Interestingly, the shell control structures (e.g., **goto**, **test**) were actually implemented as separate programs.

The Sixth Edition manual was less than 300 pages and fit comfortably in one volume. The entry for **sh** was three pages long.

By the end of 1978, there were over 600 UNIX installations. Most were universities and government facilities.

1.4   1979 – Seventh Edition

In 1979, the Seventh Edition UNIX system was released. Version 7 featured a full K&R C compiler, including, for the first time, casts, unions and typedefs. A more sophisticated shell (known as "sh" or the "Bourne shell," after one of its authors, Stephen Bourne) was provided. The system supported larger files. And the results of the porting effort were felt through a more robust kernel and new device drivers for many peripherals.

The programmer's manual for the Seventh Edition grew to about 400 pages (which still fit in one comfortable volume). The UNIX Readings became the second and third volumes, approximately 400 pages each.

John Reiser and Tom London ported V7 UNIX to a VAX at Bell Labs. This port was called UNIX 32V. In some ways, the VAX was a lot like a big PDP-11 and by treating it this way, the porting effort was made relatively easy. This is an example of a machine with an obvious hardware capability (paging) which was ignored in the interest of getting UNIX up and running quickly. Nonetheless, this nonpaging version of UNIX was used widely and for a long time within the Labs, because it had a much larger address space (4Gb) than the PDP-11. This version was made available to Berkeley, which used it as a base for further research efforts.

Whitesmith was the first commercial C vendor. Unfortunately, the licensing aspects weren't entirely clear, so the library for the C compiler deliberately used incompatible subroutine and argument conventions. Later, it was judged that there were no copyrights on the C user interface (e.g., subroutine names). Whitesmith's C is now compatible with UNIX.

1.5   Politics – Part I

At the birth of UNIX, AT&T was an assemblage of communication-related companies. These included Bell Telephone Laboratories (often called BTL, Bell, Bell Labs, or The Labs) and Western Electric Co. (WECo). Due to an earlier antitrust court decree, AT&T was prohibited from participating in particular nonregulated areas. While it could do research on UNIX, it could not possibly attempt to market any products based on UNIX. In fact, it was not clear whether computer software was allowable, but it seemed that if it became profitable (and there seemed little hope of that), AT&T would run afoul of the earlier consent decree. Either way, UNIX seemed a lost cause as a commercial product. Naturally, management was not inclined to sponsor development on an unmarketable product. This, then, was what faced Ken and Dennis and UNIX in the early '70s.

Dennis and Ken were located at Bell Labs in Murray Hill, NJ, where the actual UNIX research was done and they didn't particularly care about product development. They were having far too much fun playing with their new baby. However, it was strange to have something that was becoming very popular throughout the Labs that could not be distributed outside. Plus, no one had the direct responsibility of supporting UNIX externally. According to Tannenbaum:†

> BTL didn't really have a distribution policy in the early days, you got a disk with a note:

> Here's your rk05, Love, Dennis.

> If UNIX crapped on your rk05, you'd write to Dennis for another.

Eventually, Bell succumbed to the pressure for distributing UNIX. It developed a simple licensing policy: No support, no trial period, no warranties, no advertising, no bug fixes, and payment in advance.

However, a tremendous number of people were using UNIX at Bell internally. In order to support all these projects, a UNIX support group called USG (UNIX Support Group) was created. Unfortunately, USG was allowed only to provide support, not to do any development. The result was that, both inside and outside Bell, users did their own development. This was further encouraged by the complete access to the source code that came with UNIX. USG created several releases of UNIX, most of them only available inside the Labs.

At the same time, PWB was doing both support and development on a different version of UNIX. Furthermore, PWB was able to be distributed outside of Bell Labs as well as inside. Needless to say, there were a lot of hard feelings between these two groups. Each one thought that what it was doing was the right thing, and that the other was wrong. For example, the PWB shell was different than the USG shell.

Yet another version of UNIX was called MERT, for Multi Environment Real-Time. MERT was similar to the virtual machine concept. UNIX (or

---

† Andy Tannenbaum, "Politics of UNIX," Washington, DC USENIX Conference, 1984.

rather, a special version of it) could run on top of MERT and take advantage of some of MERT's real-time facilities.

Outside Bell Labs, many licensees chose to use either PWB/UNIX or the research version from Ken and Dennis, while inside the Labs, users used one of USG's UNIX, MERT, or the other two. (In fact, there were actually more versions. For example, LSX was a version of UNIX (c. 1977) for the LSI-11 microprocessor.) The multiplicity of UNIX systems was already quite annoying.

By this time, many UNIX licensees had installed one or another version of UNIX on PDP-11s or ported it to other hardware. Working with UNIX was much more satisfying to most programmers than the alternatives because:

1) UNIX came with the complete source and documentation. It was self-supporting. You had the very same environment that the UNIX developers had. You could modify UNIX yourself.

2) UNIX was small. You could understand the code. Most of the algorithms were simple. You could modify UNIX with some confidence in what you were doing.

3) There was no warranty to void. Since the system came without support, you had nothing to lose. At worst, you could go to the backup tapes. At best, you could make a faster system or add a new feature.

4) The UNIX manuals were readable. They were only a couple hundred pages. And it wasn't hard to read through them all. A single person could easily grasp them in their entirety.

Several institutions which were hotbeds of UNIX activity were:

Rand, Harvard and BBN

Rand had developed the first interactive time-sharing system and was quick to see the value of UNIX. Rand contracted with Walt Bilofsky at BBN (Bolt Baranek & Newman, Inc.) to develop the first screen editor for UNIX. Known as the "Rand editor," this was the first screen editor for UNIX, and it became one of the first programs developed outside the Labs that became a "necessity" to have. You took for granted that after bringing up UNIX, the next step was to install the Rand editor. (In truth, the Rand editor came with its own set of problems. The worst was that it was a terrible resource hog in terms of CPU cycles and bandwidth.)

This kind of practice continues. One brings up UNIX and immediately loads in a lot of public-domain tools (e.g., GNU Emacs, RCS, Usenet) that have become essential to UNIX programmers. Even today, people are not satisfied with UNIX straight from the factory!

At the time that the Rand editor was written, neither Rand nor BBN actually had UNIX systems. They went to Harvard which had a Version 4 system and borrowed time on that. In return, Harvard got to use the Rand/BBN enhancements. Later they added their own, some of which were reincorporated back into Version 5. For example, Brent Byer added split I/D (Instruction/Data) space to support the PDP-11/45 which had separate mapping registers.

BBN continued doing contract work and later played a very important role in the development of UNIX at Berkeley. At this time, BBN had already been involved with the Arpanet, a network developed for the U.S. Department of Defense (DoD). BBN applied its experience and gave UNIX the ability to communicate using the DoD protocols. This work was enhanced and bundled into Berkeley's software distribution. The result was that companies using Berkeley UNIX could perform internetworking for free. This led to the early relationship between UNIX and networking.

Lawrence Berkeley Laboratory – The Virtual Operating System (VOS) and the Software Tools Project

While at Lawrence Berkeley Laboratory, Dennis Hall, Deborah Scherrer and Joe Sventek read *Software Tools* by Brian Kernighan and P. J. Plauger, and decided that the book made a lot of sense. They implemented all of the tools the book presented, including a shell. What is very interesting is that they did it on a machine that did not run UNIX!

In order to be portable, all the tools were written in Fortran 66, since this was the only language that was available on most computers. Unfortunately, Fortran was not well suited for systems programming and Ratfor ("Rational Fortran") was soon born. Ratfor was an attempt to enhance Fortran with many of the features of C (e.g., better control flow constructs). Ratfor was (and still is) implemented as a preprocessor that takes Ratfor code and produces Fortran code. The latter can be compiled by any Fortran compiler. This allowed anyone to easily bootstrap the Software Tools onto their system with minimal effort.

It didn't take long before they had ported Kernighan and Plauger's tools to several operating systems. Along the way, they learned what abstractions were valid across machines and which ones were not. In 1979, the Software Tools Project as it had come to be known, held a joint conference with USENIX (the largest technically-oriented UNIX user group). Much of the abstractions were similar to UNIX, and many people saw the Software Tools Project as a chance to bring UNIX to the less fortunate machines that they still owned.

After the conference and further porting to many machines, a specification for a virtual operating system (VOS†) was created. VOS defined a logical layer upon which the Software Tools rested. As long as a machine could support VOS, it could support the tools. While some of the VOS abstractions were hard to implement on some machines, the result was a fine portable development environment – the Software Tools.

One example of the achievement was that the Software Tools supported pipes between processes – even though many systems lacked any interprocess communication or multiprocessing. How was this done? The tools simulated pipes with temporary files. Concurrency wasn't necessary either. It was simulated with program chaining. But the effect was the same, and the user ended up with the same synergy that arises from the UNIX tools paradigm.

The VOS environment was very successful. Still in use today, it brings the good ideas of UNIX to just about any other operating system. Many vendors have integrated parts of VOS into their native operating systems. The original VOS source is in the public domain.

Berkeley

The University of California, Berkeley, Computer Science Department (known as "Berkeley" or occasionally as "Berserkeley") had already had many enjoyable experiences with UNIX early on. Much of their work had been distributed to other sites. Around 1979, Ken taught an operating systems course there while on sabbatical from the Labs. During his stay, he ported UNIX to a PDP-11/70, a very powerful machine capable of supporting many users. His presence encouraged and his work enabled many more students to become involved in UNIX development.

During the same period, DARPA (DoD's Advanced Research Projects Agency) was looking for a universal computing environment for AI, VLSI, and

---

† Hall, Scherrer, and Sventek, "A Virtual Operating System," *Communications of the ACM*, vol. 23, no. 9, September 1980.

vision research, with the intent of saving money and easing development problems. The extensibility, small size and proven portability of UNIX made it a good bet. However, it lacked networking, virtual memory management, and flexible interprocess communication. The primary contender to UNIX was VMS, an operating system developed by DEC for their VAX computers. The VAX was seen as critical – it was the first 32-bit supermini, and it supported VMS which had virtual memory.

Many people were very comfortable with DEC – their PDP-11s had been enormously popular in the research community. However, VMS did have some drawbacks, and DARPA was quite concerned over whether DEC would be responsive to their requests for changes and improvements, since it was a proprietary product. They eventually decided to go with UNIX.

DARPA looked for a place to base their UNIX development project. Besides Berkeley, CMU and BBN were also heavily considered. However, Bill Joy at Berkeley was already modifying the UNIX kernel to support paging on the VAX. While Berkeley became the primary implementation site, a DARPA steering committee composed of representatives from Bell Labs, CMU, MIT, Stanford and BBN oversaw the development of the project. Efforts from all of these institutions were important to the design of Berkeley UNIX.

Bell agreed to let Berkeley redistribute its source code as long as customers had an existing source license from Bell. In particular, you had to get a source license for any system that Berkeley chose to incorporate in their distribution. The license that was required changed several times, as Bell produced a large number of distributions themselves, each of which Berkeley incorporated to some degree.

At first, Berkeley didn't rewrite UNIX but made extensive modifications and enhancements to a version called 32V. 32V was a port of UNIX to DEC's 32-bit VAX by researchers at Bell. For simplicity, they treated the VAX as a big PDP-11, ignoring the hardware's ability to allow programs to address more memory than was physically resident. This is known as *virtual memory*, and Berkeley quickly added this capability, calling the resulting system 3BSD (and 4BSD in 1980). The VAX allowed programs to address one gigabyte of memory even when the machine had only one megabyte of physical memory.

Virtual memory was hard to resist, and since 32V didn't support it, everyone outside Bell (and most inside) ran UNIX from Berkeley. Because of this one asset, the Berkeley extensions became well-known and were considered to be essential to UNIX. In particular, the C shell, `curses`, `termcap`, `vi` and job control were ported back to Version 7 (and later System III) so that it was not unusual to find these features on otherwise pure Bell releases. Indeed, these programs were often referred to as *Berkeley extensions*, as in "our system runs System III plus Berkeley extensions." More recent Berkeley extensions (from 4.2BSD) include networking (DARPA Internet) support and automatic kernel configuration.

Berkeley added many wonderful things to UNIX, but one thing they couldn't fix was support. The university was not about to go into the computer business and provide customer support. This was supposed to be a research project after all (funded by taxpayer's money). Like Dennis' love note about rk05s, early Berkeley tapes came with a suggestion from Bill Joy that "*this is a tape of bits*," meaning there was no guarantee of anything, and that complaints should be directed to `/dev/null`.

In reality, the Berkeley people were fairly reasonable about bugs. They kept a bug list accessible via electronic mail. And they fixed many problems people discovered, as well as incorporated other people's fixes into their code. Eventually a company was formed to support the Berkeley distributions, called Mt. Xinu. Its slogan, "We know UNIX forwards and backwards" is a clever reference to "Mt. Xinu" being the reverse of "UNIX™ ."

Releases of Berkeley software remain labeled as "4.X BSD" even though the differences between them are dramatic. Berkeley wanted to relabel 4.2 as "5.0" except that university regulations would have forced it to relicense all of its "customers." As it turned out, Berkeley had to do it anyway because of code that was included from a new release of the AT&T software.

AT&T also seems to have stuck with the label of "System V" for dramatically differing versions of its most recent versions of UNIX. AT&T probably spent so much money saying "UNIX System V. From AT&T. From now on, consider it standard." that it doesn't make sense to change the name. Instead, AT&T will issue new "major releases" (e.g., UNIX System V Release 4.0).

Digital Equipment Corporation

DEC (Digital Equipment Corporation) was in a strange position. All of the original UNIX users ran UNIX on DEC hardware (namely PDP-11s and VAXen). However, DEC provided no support for UNIX. Indeed, this became a serious problem on certain types of hardware bugs. Often the DEC diagnostics and DEC operating system would run successfully, but UNIX wouldn't. You were on your own.

Nevertheless, there were people inside DEC interested in UNIX. Further, it became clear that UNIX could not be ignored in the final profit and loss statement. For one thing, UNIX gave users a lot of new freedom when choosing software and peripherals. DEC systems forced you to use terminals and software designed (usually by DEC) specifically for DEC computers and operating systems. UNIX had relatively few restrictions by comparison.

The final blow came when UNIX was ported to other machines besides DECs. DEC realized that given the choice, users would buy machines from vendors who supported the operating system they were interested in running. DEC is now fully committed to supporting UNIX (which it markets under the name ULTRIX) but it would prefer that users choose its proprietary operating system, VMS, and become locked into its hardware line. DEC, however, does not wish to refuse the large number of UNIX users that are interested in DEC hardware.

In 1986, there were approximately 6,000 DEC ULTRIX licenses, 14,000 Berkeley 4.X BSD licenses and 20,000 AT&T System V licenses for DEC's VAX hardware. Since then, DEC has picked up support for UNIX on most of its old computers and all of its new ones. Interestingly, at the same time, AT&T dropped support of UNIX on any DEC hardware.

Et Al.

Besides the ones listed here, many other universities and research institutions created important UNIX applications and extensions. Located in Canada, Australia, New Zealand, Europe and throughout the U.S., some of these institutions released their versions, or rereleased a Berkeley or AT&T version with its enhancements and name tacked somewhere in the original. Some diverged enough so that they could no longer be considered UNIX. The profusion was really overwhelming.

Many contributors did not have the interest in handling their own distributions, instead sending them on to Berkeley (which seemed to use everything). Because of this, Berkeley unintentionally takes credit for much work that was done elsewhere.

1.6   Politics – Part II

The UNIX source is considered a trade secret.   If you were to get access to UNIX source without signing a license, UNIX would no longer be a trade secret, and you could theoretically sell UNIX without paying royalties to AT&T (although you might have to pay your lawyers more than the license would have cost you, fending off legal action).   Therefore, AT&T jealously guards the UNIX source so as not to lose their trade secret status.   However, AT&T has gone out of their way to continue to make UNIX available for instructional purposes. Educational licenses are still cheap, and students do not have to sign licenses or nondisclosure agreements before they can see the source.   Nonetheless, you and your company as licenser can be held liable should someone make *"unauthorized use or distribution of the code, methods, and concepts contained in or derived from the UNIX product."*   Oh, and the UNIX manuals are protected by copyright, too!

AT&T was in the strange position of not being in the software business and yet issuing software licenses. Needless to say, its licenses were quite different than other software licenses.   Early licenses were issued by the Western Electric Co., since that was where the licensing office of AT&T was.   Now licenses are issued directly by AT&T.

The original licenses were *source* licenses. You got the complete source designed to run on a couple of different kinds of PDP-11s. You could run it on one machine. Commercial institutions paid fees on the order of $20,000. If you owned more than one machine, you had to buy *binary* licenses for every additional machine you wanted to run UNIX on. They were fairly pricey at about $8,000 considering that you couldn't resell them. On the other hand, educational institutions could buy source licenses for several hundred dollars – just enough to cover Bell Labs' adminstrative overhead and the price of tapes.

At this point, UNIX was sold "as is." And even though AT&T sold binary licenses, they didn't sell binaries themselves. Any company that wanted to run UNIX had to buy at least one source license, and find some UNIX expertise. Many companies and consultants sprang up to fill this void. The first company to commercially support UNIX was Interactive Systems Corp in 1977. Its product was called IS/1 and ran on PDP-11s (of course).

In 1980, AT&T finally created *distribution binary* licenses. Binaries covered by this license could be resold by a developer to other companies. These were much cheaper than the original binaries – distribution binaries were about $1,500. The first company to use these licenses was Onyx Systems.

Interestingly, the Onyx system was built using a Zilog Z8000 CPU – a microprocessor! This was the first commercial microprocessor-based UNIX, and it would not have been able to sell had it been bundled with a software license that doubled its price. Within a year, several more companies introduced UNIX systems based on microprocessors. With prices going as low as $10,000, these prices brought UNIX systems within the reach of many businesses which previously had only considered CP/M, MP/M or other inexpensive micro-based operating systems.

1.7   UNIX Cloning

An alternative to UNIX licensing is UNIX cloning. UNIX clones, look-alikes, work-alikes, and so on, are usually compatible at the system call level, with the kernel completely rewritten.

By doing this, vendors do not have to pay the high price of a UNIX license nor do they have to put up with AT&T's unusual licensing requirements. Many vendors have done just this and been quite successful.

The earliest system that could be called a UNIX clone was IDRIS, produced by Whitesmiths, Ltd. Since some of its employees had previously worked at AT&T, Whitesmiths was understandably worried about using proprietary AT&T information. Whitesmiths realized that many of the UNIX concepts were not proprietary in themselves, but that the code was. So it completely rewrote the kernel using original code. Further, it purposely chose different library names, order of arguments, and so on. This wasn't done simply to avoid lawsuits – Whitesmiths also thought it was correcting design flaws in UNIX. Besides, it appeared that AT&T was not going to be successful in bringing UNIX to market.

AT&T finally decided that it could not, or would not, prevent non-licensed systems from using the same calls and calling sequences. Whitesmiths eventually relented, changing most of its system and library calls so that IDRIS was compatible with AT&T's UNIX. Many other cloners joined in the fray at this point and remain there to this day.

Besides the pricing structure, there were many other reasons to avoid "real" UNIX. It wasn't supported by AT&T. AT&T did not discuss the direction or the future of UNIX. It wasn't clear that AT&T was committed to

UNIX. The pricing was high, and its structure changed frequently. Most importantly though, vendors wanted to add so many fixes and features, that it was not clear that there was any reason to start with the AT&T sources if they had to modify so much of them. In the end, many vendors felt like they were simply paying for the right to use the UNIX trademark. UNIX cloners were at the root of the UNIX standards efforts in attempts to obviate the desire to use the AT&T trademark.

1.8   The UNIX Trademark

Originally, "UNIX" was an unregistered trademark of Bell Telephone Laboratories. Early papers often noted this by placing a dagger or a ™ symbol next to the first occurrence of "UNIX," along with a footnote at the bottom of the page. The symbol ™ is actually the correct designation for unregistered trademarks, but AT&T supplied a macro with early versions of **troff** for displaying "UNIX" automatically which generated the dagger footnote. "UNIX" is now a registered trademark of AT&T. Thus, the symbol ® is correct. The appropriate footnote upon first appearance of the trademark is "UNIX is a registered trademark of AT&T." (UNIX is also a trademark of a line of audio equipment marketed by Marantz in Japan.)

Strictly speaking, a trademark permits the owner to keep others from using that mark in trade. If you are offering a UNIX product, for example, you must abide by AT&T's rules for their trademark because you are using it with their permission. AT&T distributes a brochure explaining use of the word "UNIX" in trademarks, appearance, grammatical usage ("*UNIX is an adjective, not a noun*"†) and in company names.

If you writing ordinary English discourse (such as in this book), you may treat requests from AT&T as indications of their preference, but you do not have to abide by them. For example, many people prefer "Unix" to "UNIX." Indeed, common English practice dictates that trademarks are spelled with an initial capital, unless they are acronyms in which case they are all capitals. "UNIX" is not an acronym.

Licensing has continued to get more complex with each release of UNIX. AT&T has created a complex licensing structure which varies in restrictions, use and cost depending upon the use, user, machine and version of UNIX. For example, UNIX varies in price for government, commercial or educational users. UNIX on machines with multiple CPUs costs more than on

---

† You will soon realize that we can't stand this rule.

single CPUs. And UNIX can be bought unbundled at different prices for just the kernel, the applications, or the complete sources.

Licensing is such a confusing issue that we refer you to your and AT&T's lawyers. /usr/group, a UNIX user's group, has also published very comprehensive papers on the subject.

1.9   Recent History: 1980-1986

As UNIX began to mature, its popularity in the commercial market grew enormously. One of the catalysts of this was /usr/group. /usr/group started off almost as a splinter group from USENIX. USENIX was concerned with the UNIX research and had little interest in promoting its market potential. Financial analysts, bankers, accountants, and other nontechnical people were very turned off by the USENIX attitudes which seemed to them somewhat elitist, as in, *"If you don't have the source and hack the kernel, you aren't worth talking to."*

In early 1980, Bob Marsh held a meeting of CommUNIX at the National Computer Conference. Interest from commercial users and vendors was there, and the group incorporated as /usr/group the following year, producing a regular newsletter called *CommUNIXations*, and an semiannual trade show called UniForum. These and other /usr/group activities focused on concerns of the UNIX marketplace such as standards, licensing and product information. The first UNIX product catalog, in 1981, listed 250 UNIX products from 100 companies. Within a year, /usr/group had well over 1,000 members.

The period from 1980 to 1983 saw an explosion of new UNIX companies. This was a result of two factors. One was that a growing number of graduating students were extremely unwilling to give up the enjoyable UNIX environments that they had used all through school. The second was that the introduction of several low-cost 32-bit CPUs allowed the design of cheap personal UNIX workstations.

Each of these factors would have been meaningless without the other. Without sufficient UNIX workstations, ex-students would have been forced to use whatever proprietary operating system a vendor offered, perhaps with help from the VOS project. And if the ex-students didn't exist, the UNIX vendors would never have been able to sell their products to users already entrenched in propriety products.

Porters

"It is easier to port UNIX to a new machine, than an application to a new operating system." – Dennis Ritchie

One of the attractive features of UNIX is the portability of it. It is written in C, a high-level system programming language, not tied to one computer. By comparison to other operating systems, porting UNIX to a new machine is easy. However, it typically requires several months for an experienced porter to do this task. Porting is a specialized and short-term task.

In the early '80s, specialized companies, called porting houses, were born to port UNIX to new computers. They could produce a relatively unchanged UNIX, with little development cost. With hardware costs dropping significantly during this period, it became much easier to design and market a successful computer.

UniSoft Corporation began in 1981, producing a UNIX port called Uni-Plus+. Unlike XENIX, UniPlus has stayed very compatible with the AT&T versions of UNIX. It is estimated that UniSoft has performed 65 percent of all UNIX ports to date.

At the same time, SCO (The Santa Cruz Operation) collaborated with Microsoft on XENIX, which was the first implementation of UNIX on the Intel 8086 and many other microprocessors. Today, XENIX remains the most popular microcomputer implementation of UNIX. It received a particularly helpful boost when Tandy shipped 14,000 XENIX-based systems to small businesses in 1985. The second largest shipper of UNIX systems, Altos, shipped approximately 13,000 XENIX-based systems during the same period.

With the help of these and other porting houses, UNIX was moved to an amazing number of different machine architectures. At the end of 1983, there were approximately 100,000 UNIX sites running on a wide variety of hardware.

Due to the proliferation of companies and products, it became difficult to decide what was UNIX and what wasn't. Would product X run on UNIX from vendor Y? In source form? Binary? With 2 users? 10 users? 100? How about on a UNIX clone? Just what did it mean to be a UNIX clone?

In 1981, /usr/group began the first serious work on UNIX standards. A standard was completed in 1984 and promptly ignored. To this day (and probably till the end of time), UNIX standards continue to be developed by AT&T, the Institute of Electrical and Electronics Engineers (IEEE), the International

Standards Organization (ISO), the National Bureau of Standards (NBS) for the U.S. government, and X/OPEN (a consortium of UNIX vendors). (See the Future chapter for more about standards.)

Stanford and the SUN

Stanford University had had very enjoyable experiences with the Xerox Alto. The Alto was the first personal workstation to bear any resemblance to modern UNIX workstations. Of particular interest was that it included a high-resolution bitmapped screen with a mouse, a high-speed (3Mb/sec) network, and enough memory, local disk storage and processing power to support itself comfortably. The Alto was extremely expensive in comparison to any other personal computer. (Though never offered for sale, its estimated cost was $30,000.) But for price, it clearly marked the way of the future.

With the release of the Motorola 68000 CPU, it was possible for students at Stanford to design a relatively low-cost machine that duplicated much of the capability of the Alto. It also differed from the Alto in another way – it was designed to be a multiprocessing machine, specifically to run UNIX.

Stanford licensed a single-board design which became known as the SUN (Stanford University Network) board. Codata (the first licensee), Fortune, Dual, Cyb, Lucasfilm, Sun and other companies – over a dozen in all – bought licenses and with little effort sold UNIX clones that ran either 4.1BSD or System III. The machines started at an amazingly low $10,000. These prices encouraged the dramatic spread of UNIX to the commercial markets, where it competed impressively with much more expensive computer systems.

Since the market was rather crowded, many of the companies were not able to compete and quickly withdrew. Only a handful of the original SUN-board vendors remain today. (None of them continue to use the original design which has been rendered obsolete by more functional chips.) One company continued to use the name Sun (Sun Microsystems, Inc.) and employed one of the original designers of the Sun board, Andreas Bechtolsheim.

This was the period of JAWS (Just Another WorkStation). For a while, UNIX boxes seemed like a commodity market and the survivors quickly began offering particular features that distinguished them from the others. Nonetheless, the prices remained low and the established (mainframe and mini) computer companies began to see that they were letting a potential market get away.

Gradually, the larger companies such as DEC, Data General, Gould, Apollo and Hewlett-Packard began offering UNIX systems for their own hardware, even though they already had proprietary operating systems. Additionally, they began offering UNIX workstations to compete in the desktop market place.

At the same time, mainframe and supercomputer companies like Amdahl and Cray had the foresight to support a UNIX environment on their machines. It seemed like UNIX was everywhere.

Big Blue's Blessing

In 1983, IBM joined the fray by offering UNIX on its PC (ported by Interactive), based on the 16-bit Intel 8088. This was not technologically interesting – UNIX had been created on 16-bit computers, after all. What was important about it was that the IBM announcement was the stamp of approval for UNIX. It is hard to describe now exactly how important this was, but there were many people who would not buy a product unless IBM marketed it. (Microcomputers that preceded the IBM PC were a fascinating example of this.)

Currently, it is unusual to find a computer for which one cannot get a UNIX implementation. Popular computers such as the IBM PC-AT line have half a dozen ports available. Even systems such as Apple's Macintosh and Atari's ST with their more modern user interfaces have had UNIX ported to them.

The reasons for this are easy to understand.

- UNIX programmers abound and most often come directly out of college.

- Porting UNIX to a new machine architecture is substantially easier than designing and implementing a new operating system from scratch.

- UNIX is an industry standard operating system. It is the only one that is machine-independent.

- The productivity of system programmers is much better on UNIX systems than on other commonly available systems.

It is worth noting that at the time of IBM's announcement of UNIX for the PC, there were already approximately 70,000 computers running UNIX.

2500 of them were inside the Bell System. About 1,300 universities had UNIX licenses, of which 750 were in the U.S. or Canada. AT&T estimated that there were 100,000 programmers writing UNIX software, and about 300 application packages were available from more than 90 companies.

1.10   Politics – Part III

Competition between USG and PWB finally ceased when the groups were merged. Most of the contributions of both groups were integrated into one UNIX. This merged group became known as USDL (UNIX System Development Laboratory) and introduced UNIX System III in 1982. System III also included significant support for transaction processing taken from CB UNIX, a version designed by the Columbus Bell operating company. System III was the last Bell Labs UNIX product licensed through Western Electric.

Due to a ruling by Judge Greene in the monumental antitrust case that the U.S. had brought against AT&T, it was divested of many of its subsidiaries in 1984. Also, AT&T was allowed to participate competitively in the computer business. In preparation, UNIX had finally been given its own home in AT&T's Information Systems the previous year.

In early 1983, AT&T Information Systems announced System V. At this point, AT&T radically changed the style of its marketing. It lowered the price for UNIX significantly. For the first time, AT&T offered support for UNIX. And most importantly, AT&T announced its intention to maintain upward compatibility with future releases. This brought confidence to many potential markets, since AT&T was viewed as a force as powerful as IBM, and with the chutzpa to sell coals to Newcastle. On top of this, AT&T had the complete ownership of a product that people were literally begging for. At the same time, many people expected AT&T to finally integrate some of the more useful aspects that they were using but from the unsupported Berkeley UNIX. Both groups of people were disappointed.

For the next few years, AT&T did a poor job of marketing UNIX. AT&T let others sell its product more effectively. And it failed to give any resistance to IBM while it walked away with the PC marketplace. AT&T started dropping support for DEC's hardware, including the original machines which UNIX had been developed on, in an attempt to move the market to proprietary hardware that had been developed in-house. However, strong competition from Motorola, NSC and other hardware manufacturers made this untenable. AT&T lost an estimated $1 billion in its computer-related businesses in 1986.

AT&T announced System V R.2 (Release 2) in 1984 and SV R.3 in 1986, both of which have become very popular. At the same time, AT&T cemented agreements with several of the major chip manufacturers for binary compatible versions of UNIX. In addition, AT&T agreed to merge both XENIX and Sun's Berkeley-based UNIX with System V. Clearly, the future of UNIX depends a lot on whether AT&T succeeds at its merger. We have more to say about this in the Future chapter.

1.11   Is UNIX Just History?

Is UNIX just history? No way. UNIX is here to stay. International Data Corporation (IDC) states that the UNIX market was worth $3.6 billion in 1985. This was approximately 6 percent of the total worldwide budget spent on computing.

According to the December 1987 issue of *UNIXWORLD*, about $5.5 billion was spent on UNIX systems that year, of which 10 percent was for software. This was approximately 8 percent of the total worldwide budget for computing, according to IDC.

Novon Research Group states that approximately 300,000 UNIX systems were shipped during 1987. The total number of UNIX systems in use was about 750,000. Almost half the purchases came from Fortune 1000 companies. There were an estimated 4.5 million UNIX users, and more UNIX machine hours were used than DOS hours.

It is expected that 450,000 UNIX systems will be shipped in 1990, much of the increase being due to commercial use. By 1991, UNIX market share is expected to reach 20 percent, and continue increasing.

Clearly, UNIX is a success.

Dennis and Ken have said, "*The success of UNIX lies not so much in new inventions but rather in the full exploitation of a carefully selected set of fertile ideas.*"† This is probably not what people think of when they are asked why UNIX is so successful. We have tried to state our reasons. In any case,

---

† D. M. Ritchie and K. Thompson, "The UNIX Time-Sharing System," *Communications of the ACM*, vol 17, no. 7, July 1974, 365-375.

the increasing number of UNIX releases and the apparent continuing good health of UNIX is astonishing.

1.12   Who's Who

Though we cannot hope to provide a full list of everyone who was responsible for some part of UNIX, we have listed some of the people that are frequently referred to, albeit perhaps just in conversations at UNIX conferences.

It has been difficult tracking down some of the people involved in the development of UNIX. Many have not left identifiable signatures behind, even though their work was substantial. Others made large contributions as a whole, but not to any one part that can be easily stated. (It seems as though hundreds of people have hacked on the kernel.) In any case, please excuse any omissions of credit.

Many people involved in UNIX are famous (sometimes more so) for their roles in other unrelated projects. We have not listed these non-UNIX contributions to the world – not because we are myopic – rather, these attributions would fill an entire volume by themselves.

Some people have extremely well-known nicknames, usually because they were in the `/etc/passwd` file distributed with many of the early versions of UNIX, or because their initials appear in so much source code. We have listed these also, so that when you hear people say *"dmr says ..."*, you know that they are referring to Dennis Ritchie.

Mike Accetta:	Responsible for symbolic links, `key` (later to become `man -k`) and `/dev/pty`.
Rick Adams:	Major force behind UUNET. Wrote SLIP.
Alfred Aho:	The A in `awk` and author of `egrep` and `dbm` library.
Eric Allman:	Wrote `sendmail`, `trek`, `tset` and `-me` macros. Major contributor to Ingres.
Ken Arnold:	Wrote `curses`, `fortune`, and lots of other games.
Özalp Babaoğlu:	Co-responsible with Bill Joy for virtual memory in Berkeley UNIX.

W. O. Baker:	Rejected request for DEC-10 by Thompson, Ritchie and Ossanna, leading to development of a much smaller operating system on a much smaller machine.
Andreas Bechtolsheim:	Developed initial design for SUN board.
Steve Bellovin:	Wrote first implementation of Usenet.
Walt Bilofsky:	Wrote Rand editor.
Biff:	Heidi's dog.
Irma Biren:	Mailed out all the Sixth Edition UNIX tapes.
Bruce Borden:	Worked on MH and Rand editor.
Steve ("srb") Bourne:	Created the Bourne Shell. Wrote **adb**.
Steve Bunch:	Co-wrote first Arpanet (NCP) code for UNIX.
Brent Byer:	Added split I/D-space to support PDP-11/45.
Ron Cain:	Wrote Small C, first public-domain C compiler.
Rudd Canaday:	Co-designer of UNIX file system with Dennis and Ken. Created PWB group.
Lorinda Cherry:	Writer of the Writer's Workbench (**diction**, **style**, etc.), **bc**, and **dc**. Wrote **eqn** with **bwk**.
Greg Chesson:	Past drummer for Woody Herman Band, developer of **mpx** files (forerunner to **select()**), original **uucp** packet driver, Datakit, line disciplines and adaptive control in **dh** driver.
Douglas Comer:	Wrote Xinu. Responsible for first UNIX X.25 implementation with Paul McNabb and System V **cron** with Bob Brown and Keith Williamson.
Dave Crocker:	Wrote MMDF, MS.
Bill Croft:	Wrote first UNIX internetworking implementation (using PDP-11s).

Ted Dolotta: Responsible for **-mm** macros. First director of USG.

Robert Elz: Wrote BSD quotas and autoconfiguration.

Robert Fabry: Original faculty advisor to Berkeley CSRG who got DARPA funding for project.

Stu ("sif") Feldman: Author of **make**, **f77** and **efl**. Has nice wine cellar.

Mel Ferentz: Hosted first UNIX user group meeting. Founded *UNIX News* (a.k.a. *;login:*).

David Fiedler: Founded or edited more UNIX and C magazines and newsletters than anyone else, including *The UNIX Software List*, *The C List*, *Unique*, *UNIX Review*, *The C Journal*, and *The C Users Journal*.

John Foderero: Wrote Franz Lisp.

Herb Gellis: Wrote **xargs**.

Jim Gettys: Co-responsible for X Window System.

George Goble: Did first influential UNIX port to an asymmetric multiprocessor (two VAX-11/780s).

James Gosling: Wrote UNIX **emacs**. Co-authored NeWS with David Rosenthal.

Gary Grossman: Co-wrote first Arpanet (NCP) code for UNIX.

Rob Gurwitz: Wrote BBN's TCP/IP implementation which later became part of Berkeley distribution.

Doug Gwyn: Wrote BRL's System V emulation for BSD.

Teus Hagen: Established first **uucp** connections between U.S. (**decvax**), Europe (**mcvax**) and many other countries.

Dick Haight: Wrote **find**, **cpio**, **expr**. Added named variables to shell. Major contributor to PWB.

Chuck Haley: Wrote **tar**. Co-implementor of early versions of **ex** and Pascal shell with Bill Joy.

Dennis Hall: Co-implemented first Virtual Operating System while at Lawrence Berkeley Laboratory. Founded Software Tools User Group.

Robert Henry: Wrote `error`.

Steve Holmgren: Co-wrote first Arpanet (NCP) code for UNIX.

Peter Honeyman: The Honey in Honey DanBer `uucp`. Wrote `pathalias`.

Mark Horton: Wrote `curses`, `terminfo` and did substantial work on `uucp` mapping project and Usenet.

Stephen ("scj") Johnson: Wrote `yacc`, `pcc` (Portable C Compiler), `lint` and early versions of `spell`. Assisted Dennis in one of first ports of UNIX (to Interdata 8/32).

Bill ("wnj") Joy: Wrote much of original Berkeley release including virtual memory support, networking, Pascal, `vi`, `csh` and `termcap`. Co-founder of Sun Microsystems. Designed NFS. Received 1986 ACM Grace Murray Hopper Award for work on Berkeley UNIX.

David Kashtan: Wrote Eunice.

Howard Katseff: Wrote `sdb` and `last`.

Lou Katz: First president of USENIX.

Brian ("bwk") Kernighan: The K in *K&R* and `awk`. Co-authored *The C Programming Language* which set style for how most people write C. Wrote `ratfor`, `ditroff`, `eqn` and `pic`. Shared co-responsibility for Version 7.

Andrew Koenig: Wrote `varargs` (a.k.a. `stdargs`).

David Korn: Wrote `ksh`.

Ted Kowalski: Responsible for modern `fsck`.

Bob Kridle: Founded Mt. Xinu.

Jim Kulp:	Developed original version of job control and `csh` directory stacks.
Peter Langston:	Responsible for early USENIX **go** tournaments. His friends Eedie and Eddie can often be reached at (201) 644-2332.
Sam Leffler:	Wrote `tip` with Bill Shannon. Major force behind 4.2BSD and Berkeley TCP.
Mike Lesk:	Wrote `lex`, `tbl`, `refer`, `-ms` macros, `uucp` and portable C library, precursor to stdio.
Don Libes:	Co-author of *Life With UNIX*. Little else of note.
John Lions:	Wrote first book describing and documenting the UNIX system. Often misspelled as "Lyons."
Tom London:	Co-responsible for 32V, first VAX version of UNIX.
Brian Lucas:	Co-creator of first distributed UNIX file system (4 PDP-11s served by a PDP-10).
Heinz Lycklama:	Wrote MERT with Doug Bayer. Wrote LSX, first UNIX for a microprocessor (LSI-11). Responsible for much early work on UNIX standards including first (/usr/group) UNIX standard.
Tom Lyon:	Did one of first UNIX ports (to VM/370).
Joe Maranzano:	Responsible for USG.
Bob Marsh:	Founder and first president of /usr/group. Founded Onyx, first vendor of non-PDP UNIX systems and microprocessor-based UNIX systems.
John Mashey:	Wrote Mashey shell, which later merged into Bourne shell. Major contributor to PWB.
Doug McIlroy:	Suggested idea of pipes. Wrote `tmg`. Wrote `diff` and `spell`. Research in speech processing on UNIX led to `grep`.

Kirk McKusick:	Wrote Berkeley Fast File System and portable directory access routines. Prime force behind 4.3BSD. Wrote `gprof` (with Peter Kessler).
Lee McMahon:	Wrote `sed`.
Al McPherson:	Wrote `fsdb`.
Richard Miller:	Did one of first UNIX ports (to Interdata 7/32).
Robert Morris:	Wrote `dc` and `bc` with Lorinda Cherry.
Bill Munson:	Responsible for Ultrix.
Mike Muus:	Responsible for JHU/BRL UNIX.
Alan Nemeth:	Responsible for BBN's C machine, first microcoded implementation of UNIX.
Landon Noll:	Founder and judge (with Larry Bassel) of International Obfuscated C Code Contest.
Dan Nowitz:	The Dan in Honey DanBer. Substantial contributions to original `uucp`.
Joseph Ossanna:	Responsible for `troff`.
Rob Pike:	Co-developer of Blit bitmapped terminal.
P. J. Plauger:	Wrote first commercial C compiler. Started Whitesmiths, Ltd. Responsible for Idris.
Dave Presotto:	Wrote `vgrind` with Bill Joy.
Rick Rashid:	Responsible for Mach. Designed CMU interprocess communication.
Brian ("ber") Redman:	The Ber of Honey DanBer.
Bill Reeves:	Wrote `vcat` with Tom Duff and Mike Tilson.
John Reiser:	Co-responsible for 32V, first VAX version of UNIX.
Sandy Ressler:	Who??????

Dennis ("dmr") Ritchie:

While he often denies doing as much as Thompson, he is undoubtedly half the reason for UNIX. Largely responsible for C language. For work on UNIX with Thompson, received many prestigious awards including 1982 IEEE Emmanuel Piore award and 1983 ACM Turing Award.

Marc Rochkind:

Wrote SCCS, and `bfs`. Major contributor to PWB.

Rob Rosenthal:

Co-creator of first distributed UNIX file system.

Steve Schaefer:

Responsible for `CPATH`, `LPATH`, and `MPATH`.

Deborah Scherrer:

Co-implemented first Virtual Operating System while at Lawrence Berkeley Laboratory. Founded Software Tools User Group.

Eric Schienbrood:

Wrote `more`.

Eric Schmidt:

Wrote BerkNet.

Jeff Schriebman:

Founded Unisoft.

John Seamons:

Did first port of UNIX to SUN board.

Donn Seeley:

Did substantial work on `f77`, Ritchie compiler and `pcc`.

Bill Shannon:

Implemented first overlayed kernel for the PDP-11 with Bill Jolitz. Wrote early version of BSD printer spooler.

Dick Shapazian:

Responsible for designing early UNIX licensing structure.

Kurt Shoens:

Wrote Berkeley `Mail` (a.k.a. `mailx`), `fmt`.

Richard ("rms") Stallman:

Responsible for `emacs`, GNU and Free Software Foundation.

Armando ("aps") Stettner:

Spent several years getting DEC to acknowledge the existence of UNIX.

Bjarne Stroustrup:

Wrote C++.

Joe Sventek:	Co-implemented first Virtual Operating System while at Lawrence Berkeley Laboratory. Founded Software Tools User Group.
Andrew Tanenbaum:	Wrote MINIX.
Rebecca Thomas:	Co-authored first commercial book about UNIX with Jean Yates.
Ken ("ken") Thompson:	The person to blame for inventing UNIX. For work on UNIX with Dennis, received many prestigious awards including the 1982 IEEE Emmanuel Piore award and the 1983 ACM Turing Award.
Walter Tichy:	Wrote RCS.
David Tilbrook:	Founded HCR.
Michael Toy:	Author of two great games, `rogue` and `/etc/shutdown`.
Michael Ubell:	Wrote first history prototype, later adapted into `csh`.
Larry Wall:	Author of `rn`, `patch`, and `perl`.
Larry Wehr:	Responsible for modern named pipes.
Peter Weinberger:	The W in `awk`. Wrote `lcomp`.
Peter Weiner:	Obtained first commercial UNIX license for Rand Corp. Founded Interactive Systems Corp.
Lauren Weinstein:	Responsible for Stargate.
David Willcox:	Wrote `indent`.
Chris Van Wyk:	Wrote `ideal`.
Dave Yost:	Made substantial contributions to Rand editor and MH.
Walter Zintz:	Created Uni-Ops user group.
Steve Zucker:	Created early version of named pipes.

Chapter 2: UNIX Present

"The first step binds one to the second." – French proverb

UNIX can be defined in many ways. For instance, the manual that comes with your UNIX system is one way. This entire book is another way. Yet another is Dennis Ritchie's personal opinion. There are many others. Each of them presumes a certain context. Depending upon who you are and where you are coming from, one view may be more appropriate than another.

We take several approaches to looking at what UNIX is, from the technical to the philosophical to the commercial. If you like one, consider the other views as supplemental and try and understand those too.

In a sense, the rest of this book is all supplementary material to this chapter. So is sitting down at a UNIX system, trying it out, getting to know it, and writing a UNIX program. Tell others about it and see what they think. Talk to a UNIX user, programmer, administrator or vendor. Attend a UNIX conference. Read some UNIX books and magazines. Dream about UNIX.

2.1   UNIX – A Perfunctory Definition

UNIX (yoo′niks), *adj.* **1.** *Trademark.* one of several computer operating systems developed at AT&T: *That toaster oven runs the UNIX operating system.* **2.** a computer operating system or interface that bears significant resemblance to UNIX. – **UNIX-like. 3.** associated with UNIX: *the UNIX shell.* [after the *Multics* operating system; see UNI-, MULTICS, EUNUCHS]

2.2   The UNIX Philosophy

UNIX is much more than such simplistic definitions. It is more than an operating system. It is a philosophy of programming. The main tenet is that the power of UNIX comes from the relations between the programs rather than the programs themselves. UNIX encourages one to take existing programs and combine them into a new, more useful program.

Understanding this simple idea is key to using UNIX effectively. Your work will fit better in the environment, and it will be more understandable to others who understand UNIX. It will be more understandable to anyone.

There are no hard and fast rules to UNIX. No one wrote down programming laws that all UNIX programs must follow. There are no rules. However, there are some observations that can be made.

- *Small is beautiful.*

Build a program that does one thing well. UNIX gives one the ability to connect such programs together easily. The result is a synergy – a workbench of tools that are more than the sum of their parts. Many other systems have useful tools, but they generally don't work together as readily as in UNIX.

- *10 percent of the work solves 90 percent of the problems.*

UNIX was never designed to be the system to solve all problems. It purposely ignores certain difficult problems. The result is a system that solves almost as many, much more easily.

- *When faced with a choice, do whatever is simpler.*

Simpler tools are more reliable, easier to understand and easier to use. A program with lots of special case code may find that it has unexpectedly placed the burden on the user to adapt their problem to the special case solution. After enough special cases are added, the program becomes slower than it was originally.

A good example of the previous two points is the UNIX file system. It has a single simple file access method in contrast to complex file systems of other operating systems. The UNIX file system is very efficient and works easily for almost all applications.

- *Solve the problem, not the machine.*

Build programs while ignoring the underlying machine or operating system as much as possible. Don't depend on internal data structures or algorithms. Focusing on the machine results in nonportable code. Such programs are generally not useful in different contexts and don't lend themselves to helping solve other problems.

> • *Solve at the right level, and you will only have to do it once.*

Solving problems is easy. Solving them only once is the key to UNIX problem solving. For example, file name pattern matching is only implemented once (the shell), not in every program that uses files. Screen paging is only implemented once, not in every program.

Notice that none of these guidelines are technical in nature. For example, the last example mentions screen paging. It can be implemented once in either the operating system or a stand-alone program – we don't care. The point is only that it should be done once. Then all other programs can gracefully make use of it. What these guidelines do spell out is a sense of style. In a way, they implicitly decide the technical aspects of a program. Any program which follows them is a program that would live well in a UNIX system.

Of course, these are generalizations of observations, not rules or laws. There are exceptions. For example, sometimes you absolutely have to solve 100% of the problem, or use a complex algorithm. However, these are the exceptions in UNIX, and they are rare. Their relative lack, in contrast to other operating systems, makes UNIX a system that hangs together. It is a system that is flexible and easy to use.

2.3   The User Interface

This is what most people see first when they use UNIX. And those who do not go on to do UNIX programming are often left with the impression that this is exactly what UNIX is. (If you want details on the shell, see the User Environment chapter.)

In fact, the shell that most of us use is only one way of interacting with the system. You can use a window system, or a menu system, or design your own interface. Because the shell is what most people interact with, however, we come to view it as the face of UNIX.

The shell was designed for users that were programmers, not naive users. This is ironic considering that most UNIX (and other computer) users are not at all interested in programming. Almost all commands require some creativity and programming. For example, to print the date on the lineprinter, the command:

```
date | lpr
```

combines two existing programs to perform a new function. The shell allows much more complicated expressions, as well as programs that are as sophisticated as can be done from any programming language.

On the other hand, such a complex interface carries with it the potential for overwhelming and confusing complexity, just like any language. The shell is not biased towards handholding – very little is in UNIX – and therefore you must be careful what you say.

It is easy to demonstrate that the shell is unfriendly towards naive users. A classic example is that `rm *` will silently delete all the files in your current directory, regardless of your intent. (Perhaps you just wanted to remove a file actually named `*`.)

Depending upon your point of view, this is either a feature or a bug. `rm` does not see the asterisk. The shell replaces the asterisk by a list of files and gives that to `rm`. Possibly, if `rm` knew that you had just asked to delete all your files, it would ask you if you were sure since this is a fairly unusual request.

Nonetheless, there are valid reasons for doing this. And further, there are ways of protecting yourself. We are not trying to tell you that we apologize for major flaws in UNIX. We are trying to explain that the shell is designed for programmers who have some understanding of the consequences of their actions.

After all, imagine driving in your auto. You turn the wheel so that the car is now heading directly for a tree. Does your car ask you if you are sure you wish to head for a tree? No. But even if it had the wisdom to do so, you might have a good reason to head for a tree. Or go 20 mph over the speed limit. Or even drive home in reverse.

When the UNIX shell first appeared, it was a tour de force. There was nothing comparable. While early shells are now considered primitive by comparison with modern ones, the point is that a shell remains a good tool for the programmer. Pipes, redirection, and the control features of the shell allow the programmer to write new programs quickly, often without writing any C code. Small, almost simple utilities can be easily combined, becoming yet another utility that can be used and combined in the same way.

The lack of file formats and the lack of distinctions between files and devices obviates the user and programs from having to deal with differences.

Once a program has been implemented, it can read input equally well from a device, a user at a keyboard, or the output of another process.

The user interface combined with the other tools creates a synergistic environment that allows programmers to be much more productive than other systems. And the fruits of their labor, in turn, are more immediately understandable and useful to other programmers.

2.4   UNIX, the Operating System

Many people think of the shell as the essence of UNIX. It is the part they first encountered and the part they are most likely to remember. But a programmer is more likely to remember what is underneath all that – the infrastructure, so to speak.

The kernel, the system calls and the libraries, and to a lesser extent, the utilities (including the shell) are what UNIX is. But the libraries and utilities are creations after the fact. They can be rewritten, or even ignored. But what you cannot ignore are the system calls. These are the entry points into the UNIX kernel. If you could change them, you would have a different operating system than before. It would be a different version of UNIX, or perhaps something totally unlike UNIX. Everything else is written in terms of them, including every library subroutine and utility. They strongly affect the view of everything else around them.

The paradigms that are so innately UNIX are in part due to the design of the system calls, and also partly due to the UNIX philosophies expressed elsewhere in this chapter.

For example, the ability of programs to manipulate devices and files with the same code (like **mv, cat, rm**, etc.) is because the system calls also do so. One writes the following C code to open the *file* "foo" for reading:

```
open("foo", READ);
```

The following code does the same thing for the *device* "bar":

```
open("bar", READ);
```

Not only does the basic I/O system work the same for devices and files, but so do access permission and naming conventions. The results are the conceptually clean utilities of UNIX. There are very few exceptions to this paradigm, and there are none that are artificial – like other operating systems where one might use two different system calls to open files and devices, not to mention different kinds of devices, or files with different access methods, or...

Other parts of the kernel present the same type of straightforward access to the system. For example, there is only one call to bring programs into existence – `execve()`. Permissions are controlled entirely by `chmod()`. And so on.

Of course, there are potential problems with a "tight" system like this. The most important is that some things will never fit the UNIX paradigm. But people are going to try, and in two different ways. Some will make it work within the existing UNIX system, no matter how inappropriate (and slow) it is. Others might try adding a new system call, totally fracturing the consistency of the paradigm (as well as making the kernel a lot larger).

The first few versions of UNIX were written by two men sharing the same office. In that environment, it was possible to discuss future implications and ramifications that the addition or change of part of the kernel would have on any other. But once UNIX was distributed, this became much more difficult and unlikely.

Some fanatics of purity (see Minix in the Underground chapter) believe that Version 7, the last version released by `research`, is the last true UNIX.†️ Like biblical fundamentalists, the fanatics are fun to listen to but entirely impractical in this day and age. We cannot take giant steps backward, because no matter how much modern UNIX creaks, it is simply much more capable than V7.

Thompson and Ritchie knew what they wanted, and knew what they were doing. They strongly believed in the 10 percent – 90 percent rule, for example, and were willing to give up a little functionality to avoid a lot of complexity. For example, UNIX file protection doesn't provide a means of checking access on a per-user basis (unlike capabilities or authority lists). However, their applications had very little use for such fine-grain protection.

And yes, they made some design mistakes. In fact, a lot of UNIX is the result of evolution. Things that did not work out were removed (e.g., multiplexed files) or changed (e.g., file name lengths). Since the user base was small and sophisticated, there was no necessity to maintain old interfaces forever. Such modifications are rare in commercial operating systems (including

---

† Indeed, both Thompson and Ritchie had stopped putting their name in the front of the manual after V6, as if to say that they could no longer be responsible for UNIX.

recent versions of UNIX). The lack of mistakes in UNIX is as much due to divine understanding as it is to its chance to evolve without carrying around the baggage of those old mistakes.

Since Version 7, the last release of UNIX common to all others, people have created many different versions of UNIX. And while there are incompatibilites, virtually all of the UNIX kernel calls still continue to be the base upon which all other UNIX systems rest.

The kernel itself is not inviolate. AT&T has not protected the functional specification of the UNIX kernel in any way. This allows cloners to build a UNIX kernel without using any of the proprietary source code. With UNIX standards, it is possible to build a functionally equivalent system.

What is important about the kernel is its interface – the system calls. One may have a kernel that works in a completely different way from an AT&T kernel, and as long as it supports the system calls, it is still UNIX. (And here, we are not talking about the proprietary variety, but the essence.)

Some utilities have knowledge about the kernel built into them. (This is probably one of the more grievous mistakes UNIX contains.) For example, the process status command, **ps**, knows how to read through kernel data structures directly without going through any system call. When the kernel was written, Thompson and Ritchie reasoned that since there was only one program that would need this information, it wasn't worth creating a new system call. What's more, the data of interest seemed fairly machine dependent.

The result of this is that **ps** remains a machine-dependent command. While this allows vendors to not have to duplicate historical remnants of the early UNIX kernels, it introduces a small amount of nonportability into certain areas of UNIX – particularly those that require information from the kernel.

Vendors have tried to remedy this by extending existing system calls and introducing new ones. It is a difficult problem, the more so because many versions of UNIX have a completely rewritten kernel. Furthermore, vendors grow comfortable with the idea that they can add or modify system calls. This result is a divergence of UNIX systems.

Current UNIX kernels are much larger than the original one. Early kernels fit in 40Kb. Now, kernels of 400Kb are considered small, and some machines have kernels larger than 1Mb. (Of course, the early kernels didn't provide things like virtual memory, networking or large buffer caches.)

As UNIX kernels increase in size substantially, we face several problems. Large kernels require more physical (and possibly virtual) memory, in turn placing difficult demands on memory management. Such kernels are much more complex and difficult to debug. And they further isolate the user from the ability to easily change the system.

Many researchers are reexamining the concept of the modern UNIX kernel in attempts to reduce its size and complexity. For example, it is possible to reimplement parts of the UNIX kernel as user code. This has been done with the file system and other device drivers. While we normally consider these as requiring quick response to interrupts, a much smaller kernel can work so much faster, that such high-demand user code is possible. Furthermore, smaller kernels enhance reliability (less code, less errors) and give users more control.

2.5   Versions
"If you want to make enemies, try to change something." – Woodrow Wilson

While UNIX standards struggle to keep UNIX systems looking alike, commercial pressures pull in the opposite direction. Simply producing a faster UNIX isn't good enough. Vendors want products that differentiate from each other. UNIX vendors want sex appeal. In a way, UNIX's malleability may be its Achilles Heel. It is so easy to modify UNIX, that everyone does. Dramatically. It is not possible to describe UNIX as a single operating system without doing an injustice to a great many vendors. It is kind of like trying to describe an automobile. Every manufacturer tries to be different, and yet they all have to produce the same thing – an automobile.

The same holds for UNIX. There are so many companies selling UNIX that we necessarily see many, many different versions. While most of the versions can be grouped in a gross sense on technical features, there are some that resist any kind of clean classification. This is especially the case with UNIX clones.

The majority of UNIX systems are based either on Berkeley 4.2 (often abbreviated as "BSD" for "Berkeley Software Distribution"), or System III or V (often abbreviated "SV"). All of these, in turn, share a common heritage from Version 7 (often abbreviated "V7"), released by AT&T in 1978. (Older versions of UNIX are covered in the History chapter.)

Some people consider XENIX to be a version in its own right, but it is based on System V UNIX and is really not very different externally. (Early XENIX systems were based on V7 and later System III.) Internally, XENIX is different from System V – significant performance work has been done for it to run well on microcomputers. This is the largest area of use for XENIX. Because of the low prices and popularity of the microcomputers that XENIX is sold for, it is easily the most widely sold version of UNIX.

Supported by the U.S. Department of Defense's (DoD) Advanced Research Projects Agency (DARPA), Berkeley extended V7 UNIX so that it could support large AI projects in a networked environment. It added virtual memory support for DEC's new VAX 32-bit computer. And it incorporated a significantly enhanced version of BBN's implementation of the TCP/IP network protocols, developed and proven very successful in the Arpanet several years earlier.

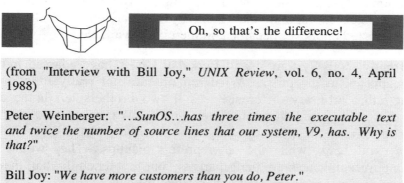

Oh, so that's the difference!

(from "Interview with Bill Joy," *UNIX Review*, vol. 6, no. 4, April 1988)

Peter Weinberger: "*...SunOS...has three times the executable text and twice the number of source lines that our system, V9, has. Why is that?*"

Bill Joy: "*We have more customers than you do, Peter.*"

Many new user and programmer interfaces were added, such as the C-shell, job control, `vi` and termcap. Some of the modifications, such as a new style of signal handling, were quite incompatible with earlier versions of UNIX. Because of the incompatibilities, the emphasis on networking and AI, and the undergraduate nature of some of the other additions, Berkeley UNIX was seen as a research project. Berkeley has expressed its intention to introduce incompatible features in future versions (or more precisely, "not to necessarily remain compatible with earlier versions"). With no intent to provide support, it is not surprising that some commercial companies avoid Berkeley's UNIX, no matter how futuristic it is. As if lack of support wasn't enough, many people have extended Berkeley UNIX (again without support) with special features, more "improvements" and rereleased it. Thus, we find a UM (University of Maryland) BSD UNIX, a CMU (Carnegie Mellon University) BSD UNIX, a JHU/BRL (Johns Hopkins University/Ballistic Research Laboratory) BSD UNIX, and so forth.

By comparison with BSD, AT&T's System III and V have remained much more compatible with their predecessors. However, some things have changed (e.g., terminal characteristics). And what they kept came with all the old bugs (e.g., signal delivery was still unreliable). AT&T chose to ignore certain areas (e.g., networking, job control, virtual memory) important to researchers and large systems, and emphasize features (e.g., shared memory, semaphores) of importance to commercial applications. Originally they lacked some modern features such as a screen-oriented editor, but now they have incorporated many of the Berkeley enhancements. More importantly, and in contrast to Berkeley, AT&T has stated that its new systems will be upward compatible with old systems (starting with System III). While System V still lacks solutions for real-time control and other problems, it is a much more appropriate choice for commercial users by comparison to Berkeley's UNIX. (System IV existed but never became commercially available.)

Currently, both System V and Berkeley UNIX have adapted much of the work that appears in the other. What remains are not really functional differences, but rather arbitrary differences, as if two brothers left home after high school and we compared them after ten years. We might find that they are both earning good money, but one might be married and the other single. One might like exotic cars, while the other prefers pickups. They would still both share strong resemblances to their parents, but not enough that their mother wouldn't notice if one of them tried to substitute for dad.

UNIX versions resemble brothers and fathers. Though a UNIX system may be based on some version of UNIX, this in no way implies that it is a subset (or even a superset) of that version. Each reseller is allowed to bundle and unbundle the software as it sees fit. Unbundling is popular with small systems. The user may not be interested in parts of UNIX (such as word processing, or program development) and may not have the disk space to store the stuff anyway. Many VARs completely rewrite parts of UNIX (the file system, for example) and then discard nonapplicable utilities (such as `fsck`).

As well as the Berkeley derivatives and AT&T derivatives, there are mixed breeds (like Apollo and Pyramid) of both Berkeley and AT&T, UNIX-like nonderivative derivatives, UNIX emulators and various combinations of each of these. Plus, there are systems like MS-DOS and OS/2 that are clearly not UNIX but have incorporated many UNIX features in them.

Trying to understand what is UNIX and what isn't is very difficult because of this diversity. It is the aim of the (unfortunately, many) standards committees to put an end to this tower of Babel. It is doubtful that this will result in a single universally accepted standard; however, some convergence is likely to occur (see the Future chapter).

There are over 100 companies offering UNIX, UNIX clones, UNIX emulators and UNIX-like operating systems on virtually every general purpose computer system from micros to supercomputers. Plus, there are several public domain UNIX systems (see the Underground chapter). It is possible to get more than one version for many popular computers. (At one point, there were five versions of UNIX available for the IBM PC.) This trend will undoubtedly continue. At the same time, there are several standards groups (see the section covering standards) that are trying to define what UNIX is, or perhaps what it was.

Fortunately, the differences between all these systems at the user level are slight. System V has gradually adopted many of the good things that were developed at Microsoft and Berkeley (gee whiz, talk about a cheap way of getting software development done). Significant differences lay at the programmers level. These can destroy the portability of the software.

2.6   Portability – Part I

One test of the differences and similarities between versions is the portability of applications. If you are an end-user of some UNIX-based product and the vendor has the same product running on both versions, then you probably don't care. If you are that vendor and you have to get your product running for that previously mentioned end user, you had better care, and take care when writing your product.

The most critical differences between UNIX versions (including Berkeley, System V and XENIX) are the areas which UNIX V7 never addressed such as real-time processing and networking.

Additionally, UNIX systems have diverged on points which UNIX V7 addressed but somewhat inadequately, such as interprocess communication, virtual memory, device control and signals.

Because of these differences, one cannot assume UNIX code written in C is portable. Writing portable software is a specialized activity that requires a lot of experience. It can be expensive and time consuming. Portability, like C, is not for everyone.

Bearing in mind the preceding discussion, it is still possible to write portable UNIX software. A particularly good tool in learning how to go about it is the book *Portable C and UNIX System Programming* from Rabbit Software. Following its guidelines will generally result in programs that easily port to most *reasonable* machines. But don't be ridiculous and complain when your Sinclair ZX81 with 1Kb doesn't run `troff`.

Of course, sometimes it is necessary to write nonportable software. Just make sure you advertise it as such. And at least make the effort to isolate the nonportable parts so that when the day comes when your software is moved to a new machine, it doesn't cause the poor programmers heart attacks when they look at your source code.

Ongoing standards work may help reduce the problems with portability. These are covered at length in the Future chapter. If and when these become official standards (and we all decide on the same one), it may be much easier to write code which is guaranteed to be portable.

2.7   Portability – Part II

A second aspect of portability is that UNIX itself is portable. This means that it works on a variety of machines from micros (the IBM PC and compatibles) to minis (PDP-11, Interdata), to superminis (VAX, 68000) to mainframes (Amdahl, IBM) to supercomputers (Cray). It has also been ported to machines with new and unusual architectures (RISC) as well as being co-resident with other operating systems (VM, VMS).

This was made possible in part because UNIX itself is written in the high-level C language which has also been ported to these machines. Most other operating systems have been written in assembler or a high-level proprietary language. Secondly, UNIX assumes little about the hardware underneath and makes few demands upon it. While this means it is possible to build faster systems than UNIX on a given piece of hardware, it also means that you will have an operating system that is much more reliable having been banged on for hundreds of man-years in many other machines. It also means that all your old applications will continue running. This is one of the reasons why UNIX provides an attractive market base, having been implemented on more different pieces of hardware than all other operating systems combined.

Besides running on many computers, UNIX supports many different peripherals. It also supports infinitely many kinds of terminals through either termcap or terminfo, systems for describing terminal capabilities in a high-level description. (See the section on terminal handling in the Programmer's Environment chapter.)

2.8   UNIX Licensing

Some of the most confusing areas of computers are the legal issues, including ownership and rights on software, hardware and firmware.   Many areas are not yet settled.   However, when it comes to UNIX, it pays to be cautious.   AT&T has staked out its turf.   It has secured patents, copyrights and trademarks on UNIX, its concepts, software and name.   And paying the lawyers in defense of an AT&T suit would probably bankrupt most companies. While AT&T has never taken a company to court, their lawyers have shown up on several doorsteps with suggestions for behavior modification.

AT&T's licensing fees for UNIX are quite confusing, varying across different machines, operating system releases, and number of users.   This is further complicated by third-party vendors and developers of UNIX.

Basically, there are two kinds of UNIX licenses, a source license and a binary license.   A source license buys the right to read the source, change it, recompile it and run it all on one machine.   Anything else costs extra (see below).   A source license includes the complete set of UNIX sources for one machine architecture.   AT&T has a small set to choose from.   A binary license buys the right to run UNIX on one machine (which includes some reconfiguration rights) and that's it.

The simplest type of license is a per-machine license, meaning that you can run UNIX on one CPU.   If you want to run the same exact UNIX on another CPU, you have to pay extra for it.   In fact, there are a number of extra charges depending upon other factors:

- The cheapest system is a single-user system.   A multiuser license costs more, and there are different plateaus.   (No, there is nothing that prevents you from running more users than you are licensed for – you are on your honor to keep this part of the contract.)

- You only get the source to one CPU-type.   If you want another, you have to pay extra for it.

- You only get the source to one version.   If you want another, you have to pay extra for it.

- You are not allowed to distribute the source or binaries to anyone. If you want to distribute the binaries (that contain AT&T proprietary code, such as a library), you must buy a distribution license (extra). If you want to distribute the source, you must pay extra for it, plus the seller must buy or have a UNIX license from AT&T corresponding to the version of UNIX that the source is from.

An excellent paper on UNIX licensing is available from /usr/group.

AT&T's Customer Communication Center will also attempt to explain UNIX licensing. Of course, since AT&T is the one who set it up in a most confusing manner, you should not expect it to be the most understandable source.

Fortunately, most people do not have to delve deeply into licensing trivia. If you buy a UNIX system for your own use, the seller generally includes the price of a UNIX license bundled with the system.

2.9   Buying UNIX

2.9.1   Making the Decision

Buying a UNIX system should be handled like buying any other computer system – with a clear, cool head. Experience helps a lot. If you have none, find other people who have systems. Even better, find people who have the same applications that you do and talk to them.

Don't be suckered by features, and especially by a salesperson's view. Ignore those benchmarks unless they are clearly for systems with similar hardware, and running your applications. Try to be application driven. Will the system do what you want? Is there an application that exists now to do what you want? Will the system meet your future needs?

Is the system compatible with other systems you own or use? Don't believe UNIX is portable until you've ported your programs and data. Realize all UNIX systems are not alike. The hardware differences are usually obvious - the software differences usually aren't.

It is nice to have a computer of your own to learn about it. But UNIX systems are expensive. And you may find out a UNIX system is overkill for what you need. If all you want to do is play games, a UNIX machine is probably not for you. Be honest with yourself. Why do you really need a computer?

See if you can borrow time on someone else's UNIX system. They are multiuser, so if you don't run big programs, many UNIX administrators will be accommodating if you explain your situation. Promise to use it only at night.

Sign up for a computer course at a local college or university. That will give you access to a UNIX machine for a whole semester.

2.9.2   The Mechanics

UNIX can be purchased in a number of ways. Unlike most programs, buying UNIX is particularly complex due to AT&T licensing requirements, as previously described.

AT&T holds the original trademark and copyrights to UNIX. Every copy sold is licensed either directly or indirectly through them. AT&T offers several different versions of UNIX (V7, System III, System V, for example). Each license is written for a particular machine or set of machines (designated by CPU), the number of maximum users, and whether it is a binary or source license. It is further qualified by the type of buyer one is (government, commercial, academic) and whether you plan to resell UNIX or include it in a product.

You probably won't deal with AT&T directly if you are buying a preconfigured version of UNIX. For example, XENIX is a licensed version of UNIX sold by Microsoft. You may buy XENIX directly from them, preconfigured for a PC and single-user operation with minimal sources.

UNIX vendors also unbundle UNIX tools and applications so that it is possible to buy, say, just the C development tools. Unbundling usually has the benefit of a lower price than that of a complete system. Because of this, however, you must be very careful to check that the system you are buying has the software components that you need. For example, if you ever expect to add a device driver, you will probably have to pay extra for the programs that allow you to rebuild UNIX.

If you are buying a UNIX look-alike, you are not paying for a UNIX license from AT&T and can expect such software to be less expensive. However, this is not always the case. Many UNIX cloners claim their products are completely rewritten, and deserve as much money as any real operating system. More in the cloner's favor is that their licensing rules are much less restrictive. For example, several UNIX look-alike systems provide the complete source with few restrictions on what you can do with it.

Unless you have bought your UNIX system directly from AT&T, you have become a customer of whatever company you purchased your system from. If you have questions or problems, you should speak to that company, not AT&T. The company will contact AT&T, if necessary.

2.10   The Dominant UNIX Sellers

UNIX is a licensed product of AT&T. Therefore, every version of the real thing is licensed from AT&T and based on an AT&T version. Now this doesn't mean it is making most of the sales, nor does it mean it is making the lion's share of the profits.

Indeed, at the beginning of 1987, Microsoft claimed that two-thirds of the 300,000 UNIX licenses worldwide were for XENIX, Microsoft's version of UNIX. Of course, most of the licenses were binary licenses, which are relatively cheap – on the order of $1 to $500. Buying even a relatively cheap UNIX box at say, $5,000, from a UNIX reseller which has to pay AT&T $100 per binary UNIX sale means that the reseller is getting the lion's share of the money. The reseller has probably bought the complete UNIX source code (around $45,000 in 1986), a one-time charge, so that has to be amortized over the income from each system sold.

Nonetheless, many computer companies have chosen to buy UNIX source code licenses, and become UNIX VARs (Value-Added Resellers). If a company sells 500 complete systems at $10,000 a piece, that amounts to a gross income of $5,000,000. Subtracting from that a $60,000 source licensing fee and the per-system binary fee of $100 times 500 still leaves a net of $4,890,000 to spend on glitzy packaging and a little value-added-development. The costs directly attributable to licensing on a per-system basis in this case would only be $220 or 2 percent of the final retail cost.

As we said earlier, Microsoft and SCO held the lead in the number of licenses sold to end-users. However, their market has in the past been aimed at the low-end single-user systems, while most other companies chose to cover high-end single-user systems or multiuser systems. ABC Corp. may have 500 UNIX users on PCs running XENIX each with their own copy of XENIX, while XYZ Corp. may have 500 UNIX users sharing five Crays. Clearly, licenses or copies of UNIX sold is not always a valid indication of number of users. We are constantly reminded of this whenever we see someone compare the number of UNIX licenses to the number of MS-DOS licenses. MS-DOS is in the millions, but each one is limited to a single-user system. (There are high-end multiuser XENIX systems, and multiuser MS-DOS-compatible systems, but these constitute a small fraction of the market.)

While Microsoft and SCO are the leaders in sublicensing agreements, AT&T is the leader in actual number of users. Informal surveys show that by number of users there is no majority; however, AT&T versions of UNIX (primarily System III and System V) account for approximately 35 percent of the market. So AT&T's claim that System V is "the standard UNIX" might be more accurately written as "the most popular standard UNIX."

System V UNIX is available on many machines. Unlike the XENIX ports, straight System V ports span the gamut from micros to supercomputers. However, XENIX and System V are slowly becoming the same thing. That is, many programs port with minor or no changes between XENIX and System V hosts. The percentage is constantly growing. AT&T and Microsoft have a binary standard for certain machines, meaning that programs will run without recompiling on both types of systems which use the same hardware.

There are hundreds of companies selling systems based on XENIX and System V. Some of the more well known include Apple (A/UX), Arete Systems Corporation (Arix), Databoard Inc. (D-NIX V), Hewlett-Packard Co. (HP-UX), IBM Corporation (IX and AIX). And while the X/OPEN effort is attracting the most attention in Europe, Japan's MITI (Ministry of International Trade and Industry) has clearly expressed its desire for development environments based on System V with Berkeley extensions.

If we add together XENIX's share of the market with AT&T's, it comes to about 44 percent of the market. What is left is primarily the Berkeley variants, the clones, and some specialized versions of UNIX.

Berkeley is the original source for all Berkeley versions of UNIX. It has distributed thousands of 1BSD and 2 (for PDP-11s) and 4BSD (for VAXen) since 1977. And it will continue this for the foreseeable future. The UNIX effort at Berkeley has attracted research grants, good students and faculty as well as raising the prestige of the computer science department. Even outside Berkeley, its UNIX dominates the research and future of the entire UNIX market because it is often the first place where new ideas appear.

It is possible to obtain UNIX directly from Berkeley, but this is a research product, not a commercial one. You will have to get support for it elsewhere. Furthermore, Berkeley does not provide (or even recommend) hardware, which you will have to obtain separately. Many companies have taken advantage of this void and offered software support (e.g., Mt. Xinu) or complete commercial systems (e.g., Sun, DEC, Wollongong) based on Berkeley UNIX. One notable company is Mt. Xinu. Since Berkeley does not support its own distribution, several Berkeley expatriates formed Mt. Xinu as a support group. It collects bugs and fixes, and redistributes them. Additionally, Mt. Xinu sells its own version (more/BSD) of Berkeley UNIX. Unlike Berkeley, Mt. Xinu will configure your UNIX for a large variety of devices and computers, easing some of the necessity of having a UNIX guru around.

There are fewer companies selling Berkeley ports than System V and XENIX ports. Nevertheless, these companies are doing quite well. Sun Microsystems, for example, is the leader in total workstations sold. This is illustrative of the market that Berkeley-based vendors have targeted. Their market is more oriented towards scientific/engineering/academic applications, which finds healthy acceptance of Berkeley's UNIX. They make up about 20% of the UNIX user base.

Some companies that sell Berkeley-based UNIX are: Convex Computer Corp., Digital Equipment Corp. (Ultrix), National Semiconductor (Genix), and Sony Microsystems. It is not surprising that fewer vendors support Berkeley UNIX. Berkeley's attitude toward support and future direction is not something that everyone is prepared to deal with. Furthermore, the system as delivered requires substantial modifications to make it into a commercial product. While BSD is definitely not a toy, it isn't cellophane wrapped either. Keen programmers don't seem to mind this. Indeed, Berkeley UNIX is more in tune with what many programmers want, and it follows that Berkeley UNIX flourishes in research institutions. But it is more work for companies to finish it off as a commercial product.

Like XENIX, there is much market pressure to merge Berkeley UNIX with System V. Unlike XENIX, however, Berkeley UNIX (at least at Berkeley) will remain distinctly different – forever a research project exploring new ideas, and necessarily incompatible approaches with existing systems. However, commercial implementations of Berkeley UNIX have tempered the original brashness of Berkeley UNIX. And we find that Berkeley UNIX is slowly merging with System V (just like XENIX).

Of course, some think the speed of this merging is akin to plate tectonics. Thus, many vendors have taken to offering multiple versions. Referred to as *dual universe* systems (coined by Pyramid), many vendors have ingeniously figured out how to supply systems that can run both Berkeley and System V programs. Some of these vendors are: Apollo Computer Inc. (DOMAIN/IX), Pyramid, Sequent Computer Systems, Inc. (Dynix), Sequoia Systems, Inc. (TOPIX), Sun Microsystems (SunOS), and The Wollongong Group (Eunice SV/BSD).

At the other end of the spectrum are vendors who have purposely sacrificed compatibility with AT&T's or Berkeley's UNIX, for one reason or another. For example, most commercial UNIX versions do not support real-time computation. In the past, this has meant that vendors of such products have had to make significant modifications to the UNIX system. Many have chosen simply to ignore compatibility problems resulting from such extensions. Since the only standards were old and weaker de facto standards, this was understandable.

2.11   The Dominant UNIX Hardware and Porters

It is possible to buy UNIX from any number of the porters if you have fairly common hardware. For example, in January 1987, it was possible to get UNIX for the PC/AT from Mark Williams (Coherent), Interactive Systems (IN/ix), Microport Systems, Inc. (System V/AT), Microsoft (XENIX Version 5.0), Opus Systems (Opus5), Prentice-Hall, Inc. (Minix), Quantum Software Systems Ltd. (QNX), Santa Cruz Operation, Inc. (SCO XENIX System V), VenturCom, Inc. (Venix System V), and Whitesmiths, Ltd. (IDRIS).

Additionally, there are many companies reselling these same systems for the PC with minimal changes. For example, IBM sells SCO's XENIX, Microsoft's XENIX and Interactive System's IN/ix.

The PC is a computer based on Intel CPU chips. These chips strike a good balance between dollar value and CPU power. On PCs using more powerful chips, such as the Intel 80386, they easily support the straightforward multiprocessing architecture presented by UNIX. These are typical of chip sets that have grown favor with UNIX vendors.

These chip sets are characterized by being relatively cheap and fast. They have good support for multiprocessing operating system architectures and the ability to address at least 2^{32} bytes of virtual memory. And, they can physically support at least 4Mb of physical memory. The following table lists some of the vendors selling UNIX or UNIX systems based on common chip sets.

Multiple Vendors Selling UNIX for Popular Chip Sets (c. 1987)		
Chip Set	Berkeley	System V and/or XENIX
Intel		Interactive, IBM, Opus, Norand, SCO, Microport, AT&T, Venix, Intel, Sphinx, Compaq, Microsoft, Altos, Systime, ITT, Lee Data, Scientific Micro Systems, Tandy, WiPro Information Tehnology
DEC	Eakins, Wollongong, Mt. Xinu, DEC, Berkeley	Interactive, Wollongong, NUXI
Motorola	Sun, Scandia Metric, Masscomp, Integrated Solutions, Apollo, Gould, Sony	Alcyon, Motorola, AT&T, Unisoft, Armstrong, Dual, Aston, HP, Integrated Micro Products, Scandia Metric, Masscomp, Sun, NCR, Heurikon, Isotron, Plexus, Convergent, Microbar, Sperry, PTL Software, Stride, Wicat, Counterpoint Computers, Tadpole Technology, Honeywell, Silicon Graphics, Apollo, Macq Electronique
NSC	NSC, Zaiaz, Competitive Computer Systems	Zaiaz, NSC, AT&T
Generic Ports	Berkeley	AT&T, SCO, Microsoft, Unisoft, Interactive

This table is a snapshot of UNIX offerings from early 1987. It is not complete. Rather, it is simply meant to illustrate that there were a large number of vendors offering UNIX systems on hardware based upon a very small number of different chip sets. Also, notice the large number of vendors that chose to use AT&T or XENIX over Berkeley UNIX.

UNIX has been implemented on just about every possible type of computer system. It would be pointless to list them all. For any given hardware, either the hardware manufacturer offers UNIX (sometimes in spite of having an already existing proprietary operating system), or a third-party vendor can provide it.

It may seem strange for a company to sell both UNIX and a proprietary operating system. But they do not necessarily compete with each other. Some operating systems specialize in an area that UNIX does not address. However, supporting two different operating systems is expensive, so most companies avoid it. Companies that started with a proprietary operating system have invariably extended support to UNIX. The demand is just too great to ignore, no matter what duplication of resources is required by the company to provide UNIX.

Some companies that provide both proprietary operating systems and UNIX for their hardware are DEC, IBM, HP, DG, Apollo, Amdahl, Microsoft, Intel, Motorola, Gould, Unisys, NCR, IBM, Data General, and Cray. There are hundreds of others.

Many new companies that started by offering systems beginning with UNIX do not have to worry about supporting a proprietary system. On the other hand, they do have to worry about the competition. Since they are using a common operating system, it is much easier for an unhappy user to simply pick up their code and move to another system that runs UNIX. Thus, UNIX vendors must be more responsive to their users.

Some companies that provide UNIX-based systems exclusively are Sun, Silicon Graphics, Wollongong, Unity, LPC, Venix, Multiflow, CAE/SAR, Convergent Technologies, MIPS, Pyramid, Ridge, MAD Intelligent Systems, and Fortune. Each of these companies has an edge in some respect. Some cover the low end of the market offering very good prices. Others offer unusual features such as real-time support, or support for multiple versions (Berkeley & System V).

Earlier we observed that most companies using the popular low-end UNIX chip sets were using System V or XENIX implementations. This does not generalize as we move into the proprietary one-of-a-kind hardware systems. One reason why is that early versions of System V and XENIX did not support the requirements of these hardware systems while Berkeley did, or could easily be made to do so. For example, Berkeley supported virtual memory for several years before it appeared in other commercial UNIX systems. This was an absolute requirement for applications that demanded systems with large memories, such as mainframes or superminis.

The last line of the preceding table lists companies producing generic ports, or ports to multiple architectures. Berkeley barely counts since it is not a commercial company, but it is the only one which continues to port Berkeley UNIX to many different architectures. The four companies listed on the right are responsible for the majority of implementations listed above them in the table, as well as many not listed.

Unisoft has produced the most ports, estimated at 65% of all of them. Unisoft calls its port "Uniplus+"; however, it has always been so closely based on the most recent AT&T version that we view it as one and the same.

SCO has done many ports including porting XENIX to the 8086. SCO and Microsoft have a joint agreement towards development of XENIX. SCO is the official second source of XENIX.

If you need UNIX ported to a new piece of hardware, you can contract directly with SCO, Unisoft, Microsoft, Interactive, AT&T or other porting houses. Porting UNIX to "reasonable" hardware might cost in the range of $100,000 and take three to six months. In contrast, most other operating systems cost ten times as much money and involve much longer times in development.

While all of these companies provide only System V ports, they all come "*with Berkeley enhancements*" such as the C-shell, job control and virtual memory management. For example, AT&T now supports the **vi** editor (which came from Berkeley) as the official editor of System V. Unfortunately, the phrase "*with Berkeley enhancements*" is not strictly defined, and thus you should inquire exactly what its interpretation is.

2.12   The Dominant UNIX Cloners

The UNIX-compatible (hereafter called simply "clone") market began even before AT&T sold its first copy of UNIX (see the History chapter). While many of the original reasons (e.g., lack of UNIX support) for clones have disappeared, some remain. For example:

- *Clones don't require an AT&T license. Clones don't have to follow AT&T pricing and licensing restrictions.*

While UNIX sublicenses are cheap enough to compete favorably with other operating systems, they are still an unnecessary expense for some companies. There are also some unusual licensing practices which make licenses inconvenient. For instance, the cost of a license differs depending upon how many users are using the system at any one time. Another example is that AT&T's source code may not be redistributed. Many other companies distribute code in source form, avoiding the problems of generating binaries for different types of computers.

  • *Clones can make nonstandard enhancements.*

AT&T has set extremely restrictive policies for conformance with System VR3. For example, vendors cannot make certain nonstandard enhancements. For areas of computing not addressed by UNIX (e.g., real-time processing), this creates a problem for a vendor. They can either not address a market, or not claim their product is UNIX.

Fortunately, other UNIX standards may provide the ability to classify products so that buyers can still intelligently compare UNIX with UNIX-like products and have some assurance of knowing the salient differences.

As we have stressed many times already, UNIX is just as much a philosophy as it is a licensed operating system. Many companies have capitalized on this by offering UNIX clones, compatibles, look-alikes, work-alikes, and so on. A large percentage of the market is served well by these UNIX compatibles. Some of the UNIX-compatible vendors are: Charles River Data Systems (UNOS), Concept Omega Corporation (Thoroughbred O/S), Cromemco, Inc. (Cromix), Flexible Computing Corporation (MMOS), Mark Williams Company (Coherent), Quantum Software Systems (QNX), and Whitesmiths, Ltd. (Idris).

2.13   The Dominant UNIX Customers

UNIX customers have changed significantly through the life of UNIX. Originally, they were groups internal to Bell Labs, and then they were quickly joined by educational institutions.

As many of the students raised on UNIX graduated, they took UNIX with them to computer companies and research institutions. And shortly after that the JAWS (Just Another WorkStation) wars brought UNIX to the mainstream for scientific users. Soon after that, inexpensive hard disks and large memory chips allowed Microsoft, Tandy and Interactive to make UNIX available on microcomputers, and UNIX invaded the low-end business market as well as the high-end personal computer market.

By 1985, all the larger companies including DEC, Amdahl, Data General and notably IBM offered UNIX. This essentially brought UNIX the rest of the way into the public eye. It is now everywhere, from Hollywood to Madison Avenue, from micros to superdupers. A quick scan of the UNIX Applications and UNIX Meets the Real World chapters will clue you in that UNIX solutions exist for all problems, and that UNIX has taken root in Wall Street offices and Uncle Joe's farm as quickly as at MIT.

More and more companies (General Motors, Ford, and so on) are mandating that most of their new computer purchases must be UNIX compatible. The U.S. federal government is also following this trend. We think many companies will make the same choice for a long time to come. It is interesting to consider the reasons.

U.S. Government

It's hard to ignore the world's biggest computer user – the U.S. government. In 1987, the annual budget for internal administrative processing alone was $17 billion. And that doesn't include computers for research and defense.

In 1986, 65 percent of the government's procurements were for UNIX. One reason that the government finds UNIX attractive is because procurements are done by function and price. A specification will state that, say, 17 functions are necessary. Specifications may not include brands unless there is an adequate justification. This functional type of specification tends to qualify UNIX machines, as they are perfectly adequate for most types of computer usage. And by comparison with most proprietary systems, they are cheaper.

The government plans to make use of the IEEE POSIX standard (see Standards section in Future chapter) in many future computer procurement specifications. POSIX is, of course, remarkably similar to UNIX.

Government Procurements

During 1988, the Department of Defense had several outstanding procurements for UNIX machines worth an estimated $4 billion. Spearheaded by one from the Air Force for 20,000 machines and another from the Army for 75,000, many other defense and civilian agencies opted in to these contracts using the same specifications. The prospect of landing such a contract made every UNIX vendor salivate, and read the specs *very* closely.

For more information on how the government buys UNIX, read "So You Want to Be a Government Contractor" in the September 1987 *UNIX World*. *Government Computer News* also carries major news on government procurements.

Computer Companies

Computer companies are different from other companies. They supply software and hardware for everyone else. They respond to market demands, and at the same time, try to press ideas of their own that they think are good, either for technical or market reasons.

We are now seeing the results of this. Most companies offer UNIX on their own systems. If they don't offer it, someone else will. Many older companies continue to offer alternative proprietary operating systems in the belief that they are better (although whether for the customer or the company is not always obvious). It is easy to lock users in, once they have made a big investment in nonportable software. At the same time, most vendors have complemented their proprietary operating systems with UNIX-like features. This is partially a marketing ploy, and partially because there are some good ideas that can be used in their own system by doing this.

Computer companies also faced the pressure of UNIX from within. While looking for employees in the '80s, most found that potential candidates knew more about UNIX than any other operating system. A company would go through a phase where the programmers insisted that they needed a UNIX machine to get their work done – to program – even if it was to develop their company's proprietary products! UNIX was often a better environment for programming than what the vendor offered on their own system. Rather than buying a competitor's system, the vendor would support the development of UNIX internally. Eventually the system would be offered to customers.

End Users

There are really two kinds of end users – those who do their own program development, and those who want turn-key systems.

End users with turn-key systems could care less if they are using UNIX or SomethingElseWare. They are application driven and will buy whatever operating system and hardware support their application needs. They won't use the UNIX shell, or any of the other UNIX utilities. The only kind of shells they want to see are the ones on the beach in Hawaii.

Thus, it may seem strange that users are buying turn-key systems that run on top of UNIX systems. After all, they are paying for a wonderful programming environment and not using it. Right? Not entirely. UNIX is now sold *unbundled*, meaning that it can be sold in separate pieces. In fact, according to SCO, around 80% of the XENIX systems do not include the development tools, such as the C compiler, `lex` and `yacc`. They are little more than UNIX-based executives (see the Real World chapter).

In some sense, these users are the most important ones of all. They are really using computers, unlike the rest of us who are "just" playing or experimenting or whatever it is we do on our programming workbenches. All of the things we discuss in the Application and Real World chapters are what these users do, from computer-aided design and engineering to manufacturing and point-of-sale transactions.

Unlike turn-key users, other end users are using the full power of UNIX – to develop their own specialized systems. As we mentioned earlier, many companies, including trend-setters like GM and Ford, have settled on UNIX for development and engineering systems. They know that the investment in UNIX will pay off in the future. Their software will continue to run as they upgrade to new hardware. They are not locked into one vendor for either hardware or software. And they can find a ready source of UNIX programmers in the field and from colleges and universities for many years to come.

Universities and Research Institutions

Interestingly, educational and research institutions are where UNIX is faced with more objective scrutiny than anywhere else. Students, faculty and researchers are continually exploring new ground – new operating systems – new realms where operating systems are not even meaningful.

These people have much less of a need to depend on the past and are the first to accept new technology with open arms, no matter how theoretical or pie-in-the-sky it appears. The payoffs in computing – whether cheaper, faster, or more stable – are enormous. Certainly enough so that new approaches are continually attempted.

It is indeed ironic that UNIX faces some of its heaviest criticism from the people who accepted it before anyone else. But that is to be expected. It was accepted only because other environments really were inferior to it. This is no longer the case.

Nonetheless, UNIX is now an accepted part of the educational system. Virtually all computer science departments in the U.S. have UNIX systems, and more students understand the concepts of UNIX than any other operating system – by a wide margin. UNIX is now the metric by which many operating systems are taught and judged.

Everyone

No one wants to be locked into a proprietary system. If you buy a computer using proprietary hardware or software, you must seek upgrades and support through channels that your vendor has approved. If you want to buy a faster machine running the same software, you're going to have to buy it from the same vendor. Too bad if it doesn't have one you like. Forget about competitive pricing.

While UNIX is licensed by AT&T, it is possible to find an implementation on virtually every computer system. At the same time, users want to unify their environment in an effort to reduce training and overhead support for different systems. These two goals conflict except in a standard system like UNIX.

Lastly, UNIX is a suitable system for doing the great majority of computer tasks. Distributed directly from AT&T, "virgin" UNIX is capable of performing most tasks with no modifications.

One reason for buying a non-UNIX system is that it runs an application which is dependent upon that operating system. However, this is an extreme disadvantage to application developers, since it effectively locks them into a smaller percentage of the market than is necessary. If an application is written to run under UNIX, the application can be ported to any computer because UNIX can be ported to any computer.

The pressures all point towards choosing a standard system. The buyers want it, the developers want it and the government demands it. Furthermore, the hardware people find that it opens up more avenues to the customers. UNIX is the only system that is standard enough, sophisticated enough, capable enough and common enough to meet the needs for such requirements.

Of course, new systems are being developed every day. Although it is unlikely that a new operating system will ever gain the popularity that UNIX has, systems other than UNIX will be bought and used. However, we claim that only systems decidedly superior to UNIX will survive its head start.

We may sound quite prejudiced, but that is not entirely accurate. We like UNIX more than other systems because we think it is better. However, we are very interested in using the best computer systems possible, and we don't care what operating system they run. (If we never use UNIX again, we will be quite happy.) However, it will take more than slick advertising to replace UNIX.

2.14   The Dominant UNIX Competitors

The truth of the matter is (and we shudder to think this), UNIX is not the dominant operating system in the world. Most of the major computer vendors offer proprietary operating systems. Some of these systems are geared for particular applications, such as large databases, fault-tolerant operation and real-time applications.

It has been said that *"UNIX is supported by IBM, like a hanging man is supported by rope."* IBM does indeed sell UNIX-based systems, but it is clear that it is not particularly interested if UNIX succeeds. Open systems like UNIX destroy the ability of vendors to lead customers their way.

IBM's success in the past has been in keeping proprietary systems closed, and forcing its customer base to follow them. Monopolistic business practices were used to lock customers to proprietary products, even in the face of equivalent or superior products from competitors. This was well documented in the multiple antitrust suits brought against IBM.†

Many other computer companies have studied IBM closely and learned their lessons well. Indeed, many of them are more competent than IBM. IBM does not have an operating system that runs across their entire line of machines, nor are their operating systems considered technically superior. IBM has only opened the doors to UNIX, and reluctantly so, because of incredible market demand.

Another vendor in a similar position is DEC. Discussed at length in the previous chapter, DEC managed to ignore UNIX for several years while customers bought their machines, left DEC's operating system on the unread tapes, and brought up Berkeley UNIX. In response, DEC refused to support the machines running UNIX. If UNIX reported a machine fault, DEC wasn't interested unless you ran its operating system and diagnostic programs to find it.

VMS, DEC's operating system for their VAX line of computers, is a typical example of an operating system that competes against UNIX. VMS attempts to be all things to all people – it is quite a bit more complex than

---

† Richard T. DeLamarter, *Big Blue: IBM's Use & Abuse of Power*, Dodd, 1986.

UNIX. At the same time, it lacks the ease and programmer orientation of UNIX. After watching their market drift away to UNIX, DEC finally began offering many of the UNIX tools for VMS, including **make**, **sccs** and a UNIX shell.

VMS was not designed to be portable and only runs on the VAX architecture. (Large parts of it are written in assembler.) Unless a vendor duplicates most of the VAX hardware, running VMS is essentially impossible. Porting VAX/VMS programs to other machines is extremely difficult because of the resulting VAX and VMS dependencies in the code.

Interestingly, DEC has announced its intention to produce a POSIX-compatible VMS. No matter what its argument, we take this as a sign that it has realized the utility of the UNIX environment. It is not going to be easy, but it looks like the way of the future for DEC and many other vendors in the same position. Proprietary systems are becoming the dinosaurs of a past age.

Our last examples are DOS and OS/2. DOS is an operating system for the IBM PC family and compatibles. It is reasonably adequate as a successor to the primitive CP/M; however, it doesn't stand up well to modern demands.

DOS is single tasking, meaning that it cannot run two programs simultaneously. It has many inherent restrictions such as a maximum of 64Kb memory segments and 32Mb disk partitions. And it is dependent upon a small family of microprocessors, meaning that you are locked into the DOS world. Anyone who believes DOS to be an "open system" is kidding themselves.

OS/2 is an up-and-coming replacement for DOS. Unfortunately, it won't run on the older PC equipment, nor will your DOS programs run in the normal OS/2 protected mode. You pay a heavy price for such a "replacement."

On the other hand, OS/2 is multitasking and has far fewer arbitrary restrictions than DOS had. OS/2 has virtually all of the features that UNIX has including pipes, signals, forks and a hierarchical file system. It also has all of the newer features such as common memory and semaphores. Plus it comes with built-in support for multithreaded processes and other things that were never bundled with UNIX.

Of course, to support all this requires the bulk of a UNIX kernel and utilities plus whatever extra OS/2 needs. OS/2 requires 2Mb of main memory, but is more comfortable with 4Mb. 20Mb disks are as uncomfortable for OS/2 as they are for UNIX. 75Mb disks or larger networked disk servers are a necessity.

OS/2 looks very much like UNIX. The system calls are very similar (in a theoretical sense). The level that the programmer sees borrows most of the UNIX environment, just as DOS tried to borrow as much as it could. It is not hard to write programs that are portable between OS/2 and UNIX. However, it is also easy not to, particularly because OS/2 is designed for one hardware architecture. Nonportable code will have the same problem that DOS code had – hardware dependencies. Gee, we haven't learned anything, have we? In fact, it's even worse, since OS/2 only runs on PS/2 systems and IBM is trying much harder to prevent PS/2 cloning. Once again, the result is nonportable applications and systems – a closed system.

What about the Apple Macintosh? Well, the Macintosh can hardly be called a competitor. Apple's A/UX operating system for the Mac II is UNIX with an Apple front-end. This could only help UNIX for the future. (See the Future chapter for more about this.)

Chapter 3: UNIX Future

"If it keeps up, man will atrophy all his limbs but the push-button finger."
– Frank Lloyd Wright

It has been said that we may not know it but our toaster at home may already be running UNIX. While this is rather unlikely, the primary reason is not one of overkill, but rather of licensing costs (since the cost of a UNIX license would probably quadruple the final cost of the toaster). Nonetheless, with UNIX standards obviating licenses and UNIX systems in ROM, it may yet happen. So if you detect a funny smell over your coffee one morning, be sure and check the toaster for a burnt core dump.

Where do we go from here? What does our crystal ball reveal out in the not so distant 20 minutes into the future? Well for one thing, an incredible amount of activity. No longer the domain of a few long-haired, t-shirt wearing hackers, UNIX is out in the real world. Heaven help us. Real live businesses actually do things like manage accounts and keep databases with important data on UNIX machines. Aside from the industrial strengthening of the system, what of the new environments and the capacity to change, distribute and innovate? Stay tuned...

3.1   Standards

"The nice thing about standards is...there are so many to choose from!" – Anon.

In 1984, /usr/group successfully completed work on the "1984 /usr/group Standard." The standard defined a subset of System III kernel and library calls plus a record-locking primitive. It was immediately ignored and, for all practical purposes, useless. The problem was that /usr/group had tried to standardize an area that was still rapidly evolving. At that time, Version 7 UNIX was still popular. But BSD had made substantial changes, and AT&T had recently reentered the picture with System III. Even worse, the UNIX compatibles were springing up everywhere. Was XENIX UNIX? Was Coherent UNIX? Was anything UNIX?

Since that time, there have been no successful standards set in either UNIX or C, although as this book is being completed (early 1988), it appears that we will be seeing some useful standards set in the near future. In the meantime, there are several de facto standards which are being used while being pushed for adoption as real standards.

While not so directly related, many non-UNIX standards bear impact on UNIX users. For instance, if you are building a network of UNIX systems, you should pay attention to communication standards, since you will have to deal with equipment following one or another of these networking standards. This is typical of the hundreds of standards that are not UNIX standards but are clearly of interest to UNIX users. Unfortunately, we cannot possibly attempt to cover all standards that indirectly relate to UNIX. Instead, we discuss the standards that directly impact us all, namely the UNIX and C standards.

If you have access to Usenet, you may keep current on UNIX standards issues by reading the USENIX-sponsored moderated newsgroup `comp.std.unix` or the mailing list `std-unix@uunet.uu.net` or `uunet!std-unix`. (Send requests to be added to the list to `std-unix-request`.) Most of the standards organizations have members who read and contribute to this forum.

3.1.1   C Standards

K&R

The C Programming Language (First Edition) by Brian Kernighan and Dennis Ritchie was the first book written about C. It included a reference manual for the language, which came to be accepted as the standard for "*K&R* C", after the authors.

Fortunately, *K&R* was extremely well written and left few dark corners in the language definition. However, there were several inherent problems in the design of *K&R* C. Furthermore, the language had many commonly accepted extensions that were not described in *K&R* (e.g., enumeration types).

In a way, *K&R* was a little like the *Bible*. There were the fundamentalists, who used the book faithfully when implementing C. There were the spokespersons who reinterpreted the divine teachings, producing an admittedly "not quite *K&R* C." There were the heretics who grossly misstated the issues, producing mongrel dialects that they passed off as C, confusing inexperienced programmers to no end. And of course, there were the new-age cultists offering us C++ and other alternative dogmas for salvation.

PCC

While *K&R* left little doubt on most issues, there was yet a higher authority available – the C compiler itself. When UNIX ran on PDP-11s, there was indeed only one C compiler – Dennis Ritchie's compiler. The *Ritchie C Compiler* was used from UNIX V4 through V7.

As interest in UNIX and C increased, several new C compilers were written, both in and outside the Labs. Of particular note was one by Steve Johnson. His C compiler was specifically designed for portability and was called the *Portable C Compiler*, or **pcc**. In contrast, the Ritchie C Compiler was not particularly portable. It had clearly been modeled for the PDP-11. And while it was reliable and produced efficient PDP-11 code – indeed, better than **pcc** – **pcc** became the standard C compiler for many systems, including System V and BSD.

The Future is Hard to Predict

The original expectation of Prentice-Hall was that an average of nine copies of *K&R* would be sold to the 130 UNIX sites that existed at the time the book was first published. By January 1988, over a million copies of the First Edition had been printed!

pcc was distributed with UNIX for several years and was used as the primary model for C compiler ports to many other machines. Thus, C compilers on different machines behaved remarkably similarly to one another. Even **pcc**'s bugs were propagated consistently!

When there was a question as to correct behavior, the answer was to see how **pcc** handled it. Unfortunately, when it was clearly wrong, you had to face the question of whether to be consistent and wrong, or inconsistent and right.

The answer, of course, was that there was no absolute right way. Each answer had its advantages and disadvantages. And after a while, it was impossible to be right or consistent, no less both. New C compilers were being written all the time. The popularity of C grew substantially when compilers for CP/M and MS/DOS became available. C was ported to many other non-UNIX environments and used for many applications that it was never designed for.

It is inevitable that there would be more and more disagreements over the definition of the C language. Analogous pressures have been placed on the libraries, although the strong bias in C applications towards UNIX has kept them fairly cohesive. However, there are so many people using the C language now, and so many companies requiring C compilers, that a real standard which is accessible to everyone is called for.

ANSI X3J11

To cure the quandary of multiple C languages, the ANSI X3J11 committee has taken on the task of defining a C standard. The aim is to produce a complete and unarguable definition of the language, with the goal of increasing portability. The result will be less guesswork, both when writing new C applications, and when creating new C compilers.

Of course, believing that a standard will cure all the world's problems is somewhat naive. While standards have their benefits, there are drawbacks as well. For example, standards may not allow easy use of a vendor's proprietary enhancements. Standards can also discourage the adoption of new and better designs.

The primary concern of the X3J11 committee is to codify the C language as it exists today with some very minor extensions. The committee has taken the wise tactic of attempting to standardize existing conventions and practices wherever possible rather than coming up with new conventions.

The committee will not fix design errors in the language because that would break a lot of code. (So don't bother suggesting that it change = to := and == to =.) It will not define too many extensions because then no one would have conforming compilers. X3J11 will simply define C rigorously, as it exists, warts and all. For a copy of the standard or information relating to it, contact Global Engineering Documents.

If you want to fix, improve or add to the C language, you would be well advised to look at C++. This will undoubtedly go through the same standards process in a few years that C is going through now.

ISO WG14

ANSI is an American standards organization. It is politically undesirable for many non-American companies to follow American standards, so the ISO (International Organization for Standardization) is also creating a C standard. It is not trying to be different; rather, it exists only to make the ANSI standard acceptable to many non-American countries and companies. The ISO standard is purely a political convenience.

Officially called the ISO TC97 SC22 WG14, the ISO Working Group on C is trying to ensure that its standard is identical to that of ANSI X3J11. It would be a tremendous failure if the ANSI standard could not satisfy the ISO, resulting in two C standards.

3.1.2   UNIX Standards

The area of UNIX standards does not fare as well as that of C standards. This is because UNIX is much more complex, and it was never defined as rigorously (see the source). In a sense, UNIX's extensibility is its own Achilles heel. Because it has been so easy to modify, virtually every company that resells UNIX has made its own extensions to it. At the same time, the concept of application code portability must survive if UNIX is to remain as attractive as it is.

The UNIX standards will undoubtedly come to pass despite the many variants of the system, simply because of the amount of money that is at stake. No standards mean large amounts of time and money wasted porting software. It also means that UNIX vendors cannot be assured of meeting competitive bids for products that require a particular brand of UNIX.

Interestingly, there are several different bodies developing UNIX standards. It remains to be seen which will turn out to be the most influential. It is possible that some of them may merge standards together. (For instance, both AT&T and X/OPEN have expressed their intent for their standards to be POSIX conforming.) Although this can lead to a much more complicated standard, the fewer standards the better.

Currently, there are many organizations attempting to produce UNIX standards. Each standard is different, as each organization has different goals in mind. None of these standards attempts a complete definition of UNIX, as it is still evolving. Thus, there are smaller but additional proposed standards for subsystems (e.g., windows, network file systems, and so on) in addition to the first three mentioned.

POSIX

Based on the 1984 /usr/group Standard, POSIX is a standard being developed by ANSI and IEEE. The full name of POSIX is the IEEE P1003 Portable Operating System Interface for Computer Environments. POSIX defines a UNIX-like system by a set of system calls, libraries, tools, and some other interfaces. While there are many things not defined by POSIX, it has the narrowest scope of the standards discussed. This is not necessarily bad, since a least common denominator can support a large percentage of UNIX code without extensions.

```
P1003.0 — POSIX Guide
P1003.1 — Systems Interface
P1003.2 — Shell and Tools Interface
P1003.3 — Verification and Testing
P1003.4 — Real Time
P1003.5 — Ada Binding for POSIX
P1003.6 — Security
```
Parts of P1003 (POSIX)

Most of the U.S. UNIX developers have announced their support of the POSIX effort, and many have representatives participating in the standardization process.

The POSIX effort is also supported by NBS (U.S. National Bureau of Standards). NBS has already produced a FIPS that is based on the 1003.1 effort. They did not wait for the final form, due to pressure from various federal agencies for a standard (of any kind). It is likely that when POSIX is finalized, the NBS FIPS will be revised to meet it.

NBS provides a test suite for conformance testing. It is expected that most government procurements for UNIX systems will require POSIX compatibility. It is likely that the U.S. government will base several multibillion dollar procurements on the POSIX standard. With this kind of incentive, we expect vendors to pay a lot of attention to POSIX.

POSIX has also been recommended as an international standard to ISO. The draft proposed standard name is TC22 WG15.

For more information about the IEEE Portable Operating System standard, contact the IEEE Computer Society and ask for the "1003.1 Posix Full Use Standard." For more information about TC22 WG15, see TC22 WG15 in the addresses Appendix.

SVID

AT&T has its own UNIX standard, called SVID (System V Interface Definition). It is also referred to as the *purple book* (the color of its cover). The SVID is more comprehensive than POSIX and defines more libraries and command interfaces. Not blind to government dollars, it is expected that AT&T will make sure that its standard is upwards compatible with POSIX. AT&T provides conformance testing for its standard. SVVS (System V Verification Suite) is a test suite which will verify if a system complies with SVID.

Beginning with System V Release 3, AT&T took a very strict approach with its standard, tying the use of the name "UNIX System V R3" to SVID conformance. In particular, any system which claims to be "System V R3 based," "System V R3 compatible" or even including "System V R3 enhancements" must comply with the SVID "base system." This can be a problem for vendors who want to modify the system in certain ways. For example, adding some of the Berkeley enhancements can produce a noncompliant UNIX. Many vendors who sold modified releases of earlier AT&T UNIX are faced with the choice of either removing extensions (and causing problems for their customers) or not upgrading to the latest releases of System V. Of course, there is nothing to prevent vendors from incorporating parts of SVR3, but not claiming SVR3 conformance.

Another disadvantage to SVID is that it is not a vendor-independent standard. Clearly AT&T has an advantage over every other company that uses AT&T's standard. While AT&T has not been known to make capricious changes, there is nothing to prevent them from doing so. And it is unlikely that the SVID will not grow to accommodate any change necessitated by a new release of System V. Indeed, if SVID tracks System V rather than the reverse, all the other System V-compatible vendors will continually be one step behind AT&T in their effort to be compatible. For these reasons and the ones given in the previous paragraph, vendors may market SVID-compatible products, but choose not to advertise them as such.

For more information about the AT&T SVID, contact the AT&T Customer Information Center.

X/OPEN

By far the most encompassing standard is that of X/OPEN. This is a standard produced by representatives from many European companies as well as U.S. companies (including AT&T) and is the best contender for an international standard. X/OPEN is based on SVID and is a superset of POSIX. However, it also defines many libraries, command interfaces, the C language, indexed sequential access method (ISAM), the SQL database language, and several extensions for international use of UNIX. Of course, X/OPEN has a test suite, too. It is called XVS for X/OPEN System V Specification.

For more information about the X/OPEN standards, contact Elsevier Science Publishers Co., and ask for the *X/Open Portability Guide*.

WeirdNIX

In a rather open-minded moment, the P1003 committee ran a contest, called WeirdNIX, to find problems with the POSIX standard. Contestants competed by submitting the "most demented" legal interpretation of the POSIX standard which violated the intuitive intent. First prize was an HP calculator and mention in the standard itself. Who ever said standards are dull?

As we said earlier, there are many related standards, de facto standards and working groups that are of interest to UNIX users. Besides the ones already listed, some other important ones are:

Networking Standards

TCP/IP – Contact Arpanet Network Information Center.
OSI – Contact International Organization for Standardization (ISO).
GM MAP/TOP – Contact General Motors, Corp.
PN1 – Contact /usr/group Working Group on Network Interface.

Windowing Standards

X Windows – Contact Massachusetts Institute of Technology.
NeWS – Contact Sun Microsystems, Inc.
/usr/group – Contact /usr/group Working Group on Graphics/Windows.

Network File Systems

NFS – Contact Sun Microsystems, Inc.
RFS – Contact AT&T Customer Information Center.
/usr/group – Contact /usr/group Working Group on Distributed File
                       Systems.

Internationalization

JAE – Contact the AT&T Customer Information Center.
X/Open – Contact Hewlett-Packard, Co.
/usr/group – Contact /usr/group Working Group on Internationalization.

/usr/group also has a number of other working groups:

/usr/group Working Group on Realtime
/usr/group Working Group on Database
/usr/group Working Group on Performance Measurements
/usr/group Working Group on Security
/usr/group Working Group on Super Computing

3.2   Merging System V with BSD with XENIX

Whether or not UNIX definitions are standardized, there will be products that become de facto standards. This happens a lot with UNIX because there are a small number of UNIX developers that resell UNIX to a large number of VARs.

The largest developer is clearly AT&T. Everything they do has potential for impact on the future of UNIX. (Actually, there are several developers in this position, including IBM, Sun, Microsoft and major research institutions such as Berkeley.)

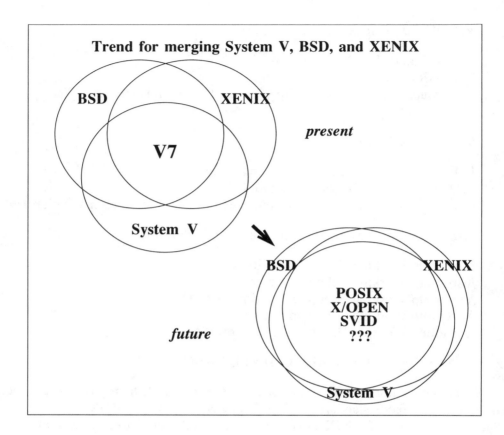

AT&T is clearly trying to incorporate important features of XENIX and BSD into System V. They have made agreements with the major XENIX and BSD vendors to produce unified versions of UNIX. We expect this effort to succeed. Other vendors (see the Real World chapter) have already done this and it has proven very popular. If AT&T provides a unified version of UNIX, this will undoubtedly become more prevalent than any other UNIX.

3.3   Mach

As we have mentioned, many people have made extensions to UNIX. One of the most important, in terms of the future of UNIX, is Mach. Mach is a modern version of UNIX. Mach was specifically designed to support multiprocessor and parallel computation while retaining the features of UNIX. With a completely rewritten kernel, Mach is potentially a UNIX for the next generation.

Like UNIX, Mach is designed to be portable. It does not require a specific machine feature (such as a memory management unit or a LAN). And because the kernel communicates by message passing, Mach can deal with multiprocessor architectures as easily as uniprocessor architectures. What Mach does is to provide a consistent model of communications and multitasking primitives, upon which can be built higher-level models such as common memory or message-passing communications. Mach can be thought of as a "UNIX brought up to date" with modern computer operating system principles. We think it will become a very popular base for multiprocessor UNIX systems.

Mach was developed at Carnegie-Mellon University where research continues today. Mach is able to run 4.3 BSD UNIX object code without modification, as well as supporting its own environment.

Mach has been ported to more than a dozen dissimilar computer systems, including the IBM RT, the Sun 3, the 16-processor MultiMax, the 30-processor Sequent Balance 21000, and nine members of the DEC VAX family of uniprocessors and multiprocessors. An implementation of Mach for the BBN's Butterfly Parallel Processor is discussed in depth in "Variations on UNIX for Parallel-Processing Computers" by Channing Russell and Pamela Waterman in *Communications of the ACM*, vol. 30, no. 12, December 1987.

And the best part of all, is that Mach is available free from CMU (although you need a System V and Berkeley license). It is copyrighted, however, and no one is allowed to resell it without permission. You can read more about Mach in "Mach: A New Kernel Foundation for UNIX Development" by Accetta, Baron, Bolosky, Golub, Rashid, Tevanian and Young, in *Proceedings of Summer USENIX*, July 1986.

3.4   Berkeley 4.3 and BRL

Research on UNIX continues at Berkeley though at a much slower rate than before. With the release of 4.3 BSD (Berkeley Software Distribution), many of the people instrumental in the creation of the Berkeley work have tired after working for several years at student wages with few benefits other than recognition at UNIX conferences. Many formed startup companies to sell UNIX products. Others went to work for large UNIX-hungry companies that were paying high salaries. And a few even went back to school and graduated.

While Berkeley will continue to produce new releases of BSD, albeit at a slower rate than in the past, many companies have stepped forward to pick up the reins. One interesting development is that the Department of Defense (which funded Berkeley's 4BSD research) has decided to fund the Army's Ballistic Research Labs (BRL) so that it can maintain BSD UNIX. Maintenance and support was something that Berkeley never provided. BRL is well known for having provided many bug fixes to the Berkeley releases. BRL has also rereleased the Berkeley 4.2 code with a System V compatibility package. BRL has also released a version of 4.3 BSD and is continuing work on it.

3.5   Changing Technologies

The future of UNIX will, to a certain extent, be governed by the future of computer science. New computer architectures that are being created and refined, such as multiprocessors, will suggest new environments for UNIX. UNIX is extending its influence throughout the range of computing hardware from supercomputers to micros. As new ones are being designed, UNIX is being ported to them. And while UNIX may never run on certain specialized hardware, such as neural nets, UNIX will certainly contain an interface to one as a peripheral.

At the same time as micros grow smaller and even more capable, super-computers grow even faster, approaching incredible speeds. The possibility of room-temperature superconductors, for example, will increase the processing rate of our fastest computers many-fold.

We will see workstations capable of 100MIPS performance in a desktop package by 1992. As memory package size decreases, we can expect that these workstations will have memory on the order of 100Mb and a small local disk of, say, 500Mb. This will enable the use of *really* smart interfaces, such as natural language understanding systems that replace the old-style shell, and AI problem solvers which use the tools optimally, or replace them with more appropriate tools dynamically.

Larger computers such as mainframes and network servers will have even larger physical memory sizes than workstations. And disk storage of network servers will easily be in the multiple Tb range. By using WORM (Write-Once Read Many) optical disk technology, backups will be continuous.

3.6   User-Friendly UNIX – The Macintosh/Smalltalk Influence

If UNIX is to survive into the next decade, we are going to have to do something about its user interface. From day 1, UNIX was designed to be used by programmers and not by naive users. This has changed little. And although there are menu-oriented shells, window systems, and other aids on many UNIX systems, the UNIX tools are still an essential ingredient in using UNIX effectively.

And that is what makes UNIX a poor comparison in this age of user-friendly interfaces. UNIX does not stand up well to comparisons with slick front-ends like the Apple Macintosh finder or Xerox's Smalltalk browser. And it is clear that the world is headed towards this kind of interacting.

UNIX revolves around pipes and filters. Take the output of one program and feed it into another program. Hook a bunch of programs together that don't know anything about each other.

The Macintosh model, on the other hand, is the exact opposite. The system doesn't deal with character streams. Data files are extremely high level, usually assuming that they are specific to an application. When was the last time you piped the output of one program to another on a Mac? (Good luck even finding the pipe symbol.) Programs are monolithic, the better to completely understand what you are doing. You don't take MacFoo and MacBar and hook them together.

Undoubtedly, we will see implementations of Mac-like front-ends on top of UNIX systems. Indeed, the Mac II running A/UX (Apple's release of UNIX System V with Berkeley enhancements and NFS) holds great promise for integrating the best of the UNIX and the Macintosh worlds. We can't wait to hypercard our way through file systems with a mouse, looking at pictures of garbage cans, tape drives and shells.

The object-oriented model presented by Smalltalk is much closer to UNIX ideas, although UNIX doesn't do it as well (or to such extremes) as Smalltalk. Think of UNIX I/O as a good example. You can write data to a disk, tape, or frisbee, and the individual driver takes care of the work. But, `write()` works the same way in every case.

Smalltalk's front-end ("the browser") enables navigation through huge unknown environments. As UNIX incorporates more and more tools, interfaces, and ... well, uh ... crud, it becomes very difficult for anyone to master, no less a new user. Browsing through capabilities – picking and choosing what to look at or what to use – is going to be the only way of staying on top of the massive choices that UNIX presents us with in the future.

Until then, we will have to make do with doldrums of reality. While making all sorts of incredibly complex pipelines, shell scripts and combinations of 20 processes to implement a spell-checker, we will continue to dream about a vision of personal computing with integrated audio, video and communications expressed so well by Alan Kay's Dynabook.†

3.7   C++

C++ is a language based on C. However, it is definitely a new language. The name is a pun on the C increment operator (++), which when applied to a variable gives you one greater. Hence C++ sounds like it is the next release of C.

C is actually an old language. From the day it was born, many people have tried to improve it. However, it was so precisely described by *K&R* that it has resisted most of those suggestions and has evolved very little. The evolutionary steps it has taken are minor. They are described by Larry Rosler in the "The Evolution of C – Past and Future," *AT&T Bell Laboratories Technical Journal*, vol. 63, no. 8, October 1984. The ANSI C standard is the next step in the maturity of C.

C++ is an attempt at producing a language which retains all the good ideas of C while adding many more new ones. In fact, C++ is upwards compatible with C, meaning all C programs will compile in C++. (Well, almost all.) While some faults of C remain due to the desire to retain compatibility, many have been fixed.

C++ really is a superior language to C. Among C++'s most notable features are better type checking, better facilities for data abstraction, operator overloading, and built-in support for object-oriented programming. The result is a language that is much easier to use than C. C++ retains much of the flavor of C, and can still be used for system implementation. But it is easier to structure code. You are less likely to produce buggy code. You can reuse subroutines more easily, and the resulting code has a better chance of being more efficient.

Implementations of C++ are characteristically written as preprocessors to a C compiler. However, there is nothing inherent about this in the definition. C++ is available from a number of vendors (see the Applications chapter). You can find more information about the language in the book *The C++ Programming Language* by Bjarne Stroustrup (who designed the language while at Bell Labs).

---

†Alan Kay and Adele Goldberg, "Personal Dynamic Media", *IEEE Computer*, March 1977, 31-41.

While implementations of C++ have actually been available since 1983, we think it will be some time before the majority of C programmers will move to it. However, we hope that at some point, most C programmers will accept this new language as their own. (There are alternatives such as Ada and Modula-2, but we think C++ has a much better chance of capturing the audience of programmers and applications that C currently has.)

3.8   The Networking Influence

The boundaries between machines are disappearing. Networking software provides us with the illusion that the our local resources are those of our local area network. Currently we simply mount another network disk whenever we need more space or access to a file that isn't local. In the future, all disks will appear as a global resource. We don't really care where our data is as long as we have easy and reliable access to it. By easy, we mean that the access procedures are identical to the ones we've been using for local disks and devices. Reliable may mean that there are multiple copies distributed at various servers. A similarly analogy holds for processes. If we need more cycles, we obtain some from another machine. The future will remove even more boundaries so that our domain encompasses *wide* area networks. The concept of *local* area networks is a prehistoric hangover from the early days of networking. Its boundaries and limitations no longer relate to our interest in communications.

The trend toward network-wide resources is attractive from many points of view not the least of which is cost. If we need only buy one expensive peripheral and easily use it from any place on the net, we can save lots of money. We have done this with printers and tape drives for years. Now it is easy to do the same thing with other types of peripherals. For example, it is possible to have a database machine attached to the network as the base of a distributed data system. Another possibility is a one-of-a-kind supercomputer as a back-end compute-engine.

The U.S. Defense Department's Arpanet was an experiment in expensive computer resource sharing. It was successful, but in ways that were totally unexpected. For example, the original implementation never called for more than several hundred computers to be on a single network. And the design did not allow for more than a small number of networks. Now there are thousands of networks, not to mention hundreds of computers on many of the networks.

The design specifications for the original Internet (as the Arpanet is now referred to) have been revised many times to handle the tremendous explosion of internetworked computers. While the Arpanet continues to face the ever increasing number of computers that want to communicate, there are many projects that are attempting to face the problems of scale, with the expectation that there will be no limit to future growth.

Two research efforts that intentionally decided to address the problem of scale in UNIX are Project Athena of MIT, and the Andrew system of Carnegie-Mellon's Information Technology Project. Each of these is building networks with tens of thousands of UNIX computers, and many more users. What happens when you have a password file with 100,000 entries? Can you access your files as if they were locally resident from any workstation on the campus? In the world? Does being the superuser on one machine entitle you to be superuser on others? Which others? These are just some of the questions faced by these projects. Answers to these questions and hundreds of others, have the potential for repercussions in many UNIX concepts.

3.9   Portables and Laptops

So you and your UNIX workstation are integrated into your local area network, and you share files and peripherals with your coworkers across the corridor. But what do you do if you need to take to the road?

Formerly, the only option for travelers was to travel with a portable terminal, and use telephone lines to connect to a larger system at home. The first *transportable* computer systems were microcomputers weighing 20 lbs or more (some people called them "luggables") and costing about $10,000. (Technically, the most accurate definition of a transportable is that it is a machine that is easily moved from place to place. Unfortunately, this is a useless working definition.) In 1985, Hewlett-Packard introduced the first transportable UNIX machine. It cost $5,000 and had the operating system in 500K of ROM.

Portables were distinguished from transportables by weighing less than 20 lbs, and having minimal setup time. Portables under 10 lbs are often referred to as *laptops* because they are light enough to rest on your lap for long periods of time. Some portables are also battery powered, allowing use on, for example, airplanes. However, while many of us have gotten used to writing articles at 35,000 feet, debugging a new kernel modification seems like something better left for the calm and cool environment of a hacker's basement.

Portables were originally the realm of primitive operating systems like CP/M and DOS, but continuing advances in technology have provided the means to support a UNIX environment on such a system. Low-power memory chips are available that provide 4Mb of memory in a compact module. Physically small disks now have large enough capacities that they can hold all of the UNIX systems. CD-ROMs can store immense databases, be carried in a shirt pocket, and popped into your portable as easily as a floppy. Lightweight plasma and LCD displays provide bitmapped screens for multiple windows.

Naturally, there are many companies offering laptop UNIX systems including Grid Systems Corp., Hewlett-Packard, and Toshiba America Inc. It is also possible to buy UNIX on many of the laptop systems designed for DOS and built with adequate processors such as the Intel 80386 or the Motorola 68020. With their small screens and keyboards, laptops are not for everyone. But if the system is compact, lightweight and can handle being jolted about, it will be welcome on a trip. However, we are still waiting for a system that has an inflatable keyboard and display. But we know as soon as we put our money down, they will be made obsolete by neural wetware devices embedded in your shoulder.

The future of portable systems seems clear. They will continue to decrease in price and weight. They will increase in power and functionality. Lastly, expected future increases in data transmission rates over dialup lines will provide portables with the ability to network with geographically distant LANs.

Where'd it get that number?

The naming convention followed at Bell Labs is to name the version according to the edition number of the manuals. We have already started to read about results from the Eighth Edition of UNIX. A talk at the 1987 Phoenix Usenix conference reported results from the Ninth Edition. Following tradition, this implies that the manuals have already been printed, and Dennis is working on the Tenth Edition. Hold your breath.

3.10   UNIX: The Standard Operating System

It is clear that UNIX is the standard operating system of the 1980s and that it will continue to be the dominant operating system, as long as there are operating systems (and incredibly large government procurements).

Many people believe there will never be another UNIX. What they mean is two things.

The first is that for an operating system to be popular, it must do things much, much better than UNIX. UNIX has such a critical mass now that it will be difficult to displace even if another operating system is clearly better. And there are better operating systems. Some interesting ones are Xerox's CEDAR environment, Brown University's PECAN system, CMU's GAN-DALF project and Tektronix's MAGPIE system.

Also, we recognize the lucky break that UNIX had from being introduced and developed noncommercially the way it was for so many years. It is unlikely that this could happen to any new system. Research projects that have any viability of success are detected and commercialized as quickly as possible nowadays.

The second meaning of the statement is that operating systems as user interfaces are disappearing. Even now, most users think of UNIX as the shell rather than the kernel. Only a tiny percentage really understands the fundamental concepts of UNIX discussed throughout this book. Most people, and rightly so, are interested in dealing with computers in a declarative way. This means that the computer should figure out the method as well as execute it. Languages such as Prolog and interfaces such as the Macintosh Finder illustrate this. While UNIX will be with us for a long time, we believe it will be The Last Great Operating System.

One of the reasons that UNIX has become the most widespread operating system is that it was written in a high-level language, and as new CPUs and systems were created, porting of UNIX was "relatively" easy. Once the porting job was finished, you immediately had lots of software available to your new machine (with the associated ports of that software being minimized). As more powerful and different types of systems come into existance, notably RISC, parallel and distributed architectures, you can bet that people will port and modify UNIX to run on those machines. Perhaps one of the true UNIX legacies will not be the operating system and utilities themselves but the fact that the environment encouraged its own evolution into something new.

The amount of money necessary to create a new operating system or to port an existing non-UNIX operating system to another architecture is so high that UNIX remains the only acceptable choice. Other operating systems (e.g., Mach) are either so heavily based upon UNIX that they can be considered a half-breed of it, are so heavily machine dependent (i.e., VMS) that they are not acceptable on most other machines, or don't resemble an operating system at all (Lisp, APL, Smalltalk).

This last category is perhaps the ultimate future. Many computer scientists recognize that operating systems are just warts on the machine. Just as we have left the era of the 1960s where we dealt with file allocation problems and blocking factors, we hope to leave the era of dealing with file names, or files at all, for that matter. Some day we will look back at UNIX and C with the same fondness that we now look back at JCL and Fortran. Discussing operating systems will be akin to discussing dinosaurs. Don Knuth said it best when he remarked that "*An elephant is a mouse with an operating system.*"

3.11   A Foundation for Innovation

The architecture of the UNIX system is perfectly designed for exploration of new computing worlds. UNIX is a continually self-improving foundation from which innovative software and hardware arises.

Software innovation is catalyzed by the ability of UNIX to span new compute-engines from micros to supers, from parallel and distributed systems to toaster ovens. Hardware innovation is encouraged by the relative ease of porting UNIX to computers still on the drawing boards. Porting UNIX to a new machine or integrating a new device is much easier than with a new or proprietary operating system.

UNIX is a wonderfully open system. Openness isn't something bestowed or permitted – it is an attribute of the underlying architecture of a system. While many systems claim to be "open," UNIX pioneered the concept even before the word was coined.

UNIX lends itself to tinkering. New tools and applications are easy to write. New languages are easy, too. The source is there to study. Many books and magazines are available and courses are taught on the subject. It's easy to play with, modify and rewrite to any degree one wants.

Of course UNIX isn't everything. It doesn't solve all the problems but it gives you the best platform on which to solve the next problem. This ability of UNIX is demonstrated by the many-fold expansion in its power since it was first released in 1973. It is inevitable that further research and experimentation based on the UNIX ideas will pay off with worthwhile ideas and practices. Since the birth of UNIX, we have seen a continual growth of innovative ideas appear on UNIX machines. It is obvious that this will continue for many years to come.

Section 2

UNIX

Information

Chapter 4: Printed Information

"... the whole documentation is not unreasonably transportable in a student's briefcase." – John Lions describing UNIX 6th Edition

"This has since been fixed in recent versions." – Kernighan & Pike

This chapter describes printed information available on UNIX. Knowing where to look is the key to successfully using UNIX. One of the differences between the experienced UNIX user and the beginner is knowledge of the available manuals. However, the manuals are only one piece of documentation in the universe of the written UNIX word. Other sources of information include books, periodicals, and source code. We describe this overwhelming collection of UNIX information and put the manuals in their proper place.

4.1   The UNIX Manuals

"Acts oddly on nights with full moon." – BUGS section for **catman** from 4.2BSD UNIX Manual

4.1.1   A Little History

In many ways, UNIX manuals are a reflection of the UNIX system itself. Originally written by the UNIX implementors (rather than a documentation team), they only contained information appropriate to the UNIX system programmer. The most severe drawback was that this often presumed a comprehensive knowledge of all other parts of the system.

For example, utilities did not explain the use of pattern matching since this was provided gratis by the shell. However, a naive user might get the idea that pattern-matched arguments were not acceptable to a utility because it was not specifically mentioned on that particular manual page.

The benefit was that the manuals were extremely concise. With a minimum of words, they described each part of the system precisely. It seemed like the authors used the same sense of style writing the manuals that they used in designing UNIX. They also had a sense of humor about the failings of some of their programs.

The style of the UNIX manuals is easily traceable to the *UNIX Programmer's Manual, Sixth Edition* by Ken Thompson and Dennis Ritchie (Bell Telephones Laboratories, 1975). It was approximately 300 pages long and fit comfortably in one volume. It was typeset with `troff` and included a permuted index of every entry. The *Seventh Edition* was a set of three volumes. The first volume was an expanded (by 100 pages) *Sixth Edition* manual. The other two volumes were sets of *readings*, each describing a different aspect of the system at length. This increased the documentation to about 1,200 pages. (Actually, the readings existed before the Seventh Edition as Bell Labs internal memoranda or Computer Science Technical Reports, but they had never been bundled with the manual before.)

The readings included an "Introduction to UNIX" by Brian Kernighan which provided a brief but beautiful introduction to the power and simplicity of UNIX. Similarly, there was a document titled simply "UNIX Programming" by Kernighan and Ritchie which devoted another short explanation of the entire philosophy of UNIX system programming, complete with lucid examples. "Password Security: A Case History" by Robert Morris and Ken Thompson was another reading demonstrating the open and honest attitude that the developers had about the shortcomings of their system. At the time, getting this kind of information from a commercial vendor would have been a fantasy.

There were many other readings – all short, concise, and amazingly easy to read and understand. Tutorials also existed for several applications such as `troff` and `ed`.

The early existence of these well-written documents is undoubtedly why so many people felt UNIX to be a very accessible system.

When UNIX reached Berkeley, the documentation enlarged again, partly by the addition of a third volume of readings. At this point, the UNIX manuals, like the UNIX system, began to become bloated in an attempt to be all things to all people.

Further, UNIX was no longer used simply by system hackers who had easy access to the source or a guru. UNIX was used by mere mortals, who wanted completed answers and explanations that could be understood without having a degree in computer science.

Nonetheless, a large part of current UNIX manuals remains substantially unchanged from the way it first appeared. We credit this primarily to the original style which we have already praised so much. In fact, the lowest-cost UNIX license you can get, comes with no documentation at all. (The documentation is probably available at your local library). It has long been published by several publishing companies. Many vendors just supply code, with some supplementary notes on software differences and hardware peculiarities.

4.1.2   Obtaining Manuals

UNIX manuals usually come with your system. Since most UNIX vendors modify the systems from the way AT&T distributes them, it is more likely that the vendors' manuals are more realistic than AT&T's.

There are reasons why you might want to get manuals without having a system, however, and it is possible to do so. For example, you might be trying to write a UNIX clone. Or you might want to write a program that is portable to multiple versions of UNIX. In that case you can obtain UNIX manuals from the larger UNIX sellers.

AT&T and Prentice-Hall sells System V manuals.

Prentice-Hall sells X/OPEN specifications.

IEEE sells POSIX specifications.

Microsoft Inc. sells XENIX manuals.

USENIX sells Berkeley UNIX manuals.

4.1.3   Organization of the Manuals

The organization of the manuals has remained much the same as when they were originally written. Few UNIX resellers reorganize or rewrite the bulk of the documentation. This is a real testament to Dennis and Ken's foresight and style.

The manuals are organized in two levels. The top level is divided into eight sections. The sections are:

Section   Description

1. *Commands & Programs:* User-level programs and commands.

2. *System Calls:* System calls; i.e., functions directly supported by the kernel.

3. *Libraries:* Subroutines and subroutine libraries.

4. *Devices:* Devices and device drivers.

5. *File Formats:* Formats of system files; e.g., **/etc/passwd**, **/etc/group**.

6. *Games:* The most important section of all.

7. *Miscellaneous:* **troff** macros, ASCII listing and other miscellany.

8. *System Maintenance:* Programs and documentation useful to the system administrator.

UNIX Manual Sections

It may not be obvious in which section to find the information you are seeking. And even if you know which section, you may not be sure what entry to look at. A particularly useful aid is the permuted index at the front of the manual. The *permuted index* lists the title of each index in the manual by every single word in the title. So if you want to know about commands to read and write tapes, you can look under "tape" and find out about **tar**, **cpio**, **dump**, and so on. Of course, you will have to read the individual entries to find out which is more appropriate to your needs.

Manual pages are usually called "man pages," after the command of the same name which prints them at your terminal. Each **man** page is divided into a small set of subheadings. Common to all are **NAME**, **SYNOPSIS**, and **DESCRIP-TION**. The synopsis is usually a one-line example of the command. This is often sufficient to jog your memory if you've already used the command. If you need more help, there will be a much longer general description following the synopsis.

Depending upon the particular entry, there may also be one or more sub-headings such as **BUGS** (describing any known problems) and **FILES** (naming files used by the command).

An example **man** page for a mythical chess program follows:

```
YACHESS(6)                      GAMES                      YACHESS(6)
```

NAME

　　yachess – the game of chess

SYNOPSIS

　　yachess [-w] [-b] [#]

DESCRIPTION

　　Yachess is yet another computer program that plays chess.　Move pieces by selecting with the mouse and moving to the new position.

　　Optional arguments are as follows:

　　-w　　　Player will play white.

　　-b　　　Player will play black.

　　#　　　Computer will play as if it had this rating.

DIAGNOSTICS

　　"Illegal move" means just that.

SEE ALSO

　　endgame(6), othello(6), chess(6)

FILES

　　/usr/games/lib/chess.open　　　　standard chess openings
　　/usr/games/lib/chess.cheaters　　record of everyone who cheats

BUGS

　　This game doesn't work without a mouse.

Life With UNIX Release 1.0　　　　　　　　　　　　　　　　　1

4.1.4　What?!?　No Manual On the Kernel?

People who are interested in writing device drivers and making modifications to the UNIX kernel will notice that there are no manual pages for kernel-level functions.　The usual device-driver man pages are user-level descriptions, not internal descriptions.　For example, `spl()` is a kernel-level function that changes the hardware priority level.　It is common to virtually every UNIX and UNIX-like system.　Yet, there is no `spl()` manual page.

Originally, the only documentation for `spl()` and other kernel functions was the source itself. People joked that "anyone needing documentation to the kernel functions probably shouldn't be using them."

That attitude wasn't meant to be elitist, rather it referred to the difficulty of kernel programming. Making changes to one part of the kernel can easily (and usually does) impact other parts, so you really had to be familiar with most of it. And since you had to have read the whole kernel, it was inevitable that you knew what the kernel-level functions did.

Of course, we are really carrying this argument to extremes. You don't have to understand everything about the kernel to write a device driver. Furthermore, there are things that are not evident from reading code. However, the tradition lingers on, and the result is that very few kernels are well documented. Some manufacturers do a good job of documenting their kernels, while others only supply documentation if you buy the complete source to the kernel. If you intend on doing kernel programming or writing device drivers, make sure you can obtain documentation from your UNIX supplier.

There are only a few books on device drivers and kernel-level programming. A particularly good one is *The Design of the UNIX Operating System* by Maurice Bach. While generic and not detailed about a specific implementation, it describes rationales, alternate approaches and substantial code describing UNIX kernels. The only book describing the Berkeley kernel is *The Design of the 4.3BSD UNIX Operating System* by Samuel Leffler, et al.

Some good treatments on writing device drivers are put out by manufacturers, but they are not generic since they are tuned to one specific system. For example "Writing Device Drivers for the Sun Workstation" is available from Sun, and we have seen similar well-written documents from Masscomp, Microsoft and SCO. Also, *UNIXWORLD* carried a three-part series by George Pajari on "Writing Device Drivers" in January through March, 1988. Recently, we saw one manufacturer document its kernel functions in "Chapter 9." We can only hope this practice spreads.

Depending upon your system, either of the two books mentioned here combined with the manufacturer's documentation is your best bet to learning about UNIX kernel programming.

As supplementary reading, we also recommend the books *Operating Systems: Design and Implementation* by Andrew Tanenbaum, and *Operating Sys-*

tem Design: The XINU Approach by Douglas Comer. Both books include complete source to systems that are very similar to commercial UNIX systems.

man Macros

The **man** macros are a set of **troff** macros which provide a standard visual format and greatly simplify the creation of a man page. Only two macros accomplish most of the work `.TH` (for Title Heading) and `.SH` (for Section Heading). After creating your text, install the new man page in the proper directory (usually under **/usr/man** or **/usr/local/man**). The **man** command will now find your new man page and you will become famous for your amazing documented program. If you are creating the man page for some other reason and it won't be installed in the place where the **man** command looks, you can say: `nroff -man filename` to format it. PS: The best way to create new man pages is to look at the existing ones and modify them to suit your needs.

4.2   Sources Are The Ultimate

/* you are not expected to understand this */ – from UNIX V6 kernel source

The best documentation is the UNIX source. After all, this is what the system uses for documentation when it decides what to do next! The manuals paraphrase the source code, often having been written at different times and by different people than who wrote the code. Think of them as guidelines. Sometimes they are more like wishes. Of course, sometimes they are right on the money, accurately describing programs and correctly identifying limitations, bugs and workarounds.

Nonetheless, it is all too common to turn to the source and find options and behaviors that are not documented in the manual. Sometimes you find options described in the manual that are unimplemented and ignored by the source.

Originally, UNIX source was supplied with each system. This allowed programmers to reference the source and manual pages at the same time, providing both the real truth (sources) and the helpful tips and wishes (manuals). Unfortunately, times have changed. Most UNIX users don't have access to the system source. A large percentage wouldn't understand it if they did, either because they don't know C, or they are not familiar with all the components of the system.

Nonetheless, referring to the source code is still an invaluable tool for understanding parts of UNIX, or any software for that matter. It's just that UNIX source is so much more accessible. Actual UNIX source code is protected by trade secret laws. However, even with these restrictions it is not hard to get a peek at it.

Most universities and many nonprofit organizations have low-cost source licenses. By signing a nondisclosure agreement (and possibly enrolling in a course), you can read any of the UNIX source. Of course, you are not allowed to redistribute it or use it for commercial gain. By comparison, it is extremely unlikely that you will see the source code to any other commercial operating system, even in the classroom.

Many books have been published that described UNIX programs and algorithms with large sections of UNIX excerpted and well-documented. There are also many clone implementations of UNIX that are available free or at low cost (see the Underground chapter) that contain large amounts of useful source code.

The books are more completely documented later in this chapter. However, we must mention a pair of books titled *A Commentary on the UNIX Operating System* (one book is the source; the other is the commentary) by John Lions. They contain the source to V6 UNIX on the PDP-11/40 accompanied by a line-by-line explanation of the code. These books were originally written under a grant from AT&T for use in an operating systems course. Unfortunately, they are no longer being published. AT&T has taken a firm stand against publishing its proprietary code, so you will not find any other books that include actual UNIX source code, with or without a comprehensive explanation.

While there are no other annotated listings of UNIX systems, *Design of the UNIX Operating System* by Maurice Bach (see review later in chapter) is better written and more complete in its overall presentation of UNIX kernel concepts and algorithms. Also, the Underground chapter has more information about many books and source releases for UNIX-like systems.

Should you be lucky enough to find yourself on a real UNIX system with sources, you will find them living in the **/usr/src** directory. Within this directory there are several other directories. The following is from 4.2BSD. Other systems may be slightly different.

cmd: This has the source to commands. For example, `/usr/src/cmd/ls.c` is the source to `ls`, the directory listing program. Some programs live in directories of their own because they have a number of source files (and hopefully, a `Makefile`). An example is the sources for yacc which can be found in the directory `/usr/src/cmd/yacc`.

games: The sources for games are here. It is not unusual to find them in `cmd`, but they are often separated, so they can easily be removed if disk space is limited.

libc and lib: These contain the libraries and support routines for the C language. In these directories, are the following subdirectories:

crt: Standing for "C RunTime," this contains special runtime support routines, for profiling or sped-up versions of math or string routines. These are usually in assembly language.

csu: Standing for "C Startup," this contains the entry and exit points of all C routines. When your C program is executed, control is passed to the entry point defined in one of these modules, which sets up things like stdio and memory and then calls your main.

sys: This contains the source for the user-level system calls. Often these are just wrappers, selecting a parameter and calling a generic system entry point. The source that performs the real work (in the kernel) is located in `/usr/src/sys`.

stdio: This is the source to the standard I/O (hence the term "stdio") library and any other portable C library routines that require the stdio library. For example, `fopen()` and `fprintf()` live here.

gen: Contains most of the library routines in section 3 of the manual that make up the portable C library. For example: **getlogin()** and **malloc()** are here.

local: This is where locally developed source that is not normally distributed lives. Since **/usr/src** is typically contained on a separate disk that may not always be mounted on the system, many installations like to place local sources in **/usr/local/src** because **/usr/local** is always mounted.

new and old: These contain, respectively, new and old versions of command and library routines. With the availability of source code control systems, few people use the new and old directories. For trivial programs, it is conventional simply to rename the old source and binary to something like **oyacc** and leave it in the original directory. Expect to be confused by seeing all of these practices used at the same time.

sys: This contains a number of directories that are used to generate the UNIX kernel. The most important is **sys** (yes, that makes **/usr/src/sys/sys**) which contains the system entry points for all the system calls.

Of major importance when reading the source code are the *include* files. These files contain many definitions and data structures used throughout the system. Often there is extensive documentation in the include files themselves. For example, the fields of data structures and their legal values are more likely to be documented here than in the source where they are used.

The **#include** files can be found in **/usr/include**. An example is **/usr/include/stdio.h** which lives here and is the file used when the line

```
#include <stdio.h>
```

appears in a C program. (The angle brackets mean "find this file in **/usr/include**.") There are also subdirectories of include files within **/usr/include**. The most notable one is called **sys** and has include files of importance to the UNIX kernel.

We don't want you to get the wrong impression. While it is healthy to have a reasonable distrust of manuals, you should not become paranoid about the written word. Going to the source code to find out how a program works is only necessary after the manual has failed to do its job. However, many people find it very hard to live on a system that does not include the complete source code.

4.3   UNIX and C Bookstores and Publishers

Here are the stores that we are aware of that have all or most of the important titles in the field. While we recommend these stores, it is a good idea to call ahead to ask if the particular items are in stock and ask about the delivery schedule. All of the stores will supply lists of books that they regularly carry. (Complete addresses can be found in the Appendix.)

Cucumber Bookshop, Inc. — Cucumber carries all the UNIX and C books available. It does not carry magazines. Orders are taken by mail or phone with 24-hour turnaround. Credit cards and checks accepted.

Computer Literacy Bookshop — The largest bookstore of computer and electronics books anywhere. They carry most of the UNIX and C titles. Credit card and checks accepted. Overnight delivery available.

Computer Systems Resources, Inc. — CSRI sells UNIX reference and tutorial books. Checks accepted on mail orders. Phone orders will be delivered C.O.D.

Jim Joyce's UNIX Bookstore and *Uni-Ops Books* — Both of these organizations carry a good selection of UNIX and C-related books, journals, reference cards and posters.

If your favorite bookstore is out of some UNIX book and you can't find anyone else that carries it, you can always call the publisher and order it directly. However, publishers often have much longer delivery times than bookstores.

4.4   Reference Cards

Useful condensations and references for experienced users are reference cards for C and UNIX. Some of the available cards we have seen are: **ed**, **vi**, UNIX Shell, Netnews, SCCS and C Programmer's. SSC, Uni-Ops Books, Cucumber Books and ASP all specialize or have a large selection of such cards for C, C libraries, the UNIX shell and other utilities.

4.5   Books

There is an incredible number of UNIX and C books available. Knowing which to read and which to avoid is difficult, since no one can review them all. Nonetheless, there are a number of *classics* that you should be familiar with.

We refer to many of these as classics because they are often referenced by others, although not necessarily because they are superior. Indeed, some were simply the first book available on a topic and became ingrained because of that. We mention the classics to avoid as well as the ones to have on your bookshelf. We also include some books that, while not classics, are nonetheless noteworthy. Each book is rated on a scale of one to ten for the type of audience, usefulness, lasting value and readability.

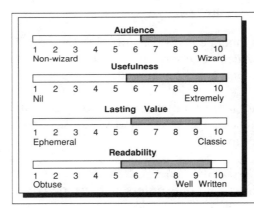

Advanced Programmer's Guide to UNIX System V

Author(s): Rebecca Thomas
Lawrence Rodgers
Jean Yates

Publisher: McGraw-Hill

A good reference for System V specific users and programmers. The book contains many good shell scripts and C code examples, especially on interprocess communications. Do not confuse this with Yates' and Thomas' *User Guide to the UNIX System*.

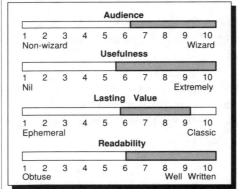

Advanced UNIX Programming

Author(s): Marc J. Rochkind

Publisher: Prentice-Hall

This superb book pedagogically describes programming at the UNIX system call level. The author covers every system call in detail and with sample code. Included are comprehensive treatments of sophisticated subjects such as signals and interprocessor communication. While little knowledge of UNIX is assumed, this book is one that all UNIX experts will want to keep handy. The book is oriented towards System V and its derivatives. However, the author discusses portability issues with specific mention of BSD, XENIX and other systems.

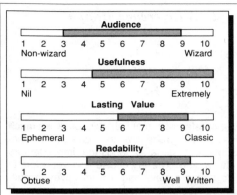

The AWK Programming Language

Author(s): Alfred Aho
Brian Kernighan
Peter Weinberger

Publisher: Addison-Wesley

This book is a long-needed answer to the many problems one encounters when looking at the original documentation on AWK. Written by the authors of AWK, we finally have an explanation of the power of AWK, a much underestimated language/tool. Filled with many examples and covering the ground from introductory concepts to full-fledged applications the authors have greatly contributed to the usability of this language which has been used from data base prototyping to report generators to recursive-descent parsers.

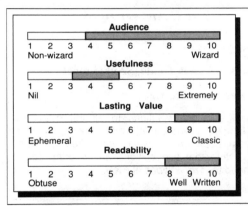

The Bell System Technical Journal 57, no. 6, pt. 2, July/August 1978

Author(s): Bell Laboratories staff

Publisher: Bell Laboratories (AT&T)
(reprinted by Prentice-Hall)

This is a special issue of BSTJ, made up of important UNIX readings. The papers describe UNIX from various viewpoints (including those of Thompson and Ritchie). There are several papers describing important UNIX applications and related works. Almost all of the papers are classics.

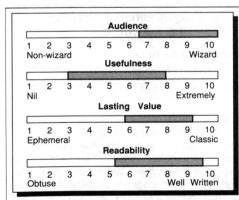

AT&T Bell Laboratories Technical Journal 63, no. 8, pt. 2, October 1984

Author(s): Bell Laboratories staff

Publisher: Bell Laboratories (AT&T)
(reprinted by Prentice-Hall)

While it has changed names, this is another special issue on UNIX of the BSTJ. As before, the papers are extremely well written and are classic essays. Many new applications and areas are covered. Unlike the earlier edition, there are several essays that include lucid reviews of the past.

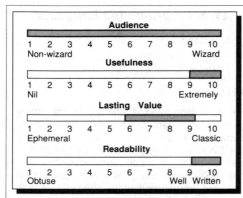

C: A Reference Manual

Author(s): Samual Harbison,
Guy Steele, Jr.

Publisher: Prentice-Hall

Ostensibly a reference manual, this book is much more. It is so comprehensive in scope that it functions just as well as a C language implementors guide. The writing style is concise and yet informal enough so that one can read it from cover to cover, picking up useful knowledge on every page. **If you only have one C book on your desk, this should be it.**

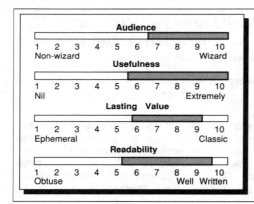

The C Answer Book

Author(s): Clovis Tondo, Scott Gimpel

Publisher: Prentice-Hall

This book provides solutions to all the questions posed in *K&R*. Additionally, many examples from the earlier book are resolved with alternate techniques. Note that two editions are in print, corresponding to the two editions of *K&R*.

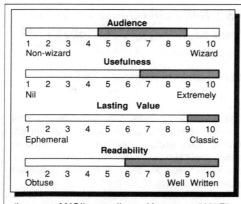

The C Programming Language, First Edition

Author(s): Brian Kernighan
Dennis Ritchie

Publisher: Prentice-Hall

This was the first C text to be published. Containing the complete C reference manual, it was well written enough that it served as the definitive C manual for many years, both for beginners and compiler-writers. It has been superseded by a second edition (see next page). C hackers should have this book nonetheless, for working with *K&R* (i.e., pre-ANSI) compilers. Known as "*K&R*" or "*the white book.*"

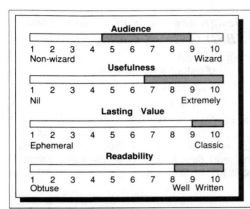

The C Programming Language, Second Edition

Author(s): Brian Kernighan
Dennis Ritchie

Publisher: Prentice-Hall

This is a complete rewrite of the original *K&R*. It is based on the ANSI X3J11 standard and includes new examples, a simple version of `cdecl`, discussions of language changes, and a `yacc`-compatible grammar. And the cover is still white. This is *the* book to learn C from. It is destined to be a classic.

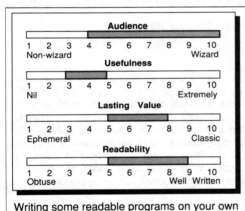

The C Puzzle Book

Author(s): Alan Feuer

Publisher: Prentice-Hall

Literally a book of C puzzles, such as figuring out what cryptic C expressions evaluate to. Many people cite this book as an aid that up-and-coming hackers can cut their teeth on, but its focus is extremely low level. We do not recommend learning the C language by reading this book, unless you want to fill your head with extreme esoterica that you will probably not use but once in a lifetime. Writing some readable programs on your own is a much healthier exercise.

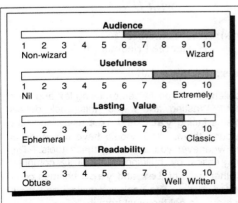

The C++ Programming Language

Author(s): Bjarne Stroustrup

Publisher: Addison-Wesley

This book describes C++, a successor to the C language. The author of the book is also the author of C++, hence it is impossible to find any differences between the book's description and the language. Indeed, the book is only barely a tutorial, but rather a reference. In many ways, this book reminds us of the seminal book on C by Kernighan and Ritchie. It will doubtless be superceded by others.

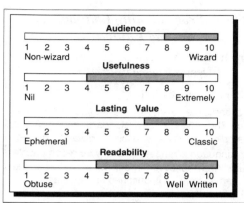

The Design and Implementation of the 4.3BSD UNIX Operating System

Author(s): Samuel Leffler
Marshall Kirk McKusick
Michael Karels
John Quarterman

Publisher: Addison-Wesley

This book is an excellent description of the internal algorithms and data structures in the UNIX kernel. It is specific to 4.3BSD UNIX.

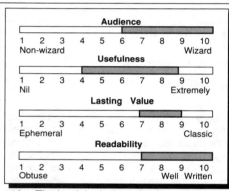

Design of the UNIX Operating System

Author(s): Maurice J. Bach

Publisher: Prentice-Hall

This book is an excellent description of the internal algorithms and data structures in the UNIX kernel. It is specific to UNIX System V, but much of it is common to most modern versions of UNIX. Unlike the Lions book, this book does not include any proprietary source code, either presenting pseudocode or rewritten code. However, it is currently the best book for learning about UNIX kernel internals. The book is designed as a textbook for a semester course on the UNIX operating system.

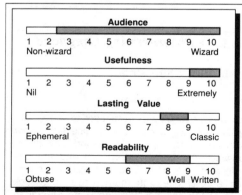

Introduction to Compiler Construction with UNIX

Author(s): Axel Schreiner
H. George Friedman, Jr.

Publisher: Prentice-Hall

This excellent book specializes on using lex and yacc effectively. Wasting few words, this book details the problems facing `yacc` and `lex` users and how to get around them. You should have this book at your side whenever you are using these tools. The book progresses by building a small C compiler. However, much of the material is appropriate towards other uses of `lex` and `yacc` besides compilers. Little theory is presented about parsing and related areas. The book is practical and readers should have a reasonable understanding of compiler theory to get the most from it.

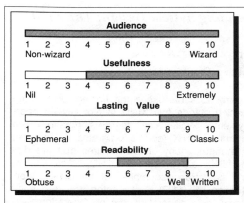

Life with UNIX
A Guide for Everyone

Author(s): Don Libes
Sandy Ressler

Publisher: Prentice-Hall

Comprehensive treatise of what UNIX is all about, from technical, market and historical orientations. Includes much rare material and unusual sections such as a Who's Who of UNIX, public-domain and underground UNIX, notable UNIX quotes and a flattering review of itself.

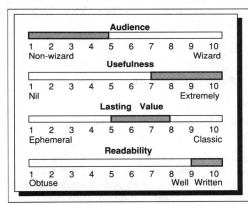

Introducing the UNIX System
Introducing UNIX System V

Author(s): Rachel Morgan
Henry McGilton

Publisher: McGraw-Hill

We give this book our highest recommendation as an introductory UNIX text. It is extremely comprehensive and yet reads easily. A separate version is available that concentrates on System V.

Nutshell Handbooks

Author(s): O'Reilly & Associates staff

Publisher: O'Reilly & Associates

An excellent series of handbooks covering topics including Usenet, `curses`, `termcap`, `vi`, and `make`. Each handbook is an extended essay on a particular area with a lot of examples, help and reference material.

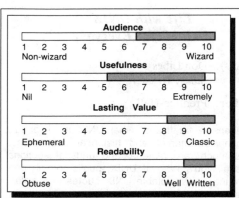

Operating System Design: The XINU Approach

Author(s): Douglas Comer

Publisher: Prentice-Hall

This superb book discusses the implentation of the XINU (which stands for "XINU Is Not UNIX") operating system. While XINU is not compatible with any version of UNIX (source programs will not run without change), many of the features that are distinctively UNIX are present in XINU. Actual code (including bootstrap assembler) of the XINU operating (on an LSI 11/2) is presented and discussed in great detail. This book is suitable as an auxiliary text for a general course on Operating Systems, or bundled with the Lions text for a course on the UNIX kernel. It also provides some insight on implementing C in the UNIX environment. An optional tape is available from Prentice-Hall which contains the XINU operating system discussed in the text.

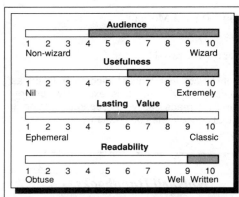

Operating System Design: Internetworking with XINU

Author(s): Douglas Comer

Publisher: Prentice-Hall

This book is a companion to "The XINU Approach". Building on the XINU system, a TCP/IP network is presented, along with a shell and a stateless network file system. As with the earlier book, the complete implementation appears and is extremely well documented. While the emphasis in both books is on practical and immediately useful knowledge, their fading timeliness will always be offset by the clarity of presentation.

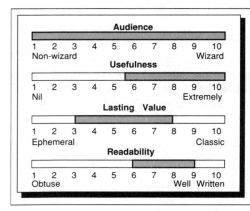

Operating Systems: Design and Implementation Minix for the IBM PC, XT and AT

Author(s): Andrew Tanenbaum

Publisher: Prentice-Hall

These books describe the MINIX system. MINIX is a public-domain rewrite of V7 UNIX that runs on the IBM PC and several other microprocessor-based systems. While internally the system differs substantially from the original V7 UNIX, this book is an excellent replacement for the no-longer-available Lions book.

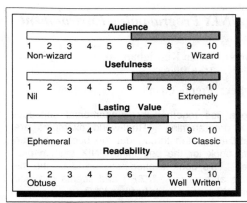

Portable C and UNIX System Programming

Author(s): J. E. Lapin

Publisher: Prentice-Hall

This book aims at providing users with guidance for creating portable C and UNIX programs. It contains a good comparison of the various UNIX versions and points out many pitfalls in creating portable code.

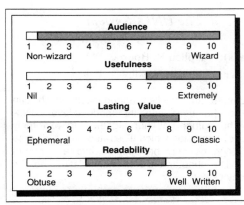

System V Interface Definition

Author(s): AT&T

Publisher: AT&T Information Systems

This book describes the AT&T UNIX System V standard. While it is only one of several UNIX standards, it was the first in common use, and thus has become a common reference.

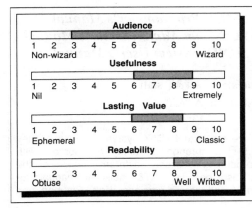

The UNIX Operating System

Author(s): Kaare Christian

Publisher: Wiley Interscience

A comprehensive introduction to the UNIX system. Somewhat of a compromise between the brevity of the manuals and the more informal *K&P*. While well written, this may be a little too detailed for a beginner to easily read.

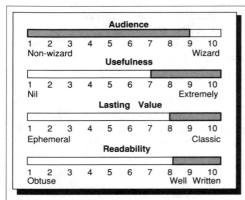

The UNIX Programming Environment

Author(s): Brian Kernighan
Rob Pike

Publisher: Prentice-Hall

This book ties together the fundamental concepts of UNIX programming. Real-world examples are used and elaborated throughout the book. It is an excellent book for the beginning UNIX system programmer. This book is often referred to by the initials of its authors (i.e., "*K&P*") and seems destined to become a classic like its brother *K&R*.

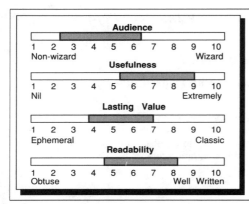

The UNIX System

Author(s): Stephen R. Bourne

Publisher: Addison-Wesley

This book is an excellent introduction which can also take the user into intermediate-level UNIX tools. The author has put together an extremely lucid set of examples which illustrates how a diverse set of programs may be coupled into a coherent system. The chapter on data manipulation tools is particularly useful.

UNIX Programmer's Manual
UNIX System Administrator's Manual
UNIX System User's Manual

Author(s): AT&T staff

Publisher(s): AT&T
Prentice-Hall

These are the actual UNIX system manuals. They are published through a variety of sources, with each producing a slightly different version of the manual (user beware). AT&T sells the manuals for System V and earlier versions. Holt, Rinehart and Winston publishes some of the manuals on AT&T's behalf.

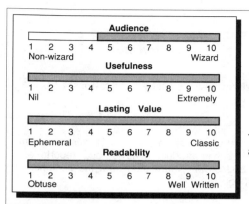

4.3BSD UNIX Manuals

Author(s): Univ. of California at Berkeley

Publisher: Howard Press
c/o USENIX Association

These are the actual Berkeley UNIX system manuals.

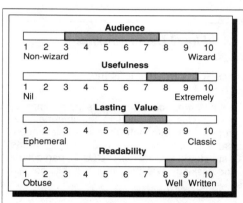

UNIX System Administration

Author(s): David Fiedler
Bruce Hunter

Publisher: Hayden Book Company

This is an excellent book on administrating a UNIX system. Keep it on your desk next to your system-specific administrative manuals.

X/OPEN Portability Guide

Author(s): Members of X/OPEN

Publisher: Prentice-Hall

This book describes how to produce portable systems and code with respect to the X/OPEN effort. While this multi-volume set is extremely comprehensive, you can expect it to change as X/OPEN standards work continues.

4.6   Periodicals

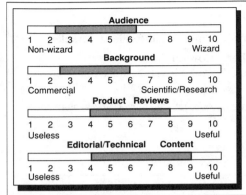

3B Journal

Publisher: Owens-Liang Publications, Ltd.

3B Journal specializes on AT&T's 3B series of computers. It has product reviews, bug reports and fixes. 3BJ covers information from the beginner to the UNIX guru.

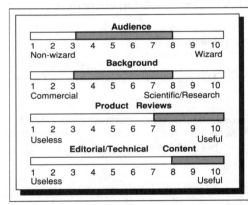

The C Users Journal

Publisher: R&D Publications Inc.

The C Users Journal covers what its name implies. Most of the articles are aimed at the intermediate-level C programmer, although there is a fair amount of technical material covering the continuing efforts of the C standards committee. *CUJ* is particularly notable for making available much public-domain software.

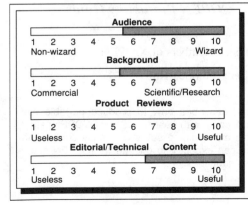

Computing Systems – The Journal of the USENIX Association

Publisher: University of California Press

This quarterly publication specializes in articles on research, implementation and analysis of advanced computing systems that involve UNIX or are based on UNIX ideas. Papers reflect a mix of theory and practical experience.

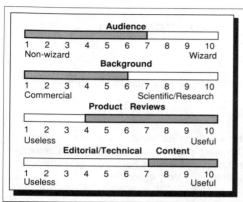

CommUNIXations

Publisher: /usr/group

This is /usr/group's monthly newsletter. It reports /usr/group activities and prints several commercially-oriented papers each month, in effect, spanning the gap between UniForum conferences. In this respect, it is comparable to the commercial UNIX magazines, except this is free when you become a member of /usr/group.

;login:

Publisher: USENIX Association

This is the USENIX Association's monthly newsletter. It is one of the oldest regularly published UNIX periodicals. Apart from reporting on USENIX activities, ;login: prints several technical papers each month, in effect, spanning the gap between USENIX conferences. ;login: is free to all members of the USENIX Association.

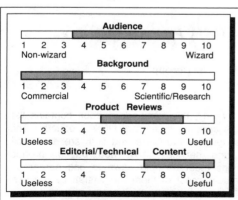

Patricia Seybold's UNIX in the Office

Publisher: Patricia Seybold's Office Computing Group

This newsletter specializes in UNIX in the office. It includes product reviews, trends and some extremely technical and in-depth analysis. Very expensive.

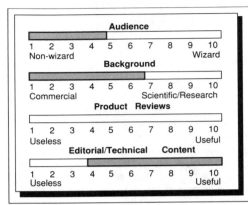

UNIGRAM • X

Publisher: Miller Freeman Publications

The only weekly UNIX newsletter. Market-oriented stories on new products, mergers, large contracts, joint-marketing agreements, analysis of companies, market trends, etc. Very expensive.

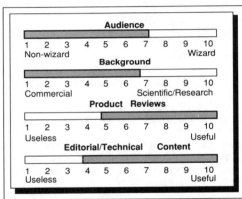

UNIQUE

Publisher: InfoPro Systems

Monthly newsletter that presents a small number of in-depth analyses of topics ranging from technical issues to product reviews to market trends. Somewhat breezy but down to earth.

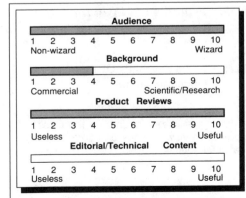

UNIX Products Directory

Publisher: /usr/group

Updated yearly, this tremendous book contains listings of all current commercial UNIX products. This includes not only hardware and software, but publications and services. At 600 pages, product descriptions must be held down to one paragraph. Unfortunately, most of them are written by the vendors.

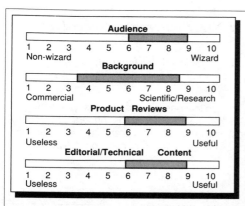

UNIX REVIEW

Publisher: Miller Freeman Publications Co.

This monthly magazine is oriented towards the UNIX programmer/hacker as opposed to the manager or seller/buyer of commerical products. *UNIX REVIEW* covers programming and items of importance to programmers. Reviews of software and hardware focus on products that can be integrated into systems rather than complete systems. Each issue has a fascinating interview with a person who has had a major influence on UNIX. The regular columns are very good, including "C Advisor" by Eric Allman and Ken Arnold, and "Rules of the Game" by Glenn Groenewold.

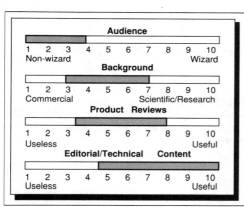

UNIXuser

Publisher: Marvin L. Rosenfeld

This magazine is oriented towards the UNIX beginner. *UNIXuser* has more subject introductions and tutorials of material than other magazines. Product reviews are aimed at first-time buyers. This magazine takes account of the fact that most UNIX users know very little about UNIX.

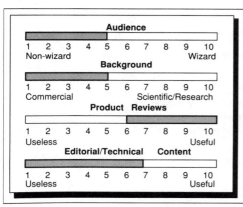

UNIXWORLD

Publisher: Tech Valley Publishing

This monthly magazine is oriented towards the UNIX user/buyer/manager. *UNIXWORLD* covers marketing and technology trends, applications, reviews and limited technical articles. Product reviews focus on complete or packaged computer systems. Its regular columns are very good, including "Inside Edge" by Omri Serlin, "The Hindin Report" by Wendy Rauch-Hindin, and the "Guest" essays.

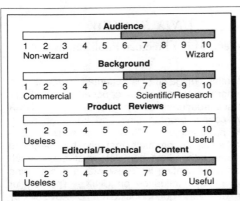

USENIX Conference Proceedings

Publisher: USENIX Association

These are collections of the papers presented at each USENIX conference. The papers are usually technical, ranging from practical to futuristic research. Many seminal papers on UNIX appear here first.

UNIX Bulletins

Publisher: International Data Corporation

UNIX Bulletins is published twice monthly. It focuses on one topic in depth, such as standards, trends or new product information, along with technical analysis when appropriate.

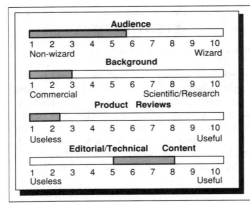

/usr/digest

Publisher: /usr/group

A news digest published bi-weekly. Consists primarily of headlines with single-paragraph briefs. A good complement to /usr/group's *CommUNIXations*.

Chapter 5: Nonprinted Information

"I never let school get in the way of my education." - Anon.

While there are quite a few excellent books covering the technical aspects of UNIX, there is a large amount of information that is not available in print. You can't find it in your library, whether you look in texts, magazines or the manuals.

Some information goes out of date too quickly. Some varies too much from installation to installation. Some (particularly product information) changes at people's (and marketing moguls') whims. Some information is simply best presented in a different form than the printed word.

In the previous chapter we have tried to point you towards sources of durable information. This chapter will cover another world of information that we have classified as "nonprinted." We consider this to include classes, conferences and user groups. (Electronic bulletin boards which do provide a wealth of information are covered fully in the UNIX Underground chapter). Each of these are excellent sources for product announcements, product reviews, benchmarks and other transient information.

5.1   Conferences

Should you go to a conference? Which one? Is it worth going across the country, or to a different country to attend a UNIX conference?

The number of annual computing conferences is truly astounding. While the number of UNIX-specific conferences is a tiny percentage, even a UNIX mavin will find it impossible to attend all of the UNIX conferences. Fortunately, however, it is not necessary to attend them all. Indeed, you might question attending any of them. Perhaps you should be attending an application-specific conference (such as SigGraph for graphics) rather than a graphics session at a UNIX conference.

One thing to keep in mind when choosing a conference is to know what you expect to get out of it beforehand. Some things conferences are good at are: meeting UNIX movers and shakers, rubbing elbows with the gurus and wizards who have the right stuff. It is not unreasonable to go to a conference, specifically to talk to several people that are normally unaccessible, secreted away in corporate basements, only allowed out for annual shows, and just this occasion.

These conferences always have job bulletin boards, where you can post your job opportunity and expect many knocks on your door later that evening. The majority of people recruited this way will be newly-graduated UNIX hackers with little outside experience, although disgruntled gurus will usually give the board a summary review just in case. Indeed, one of the first places that many startups become known (and gain notoriety depending upon the wording) is through their initial posting for employees on these bulletin boards.

Many people are under the naive impression that this is the primary activity at a conference. Actually, we have come to believe that this is the least important priority at a conference. Especially if you are a beginner, you cannot learn UNIX this way. After all, if you go to a week-long conference, how much can you expect to learn in five days? Answer: About five days' worth. There aren't any mystical concepts that require passage from the mouth of the master to understand them. With the right book, you can learn the same material, and do it at your own rate. Better yet, you can do it at a terminal and try out what you are learning, rather than watch someone put up unreadable view graphs of printouts.

Even advanced courses, such as "Writing device drivers" or "Arcane awk programs" are of limited use. Typically presented as day-long tutorials, these courses present a mass of information that is difficult to comprehend in eight hours. It is extremely difficult for instructors (who often are not professional instructors) to explain advanced concepts to people who have a range of experiences and backgrounds. Before attending such courses, make a good attempt at finding written information covering the material. For sufficiently obscure material, contact the instructor and ask for a copy of the course notes. Sometimes the conference sponsors keep a copy of the previous year's notes.

Even though we don't think highly of these tutorials, they are popular. People like to believe they can reach nirvana by immersing themselves with the material from a guru for a day or two. While our experience says otherwise, we often find that these tutorials are booked solid months in advance. Do not expect to pay at the door and be admitted to a tutorial, as they are usually full. And they have guards at the door, to make sure you don't sneak in.

In 1986, AT&T performed a survey of customer interest in tutorials and classes. The survey results (published in a letter to customers) were as follows:

1. Networking
2. Applications Software
3. V5R3 Features
4. Connectivity
5. Office Systems
6. Programming Algorithms in C Language
7. Programming Productivity
8. Porting
9. Documentation
10. Security
11. UNIX Kernel Debugging (Crash Dump Analysis)

Like most computer shows, unless you have just completed a comprehensive survey of a field in which you are an expert, vendor exhibitions are confusing, or to put it more bluntly, misleading. For example, if you are shopping for a database, you can't very well load in your data, sample applications, and try a couple of queries, to see if the thing works under a real load. Even getting a feel for the user interface is difficult under the situation of a salesperson at one side and a restless crowd surging against your other side.

At every conference, there seems to be a person who runs around from one exhibit to the next, typing in a couple small benchmarks and running them on all the systems. However, these benchmarks (as well as the people) should be taken with a grain of salt. Some vendors have machines fully loaded with memory. Some have very fast disks, which you won't be able to afford. Others bring beta-test versions of software that have loads of diagnostic information compiled into them so that they present artificially slow benchmark times.

Some of the conferences have technical sessions where research projects, experiences and issues are discussed. We find the level of such presentations quite high; however, it is often sufficient simply to read the conference proceedings to learn the same material. (Although you will miss all the questions from the audience, and more importantly, the speakers' jokes.) Indeed, it is useful to scan the proceedings before attending the talks, so you can 1) better choose which talk to go to and 2) have a better understanding of what the talk is about. Feel free to order the conference proceedings, even if you choose not to go to the conference. The conference proceedings are often where seminal papers on UNIX first appear.

There are several large UNIX conferences, each typically meeting once or twice per year. Each conference tends to have a different slant on the same subject matter. Here are descriptions of some of the conferences:

UniForum

Sponsored by /usr/group, UniForum is held once a year. They are often held in conjunction with the USENIX conferences (see below).

UniForum is aimed at the business and end-user segment of the computing industry. UniForum includes a vendor exhibit, workshops, tutorials and conference sessions. The workshops and tutorials tend to be oriented towards the commercial end user. The conference sessions are usually run by industry people and are invariably based on market issues.

UniForum occasionally holds joint conferences with USENIX. These are certainly more convenient to attend, although they tend to draw uncomfortably large numbers of people.

USENIX Conference

USENIX conferences occur twice a year, in different parts of the country. That way, at least one is in a close proximity to most users. One conference is usually run in conjunction with UniForum.

In contrast to UniForum, the USENIX conferences are aimed at the technical UNIX developer and researcher. Seminal results in the UNIX field are often reported here first. The technical sessions are based on refereed papers. The tutorials are more sophisticated, often requiring fluency in some section of the UNIX source code. (Some of these require that you be able to show a license or proof of purchase.) Attendance from universities is much higher at USENIX. You are more likely to find Ken and Dennis here then any of the other conferences. Expect more beards and shorts to be worn. No smoking, please.

One complaint many people have with the USENIX conferences is their choice of locales. They are typically southern spots in summer, and northern spots in the winter. No matter where, it is always in the off-peak season. This is designed to make it affordable to students. In 1987, students attended for $40, while USENIX members paid $120. A tutorial cost students $115 while USENIX members paid $195.

EUUG

The European UNIX Users' Group sponsors a conference twice a year. This conference is the European answer to all of the American conferences, and is a compromise among all of them. The conference includes tutorials and a vendor exhibition. Like USENIX, EUUG accepts refereed papers for presentation.

The 1987 conference was held on a luxury ocean liner, which while undoubtedly fun (it traveled from Stockholm, Sweden to Helsinki, Finland) probably was prohibitively expensive for most of the students that would otherwise attend such a conference (often by doubling up or staying with nearby friends).

While covering the same ground as its American cousins, EUUG tries to make up for the historical American bias in UNIX. Typical issues that are always in the forefront at these conferences are 1) how to adapt UNIX to international character sets, 2) date/time formats, 3) how to deal with each country's national telephone system and 4) forcing UNIX into the ISO mold.

The official language of the conference is English.

UNIXEXPO

Held every fall in New York City, UNIXEXPO, the UNIX Operating System Exposition & Conference, is a three-day conference offering commercial exhibits, talks, tutorials and computer labs, and job fair. The tutorials and computer labs are all run by AT&T.

UNIXEXPO is strictly a commercial show. While the speakers run the gamut from all the UNIX companies, there are virtually none from academia. This conference studies how UNIX gets the job done in the real world. The material ranges from the financial world to the scientific. Just because there are no academics here doesn't mean there are no highly technical talks.

In 1987, the rates were as follows: $100 for three days of conference and exhibits. There is a small fee for attending only the exhibition, but most vendors will be delighted to supply you with free passes at your request. Full-day tutorials are $300 each. Full-day computer labs are $325 each.

UNICORN

UNICORN holds open conferences twice yearly in the Washington, DC area. As might be expected, they deal primarily with issues of concern to the government or people who deal with the government. Typical issues are 1) national security, 2) customs, 3) GSA purchases, 4) FIPS and POSIX standards, and so on. Meetings are free. Certain topics may require a security clearance.

5.1.1   Conference Freebies and Other Trash

One of the most important reasons to go to a conference is to get the wonderful giveaways that so many of the exhibitors distribute, trying to capture your attention. Naturally, we have a modest collection. Here are some of them.

Buttons

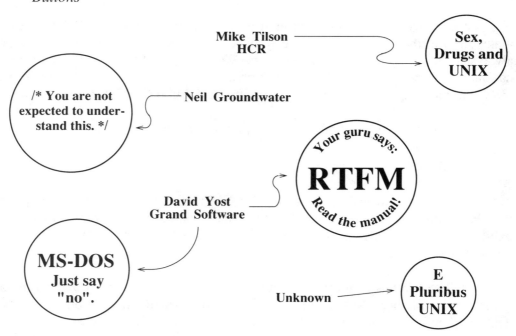

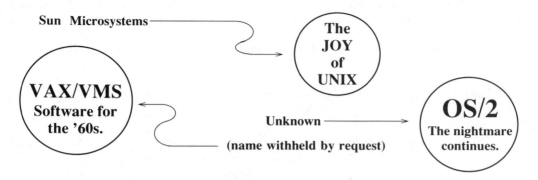

Posters

Posters are almost as good as buttons, although a little more unwieldy to wear. Some of the best ones we have seen are:

C-shell – Picture of a sea shell with various csh commands grouped by function in the partitions of the sea shell. Available from UNIX/World.

vi – Commands of the **vi** editor grouped by functions inside of big hollow v and i. Available from UNIX/World.

4.2 > V – Picture of the "Mt. Xinu/4.2bsd" rocket blowing up the AT&T death star logo. Lots of phones and telephone poles falling out of the death star. Available from Mt. Xinu.

C syntax – Graphical drawings of BNF for the C language. Available from AGS Computers.

UNIX Magic – Typical dark ages alchemist as guru wearing tall wizardly hat labeled "su." Surrounded by black cat and lots of mysterious potions like "oregano," "tar" and "grep." Available from UNITECH Software.

Other Miscellanea

10th Anniversary USENIX t-shirt – Picture of UNIX internals, consisting of lots of leaky pipes, demons running around having fun. Available from USENIX.

"Reach out and grep someone." – Found on opposite side of AT&T t-shirt.

"UNIX is a trademark of Bell Laboratories" – Found at the very bottom of a Mt. Xinu t-shirt.

"/nev/dull" – Found on t-shirts available from Jim Joyce's UNIX Bookstore.

Ratfor t-shirt – Picture of large rodent at keyboard wearing "4" t-shirt. Available from STUG.

"awk: bailing out near line 1" – Caption on t-shirt. Plane going down in background. Bird (an auk perhaps?) wearing parachute in foreground. Available from The Independent UNIX Bookstore.

Chateau NUXI - A rare vintage. Available from The Instruction Set.

Mt. Xinu Command of the Month Calendar – full of important dates like August 6th, 1983 (4.2BSD released), and amusing definitions of error codes such as **ENOTOBACCO**: Read on empty pipe, and **EWATERGATE**: Extended tape gap.

**License plate by
Armando Stettner.
Distributed by Digital
Equipment Corp.**

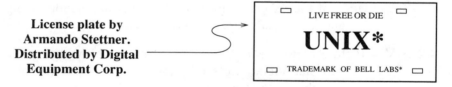

5.2   Workshops

UNIX *workshops* are meetings of small groups of people, who get together to share experiences and work out solutions in one particular technical area. Some of the past workshops have dealt with UNIX standards, C standards, graphics and C++.

Workshops differ from conferences in several ways. Workshops are typically attended only by implementors, concerned parties and others with direct experience. Typical attendance at a workshop ranges from fifty to several hundred people. There are no exhibitors. The emphasis on the talks is technical. And they remain extremely informal, partly because they often present "work in progress."

The organizer of most workshops is the USENIX Association. Workshops are announced in its newsletter, *;login:*. If you are interested in a workshop on a new subject, contact USENIX.

You may find workshops on topics such as UNIX internals, and C programming offered by UNIX vendors and other commercial companies. These are really classes. They may have the informality of workshops, but there are students and instructors, and the students learn while the instructors teach.

5.3   Courses

"The only way to learn a new programming language is by writing programs in
it." – Brian Kernighan

Large companies can often support their own instructors, or have staff members who can give occasional classes. For introductory classes, this is a good way to go. If your organization isn't that big, and there are still a fair number of people who would like to attend a similar class, your company can hire, on a one-time basis, an instructor to come to your shop and give classes.

This is preferable to your leaving work and attending a class outside, since the instructor will shape the class more to your needs or those appropriate to your company. Of course, there are plenty of classes and seminars which are open to anyone who pays the appropriate fee. In 1987, typical three and four day courses cost $1,000 per student.

Most vendors offer classes to users of their software and hardware. However, certain UNIX topics are so standard (e.g., C-shell programming) that many of these classes can be considered even if you don't have that vendor's equipment. Particular topics may require that the student be able to show a UNIX source license.

All companies listed offer classes around the country for your convenience as well as on-site classes. Several of the companies offer their courses on videotape and videodisc. Videos are the ultimate in convenience, with the one drawback that you cannot ask the instructor questions. On the other hand, videodisc courses are often interactive, and can quiz you periodically, or allow you to skip around following up just the areas that are of interest to you.

Here are some of the largest course vendors:

AT&T: As might be expected, AT&T has been teaching UNIX classes for longer than anyone else and offers the widest variety of classes (over 40 this year) and options. AT&T actually offers CEUs (Continuing Education Units). Many courses are available on videotape.

Computer Technology Group: CTG offers a large variety of UNIX and C topics, in Canada and England as well as the U.S. Courses available on videodisc.

Digital Equipment Corporation: DEC offers classes in ULTRIX internals as well as C programming.

Institute for Advanced Professional Studies: IAPS offers classes in many UNIX topics, but specializes in advanced areas.

Lurnix: Lurnix offers classes in a variety of UNIX topics as well as C programming. Lurnix offers a self-study program based on the book *UNIX for People*. (See Printed Info chapter.)

Uni-Ops: Uni-Ops offers a variety of courses such as UNIX System Security, 386 UNIX for Programmers and even Advanced `vi`.

USPDI: A nonprofit organization, the U.S. Professional Development Institute offers UNIX and C classes for CEU credit. These classes are sponsored by the DPMA Education Foundation.

Integrated Computer Systems: ICS offers courses on C and UNIX in the U.S. and Canada. ICS also offers video courses on the same material.

5.4   User Groups
"I refuse to join any club that would have me as a member." – Groucho Marx

There are several national and international UNIX user groups. If you depend upon UNIX for your livelihood, it is worthwhile for you to become a member of one of them. Your company may also want to become a corporate member or sponsor.

The user groups are most well known for their annual and semi-annual conferences, however they all provide many more services. These include supporting standards work, supporting local user groups, disseminating information and funding projects that benefit the members. Most of the user groups are nonprofit organizations.

International User Groups

The international UNIX user groups are /usr/group, USENIX and EUUG.

/usr/group is an international organization for commercially-oriented users and other end users. It publishes the *UNIX Products Directory* yearly, *CommU-NIXations* bimonthly, */usr/digest* biweekly, and sponsors annual UniForum conferences. /usr/group is an excellent source of information interpreting the UNIX problems of concern to the commercial UNIX user and marketer. /usr/group continues to do a substantial amount of work in setting UNIX standards, including sponsoring many working groups, and publishing many documents interpreting these standards. /usr/group also sponsors national and local user groups.

USENIX is an international organization for technical and academic UNIX users. USENIX publishes *;login:* bimonthly and *Computing Systems*, a refereed journal on UNIX-related papers, quarterly. USENIX also sponsors several conferences and workshops each year where many seminal papers on UNIX appear first. In general, USENIX is the first choice as a user group for UNIX developers and researchers. The organization sponsors experimental projects (e.g., UUNET, Stargate), and provides software exchange of member-donated sources. The Usenet newsgroup, `comp.org.usenix`, carries discussion of USENIX-related matters.

Historical notes about /usr/group and USENIX are presented in the History chapter. Their publications and conferences are further described elsewhere in this chapter and in the Printed Information chapter.

EUUG, the European UNIX User Group, is an international user group. However, unlike /usr/group and USENIX, EUUG makes no attempts at hiding its bias. EUUG conferences, publications and other activities are aimed at providing UNIX support to European users. (Ironically, however, the official language of EUUG's conferences is English.) EUUG conferences are held twice a year. EUUG produces a monthly newsletter called *EUUGN*. Many of the national European user groups provide automatic membership in EUUG.

National User Groups

There are many national UNIX user groups – indeed, more than one in some countries. While USENIX and /usr/group are international user groups, their directly sponsored activities (such as conferences) have traditionally been primarily in North America. National user groups such as the Australian UNIX

Users Group, and the Association Francaise des Utilisateurs d'UNIX exist to promote UNIX in their respective countries. These and other national user groups have regular meetings, newsletters and other services that complement the work of the international user groups. Other well-known national UNIX user groups include the Japanese UNIX Society, Korean UNIX User Group, National UNIX User Group/Netherlands, New Zealand UNIX Systems User Group, and /usr/group/UK Ltd. Addresses of these and other national user groups are listed in the Addresses Appendix.

NZUSUGI

NZUSUGI, the New Zealand UNIX Systems User Group, holds a yearly conference, which some claim is one of the few UNIX conferences still worth attending. It is quite informal as the attendance still numbers in the hundreds, not including sheep. (There are always a lot of sheep jokes at the conference.)

Local User Groups

Most of the national and international user groups have local affiliates. For example, there are user groups in most of the larger cities throughout the world. There are also national user groups for many of the smaller countries. The easiest way to find out about your local user group is to contact the larger user groups previously listed. They can tell you if they know of or sponsor a user group in your area.

These local UNIX user groups are a fun way of getting together with local UNIX talent and swapping UNIX and C tips, tricks and help. Most of the groups have regular meetings and newsletters. Public-domain software swapping is usually encouraged at meetings, and you can hear talks on new products or projects having to do with UNIX.

Some of the user groups have classes, and while these tend to be informal, they are much cheaper, and probably nearly as good as the commercial classes (see elsewhere in this chapter).

Besides these user groups, there are many "personal/amateur computer hobbyist groups" that can supply you with UNIX contacts also. While these user groups do not cater exclusively to UNIX or any particular software or hardware, they tend to attract enough people that they can support subgroups of interests. These usually include UNIX interests, and always include C interests. (Remember that C is a very popular language on PCs and other microprocessor systems.)

If you are interested in forming your own UNIX user group, contact one of the larger user groups previously listed. They are interested in local user groups that fit their own interests, and will help you kick it off. Typically, they will do your first mailing and supply you with lists of their members in your local area. They will mention you in their publications. And they might make available seed money for your new group.

Vendor User Groups

There are many user groups that specialize in particular vendors or products. Some of the most active ones are ADUS (Apollo DOMAIN Users' Society), DECUS UNIX SIG (DEC User Group UNIX Special Interest Group), and SUG (Sun User Group). All of these have newsletters and conferences devoted to topics concerning their respective systems. They also have distribution tapes that contain user-contributed software designed to run on their systems.

Many of the vendor-specific user groups are financially supported by the vendor itself. Thus, such conferences will not have exhibits for competitors. In other words, comparison shopping at conference exhibits will generally be restricted to products that do not compete with the vendor's. Of course, if you are looking for products that do not compete with the vendor's but run on or with their products, you may find such conferences a great marketplace.

Unlike most other user groups, the vendor user groups are generally for-profit organizations.

Some Other Groups

It is possible to spend every day of your life going to different UNIX user group conferences and workshops, while never attending a non-UNIX function (no less getting any work done). In reality, there are many other conferences and special-interest groups in professional organizations like the ACM and the IEEE which do not necessarily cater to UNIX. This does not mean that they ignore it. Indeed, they may provide a more balanced view of the world.

If you have read even a small amount of this book, you will have seen that many of our sources are not from within the UNIX world. It is in your best interest not to blind yourself to things simply because they are not UNIX. While UNIX is a wonderful system, it has freely borrowed many ideas from other operating systems and environments. It is to your advantage to be as knowledgeable about other systems as you are about UNIX. Only then will you really understand the UNIX world.

While it is not appropriate here to mention unrelated but worthwhile user groups, two user groups exist that are indirectly related to UNIX. Namely, the Software Tools User Group and the C Users' Group.

The history and importance of the Software Tools User Group (STUG) was discussed at length in the History chapter. STUG remains active although much of its work has been superceded by UNIX implementations.

STUG continues to distribute distribution tapes of the Virtual Operating System software for a large number of different computer systems, along with user-contributed software. STUG meetings are held alongside the regular USENIX meetings, every six months.

As its name implies, the C Users' Group (CUG) specializes in the C language. It produces the *C Users Journal* eight times a year, an excellent magazine for C programmers. However, CUG became known first for their distributions of member-contributed software. CUG's software is written for a variety of operating systems (including UNIX) and most of it is in C. (A little is in assembler, naturally, and some of the C programs are compilers and interpreters for other languages.)

CUG claims to have "the world's largest holding of public-domain C software," and they are quite professional in their distribution techniques. They can write media in many different formats (including `tar` and `cpio`) and will ship overnight if you request. In 1988, they charged $8 per volume, and their catalog included 135 volumes (5 1/4" floppies).

Section 3

Inside

UNIX

Chapter 6: The User's Environment

"A program designed for inputs from people is usually stressed beyond the breaking point by computer-generated inputs." – Dennis Ritchie

This chapter describes the UNIX users' environment. We describe UNIX shells and many other common tools and commands. With a minimum of effort, it is possible to do extensive UNIX programming even without learning the C language. Most UNIX users do take advantage of this and we present some examples.

Programmers will find the next chapter filled with more information about what lies underneath the UNIX environment. However, programmers are users, too, and will benefit by understanding the UNIX environment, as much as users.

6.1   Beachcombing for Shells

When asked "*What is UNIX?*", many people think simply of the *shell* (so named because it is the outermost layer of the system) and its characteristic features to control processes and files.

When the user types commands such as `cat` and `ls`, the program that is listening is the shell. The shell is the program most often used to start and control other programs, including editors, compilers, games, and so on. The shell is not a particular program but can actually be any program. Users can create their own shell. This allows one to stylize the UNIX user interface drastically on a per-user basis.

Allowing the user to substitute any program for the default user interface was an invention with UNIX. Even today, most operating systems do not let the user replace the user interface, and if they do, the program has to be a special one using unusual conventions.

To a certain extent, complaints about the arcane nature of the UNIX commands can be answered by *"Well, then write your own shell!."* However, while this is simple to say, writing a good shell takes some expertise. Nonetheless, we think that the designers of UNIX recognized the difficulty of designing an interface that would please everyone. So they left us with one that pleased themselves as programmers, and left a hook for the future.

Many people have taken that hook, and now we see UNIX systems with menu interfaces, AI interfaces, and iconic interfaces. The point is that all of these are possible.

A well-written shell can be a pleasure to use. Writing a good one admittedly takes some expertise, although the basic idea is simple enough.

```
while (1) {
        prompt("command:");
        read(command);
        execute(command);
}
```

A real shell is a good bit more complicated than this, having to deal with signals, interrupts, pipes and I/O redirection. One of the important points about a shell is that, like any UNIX program, it can have its I/O redirected. So if you redirect its input away from the keyboard to a file, it can execute a set of shell commands. This is called a *shell script*.

Shell scripts may be as simple as a set of commands to be executed. Even this simple concept allows one to tie together existing programs into new and more powerful programs. The shell is ideal for this. And because the shells all implement programming language constructs, shell scripts tend to look a lot like programs and do very sophisticated things, rather than just simply executing a set of commands. And like programming languages, choosing shells can differ with the application.

We tend to see different people using different shells. Many people use more than one shell. While this is a little confusing to the beginner, there are important reasons for being familiar with more than one shell.

sh, also known as the "Bourne shell" after Steven Bourne of Bell Labs, is the simplest shell. It is kind of a lowest common denominator of shells, having the rudiments of a programming language (similar to Algol-68), simple variables, and so on. It is popular because it was available before the other shells, and it is the only shell you are guaranteed to find on every UNIX system.

Because of the latter reason, it is common to find people writing shell scripts for **sh**, while using another shell interactively.

csh, also known as the "C shell" was written by several people at Berkeley and IIASA. While the programming language constructs of **sh** resembled Algol, those of **csh** resemble the C language, hence the name "C shell." Ironically, most people find the **csh** more difficult to program and continue to write shell scripts for **sh**, while using **csh** interactively.

While its name implies otherwise, the really noteworthy features of **csh** are job control, history and aliasing. *Job control* allows one to control multiple processes moving them between the foreground and background with single keystrokes. *History* keeps a list of previously executed commands, on the basis that you are likely to repeat commands or variants of them. Compared to **sh**, **csh** can drastically reduce the number of characters one has to type to get work done. *Aliases* are names given to command lines, which the **csh** remembers on your behalf.

csh is distributed with all Berkeley-based UNIX, and is usually included with any AT&T UNIX that says "with Berkeley enhancements."

tcsh, is a popular varient of **csh**, available in the public domain. It incorporates all of the features of **csh**, plus "command-completion" similar to the Tenex system from BBN. *Command-completion* allows one to type partial command and file names. As long as enough is given to disambiguate, the system can automatically complete the command. **tcsh** also provides **emacs**-style editing of the command line.

ksh, also known as the "Korn shell" after David Korn of Bell Labs, is the most powerful shell in common use. It is upwards compatible with **sh** and contains many of the best features of **csh** and **tcsh**, plus it has command-line editing à la **vi** or **emacs** (your choice). It is also much more efficient than any of the other shells. **ksh** is available from the AT&T Toolchest (see Applications chapter) as an unbundled product.

We expect that **ksh** will eventually be distributed with UNIX as the default shell. We enourage people to obtain **ksh** and think of it as the "standard shell." **ksh** is described in *The Korn Shell Command and Programming Language* by David Korn and Morris Bolsky, Prentice-Hall.

The shells discussed here are the most common. You are more likely to find them on your UNIX system than any other. However, there are many other shells available. Many third-party companies have begun to offer shells, sometimes optimized for a particular system. Some other shells worth mentioning are: **vsh** (Microsoft's visual shell), **deskmate** and **tsh** (Tandy), MultiView (SCO), **sysadmsh** (SCO's system administrator's shell), **dsh** (American Management Systems Inc.'s directory shell), and ATvanced Office System (Technology Research Group Inc.).

Note that describing shells can be as difficult as describing UNIX. They can be modified as easily, and they tend to change over time as authors add new features. For instance, **csh** has gained features with each new release. While **sh** was evolving, it took many ideas from other shells (including **csh**). **csh** and **ksh** continue to be enhanced, as do many other shells that we have mentioned here. Do not be surprised to find that what you thought was a feature of one shell shows up sooner or later in all the shells.

6.2   Shell Basics

All of the shells have many fundamental characteristics in common. These are described briefly in the rest of this chapter. We cannot hope to provide a comprehensive tutorial and reference guide for any one shell, no less all of them, but you should be able to come away from this with a working knowledge of

- some basic shell commands and features
- why the shell is useful
- what makes it better than most other operating system's interfaces

Let's dispose of the simplest stuff. The shell prompts you for a command. Here it uses a percent sign.

```
%
```

If you type the word "date," the shell will execute the program by that name. This prints out the current date and time.

```
% date
Tue Dec  1 17:38:30 EST 1987
```

Another command is **cat**. **cat** prints the contents of the named file to the terminal. Both **cat** and **date** are examples of programs that produce *standard output* (written **stdout** in C programs) meaning that their output appears on the terminal by default. Many commands take *standard input* (**stdin**) which means that they read from the terminal by default. Any flow of data is called a *stream*. Hence you may hear **stdin** referred to as the "input stream," and **stdout** as the "output stream."

6.2.1   I/O Redirection

    stdin and **stdout** are not exciting by themselves, but the shell allows us to easily *redirect* them. For example, you can store the output of the date command in the file **old-date** with the following command.

```
date > old-date
```

    When a command is executed, its input or output may be redirected to a variety of places. All UNIX programs understand the concept of **stdin, stdout, stderr** (standard error). **stderr** allows you to redirect a command's output without losing any error messages.

    stdout from any program can plug into **stdin** of another. It is surprising how many programs easily make use of this abstraction, and how easy it is to write programs to do so.

    I/O redirection is provided by the shell. User programs don't have to deal with it themselves. Some basic types of redirection are as follows:

< file	Use **file** as the standard input.
> file	Use **file** as the standard output.
>> file	Use **file** as the standard output, and append to it if it already exists.
<< string	Use current standard input until a line containing **string** is encountered, or End-Of-File (EOF) is reached.
`command`	Execute this command, and replace **`command`** by its standard output.

    Here are some examples. The following records the output of the **ls** command in a file called **dircontents**.

```
% ls > dircontents
```

    Since the **cat** command sends its standard input to its standard output, we can print out **dircontents** by having **cat** use it as its standard input. By not redirecting **cat**'s output, we will see it on the terminal.

```
% cat < dircontents
```

The last type of redirection is called *command substitution* or *backquoting*. It allows command output to become new commands or arguments to be executed.

```
% echo date
date
% echo `date`
Mon Feb 1 08:04:28 EST 1988
```

6.2.2   Pipes

Pipes connect the standard output of one process to the standard input of another. You can think of it as another kind of redirection. To create a pipe, list the two commands with a | between the two. (Naturally, we call it a pipe symbol.)

For example, you can count the number of files by piping the output of **ls** to the input of a word-counting program. (**wc** counts words and other things. **wc -w** will print out just the word count.)

```
% ls | wc -w
5
```

Isn't this handy? You could sort your directory by piping **ls** to the **sort** command (although **ls** does that already). **wc** will count other things – it doesn't know anything special about files. For example, using **grep** (which searches for strings with specific patterns), you can count the number of words in the dictionary that match a pattern.

First, watch how **grep** searchs for words containing the string "sue" in the file called **/usr/dict/words**.

```
% cat /usr/dict/words | grep sue
desuetude
ensue
issue
pursue
pursuer
sue
suey
tissue
```

Now, use **wc** to find out how many words there are.

```
% cat /usr/dict/words | grep sue | wc -w
9
```

Notice how we took the output of several commands and used them as the input to other commands. You can construct *pipelines* to any degree of complexity. By combining very simple programs, it is possible to create useful commands. It is easy to use existing programs in ways that the original authors never imagined.

6.2.3   Shell Scripts

Commands that are often repeated may be stored in files, so that you can just type the file name to rerun complex commands. Sequences of commands may be stored in a single file. Files with shell commands are referred to as *shell scripts*. These shell scripts can be invoked just like any other command. (They continue to use **stdin** and **stdout** if the commands inside them do.) Hence, your environment can be extended and customized very easily.

Shell scripts resemble programs from modern programming languages. In fact, the shell provides control structures so that you can write just about anything that you can in a high-level programming language. The shell supports if-then-else statements, do loops and variables.

Many people find that they rarely have to use any other language but the shell. It is that powerful. And it is easy to use. Best of all, the shell uses the same exact syntax whether you are writing shell scripts or typing commands to it directly.

Of course, different shells do things differently, so it is a good idea to state at the beginning of your shell script which shell you are writing for. (The Administrator's chapter discusses a standard way of doing this.) If you find yourself with shell scripts that you need to run faster, you can do several things. One way is to find where in the script things are slow. (Usually just one or two lines cause most bottlenecks.) Then either rewrite those lines, or replace them with specially written programs (in another language like C). We find that it is rare that we have to rewrite more than a couple of lines. (Most of the UNIX programs work efficiently enough.) An alternative is to get a shell compiler. These are discussed in the Applications chapter.

The final section in this chapter "Putting It All Together" contains some more shell script examples. The chapter on the Present also presents some more philosophy about shell programming.

Shell Example: Incremental Archive

Many users like to back up their own files using the archive program, **cpio**. However, **cpio** does not provide a way of saving only files which have changed recently. The program **find** can be used to locate files which have been changed in some number of days. By combining two unrelated UNIX commands, **cpio** and **find**, we can create a new program which produces *incremental* archives. We call it **incarc**. (Put the next three lines of code in a file by that name. Then mark it executable with **chmod**.)

```
find $1 -mtime -$2 -type f -print > $HOME/incarc.tmp
cat $HOME/incarc.tmp | cpio -ocBv > /dev/tape
rm $HOME/incarc.tmp
```

To execute it, type **incarc directory days**, where **directory** is the one to save, and **days** is how many days' worth of changed files to save.

The first line uses **find** to locate all the right files. (See later in this chapter for more about **find**.) The first and second arguments can be accessed by using the tokens **$1** and **$2**. The file names are saved in a file called **incarc.tmp** in your home directory. The following line saves the archive onto tape. Notice that the archiver reads its input from the standard input and writes to the standard output.

The last line deletes the file that we used to store the file names. If you want to, try rewriting this script so it avoids the use of a temporary file. Next, read up on **find** and fix **incarc** so that it can figure out itself how many days' worth to dump. (Hint: **-newer**)

6.2.4   Aliases
"The French for London is Paris." – Eugène Ionesco

Most shells provide the notion of aliases. *Aliases* are like shell scripts, except that they aren't stored in a file. They are stored in the working memory of the shell. They are appropriate for one-line commands. For example, if you type **ls -lt** a lot, you could alias it to the single character **l**. This would reduce your typing a lot. And if you really have to, you can alias **ls** to "list" or "directory" or whatever you think it ought to be called.

```
% alias l ls -lt
```

Although aliases are usually used for one-line commands, they can be quite complex, and have most of the same capabilities as shell scripts.

6.2.5   Environment Variables

Like any programming language, the shell has variables which function in exactly the same way. Several variables are predefined by the shell. For example, the variable **prompt** has the string which is used to prompt the user. Many people like to have their prompt reflect their current directory, although others like "fun" prompts. For example, the following works in **csh**.

```
/usr/libes/src/pacman% set prompt = "Yes, master? "
Yes, master? date
Tue Dec  1 17:38:30 EST 1987
Yes, master?
```

Besides the shell, many programs take advantage of being able to pass information through shell variables. For example, programs (such as the mailer) that use a character-graphics editor will not provide the function themselves but will call the one that the user likes. How? The mailer will look at the value of the variable **EDITOR**. If it is set to the name of a program (e.g., **emacs**, **vi**), that editor will be run. This provides the user with a familiar environment and obviates the mailer from having to duplicate the function of an editor.

Although these variables (and the aliases described earlier) can be set interactively, most are usually set in a special file that is read at login (e.g., **.login**, **.profile**), or whenever a new shell is started (e.g., **.cshrc**).

6.2.6   Process Control

UNIX is a *multitasking* operating system. (You will also hear it called a *multiprocessing* operating system.) This means that it can perform several tasks at the same time. Your shell is just one such task. There are also many other processes that run constantly on behalf of the system. The pipelines that we saw earlier were examples of commands that started the execution of several tasks at the same time.

You may never run more than one command at a time, but that would be very unusual. Most people are constantly running several processes. While one process is running, they are issuing commands for the next process. After all, if you just sat and waited for every command to finish, you would spend a lot of your time idle.

This brings up the interesting question of how to control all these processes. Early versions of UNIX had very simple mechanisms for process control. You may have noticed already that when you issue a simple command like **grep**, the shell completes execution of the command before prompting you for another command. This is called *synchronous* execution. If you put an ampersand symbol (**&**) at the end of a command, it will run *asynchronously* (or in the *background*). This means that the shell will not wait for it to complete before letting you do something else.

You can have any number of processes executing in the background but only one in the foreground at a time. The *foreground* process is the one that is getting your keystrokes from the terminal. If there were more than one foreground process, there would be no way to tell which process your keystrokes should go to.

One significant problem with early UNIX interfaces was that you could not move processes back and forth between foreground and background. For example, if you were editing a file in the foreground and wanted to look at a file (using **cat**) and then resume editing, you couldn't. You had to stop the editor, run **cat** and then restart the editor.

Originally, few UNIX programs were interactive, so there wasn't much need to move foreground processes to the background and vice versa. It was rare that a foreground command lasted long enough to be interrupted. The editor was one of those rare commands. A special command ("!") was created to execute other commands so you didn't have to stop the editor. These escapes became common in other long running interactive programs (e.g., **tip**, **cu**, **adb**, **vi**). They all continue to use the original syntax from **ed**.

Eventually, many more interactive UNIX programs were written and this brought about the need for more sophisticated control over processes. A number of different process control mechanisms are available in modern UNIX systems. Two approaches are particularly popular – job control and windows.

Job Control

Berkeley's C-shell was the first shell to use job control. *Job control* is a mechanism provided by the UNIX system to suspend and resume processes, and connect and disconnect the physical terminal to a process's `stdin` and `stdout`. The C-shell made job control look like a very simple system to swap processes between foreground and background. The C-shell reserves several control characters which could be entered at any time to suspend the foreground process, and return to the shell. Once you are in the shell, you can manipulate background processes through an extensive set of commands. Naturally, one of the commands brings a background process to the foreground.

One disadvantage of job control is that an application program may want to use the very same characters that have been reserved for job control. Another disadvantage is that job control (specifically, the Berkeley implementation) does not save all the state of a process when it is suspended. For example, the physical screen is not saved. In the case of a graphics-oriented application, this can be critical. The end result is that some applications must be aware of job control, for it to appear as though it really works with all processes. Even though job control is not entirely transparent to all applications, it is extremely popular because it works so well for the majority.

At the same time that Berkeley introduced job control, AT&T introduced *shell layers*. These supported a better degree of I/O control than simple redirection, and indirectly through that, a crude form of job control. For example, you could signal one process to come to the foreground as soon as it was ready for input. This system has largely disappeared, and Berkeley job control is supported on almost all systems whether or not they run Berkeley UNIX. System V machines with "Berkeley enhancements" usually include `csh` with job control.

Windows

It is possible to display multiple sessions at once on a single screen. The physical screen is logically divided into separate *windows*. Each window controls a different program. Unlike job control, where only one process is in the foreground, windows allow any number of processes to run in the foreground. Stated another way, every process in a window is in the foreground.

Users typically use a pointing device, such as a mouse, to manipulate the windows themselves. Of course, windows still have the same problem as job control – namely, an application may want to see the same mouse strokes that have been reserved for the window control. It does not appear that there is any way to escape this "meta" control problem.

Nonetheless, windows are quite popular. Imagine doing program development by displaying separate windows for the debugger, editor, compiler and manual. The only real disadvantage is that high-quality devices for displaying windows require more money and CPU time than do simple character-graphic terminals.

SunWindows running multiple applications on a single screen.

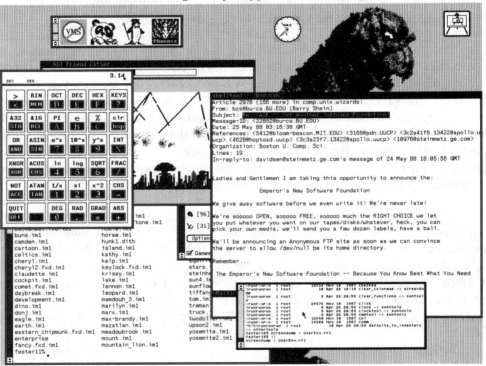

It is possible to have both windows and job control at the same time. How does that work? Running a shell in a single window, you can use job control to run several programs in the background. (And you can still use the old-style escapes that still exist in **ed** and other programs!) It is also possible, using job control, to suspend an entire set of windows by suspending the window manager itself. This is kind of like getting up from your desk and moving to a new one.

See the Applications chapter for references to particular window systems.

6.3   File Structure and Names

The UNIX file system is *hierarchical*. This means it resembles a tree (although it is usually drawn upside down) with a single root and many branches and leaves. Here is a graphical illustration of a small UNIX file system.

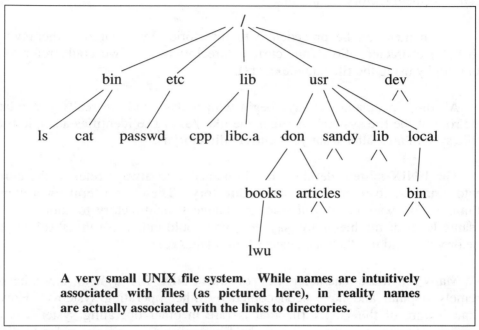

A very small UNIX file system. While names are intuitively associated with files (as pictured here), in reality names are actually associated with the links to directories.

The root of the file system is always written as a slash ("/"). Thus, we can list the files at the top of the tree by saying `ls /`.

```
Yes, master? ls /
bin
dev
etc
lib
usr
```

Files that contain other files are called *directories*. UNIX actually makes very little distinction between different types of files. Most of the commands to manipulate files can be used whether the file is a text file, a directory or some other type of file. Devices appear as files in the file system. This allows devices to be manipulated with the same commands that you use to manipulate files.

Directories are particularly interesting because they control access to other files, if only by name. You can "be" in a directory, in which case all files are accessed relative to that directory. Looking at the sample file system, if you are in directory **/**, you will see a different version of **lib** than if you were in directory **usr**. *Relative* means "relative to the current directory." The *current directory* is the directory we are in.

File names can be preceded with directories by separating them with a slash ("**/**") character. So if our current directory was **/**, we could refer to the second lib by using the file name **usr/lib**.

Absolute pathnames always begin with a slash and are really just relative to the root of the file system. A file name like **/usr/lib** identifies a single file in the file system no matter what your current directory is.

The UNIX system defines the file named **.** to always refer to the current directory and **..** to refer to the parent directory. These are useful for a number of things. For example, if you want to change your directory to another one at the same level of the hierarchy, say **foo**, you could either use the absolute pathname or you could use the much easier form of **../foo**.

Many of these characteristics of the UNIX file system have become extremely popular and have been copied by other operating systems. However, one feature of the UNIX file that is rare in other operating systems is that file names are case sensitive. Thus, the file names **foo** and **Foo** refer to different files. Virtually any character can be used in a file name. However, some characters are used by the shell for special purposes (see the next paragraph) and are unwieldy because of that. Human readers are also apt to be confused. For example, if you use spaces in file names, the name "**foo bar**" might appear to reference two files. Use your judgment.

By using regular expressions, users can specify a file name or groups of file names by a pattern, rather than spelling them out. *Regular expressions* are a theoretical classification of certain patterns – it is not necessary to know the theory, but the end result is extremely powerful.

To implement regular expressions, the shell reserves certain characters. For example, while the string **foo** matches the file name **foo**, the string **f*o** matches the file name **foo**, **fooo** and **foooo** as well as **fao** and **fhelloo**. That is because an ***** is defined to match any string.

Brackets are used to match a set of characters (any one between the brackets). Two characters inside brackets separated by a hyphen matches a range, and characters preceded by a caret ("^") matches anything but those characters. A question mark matches any single character. For example, imagine a directory with several files:

```
% ls
abra.cadabra     baby     bozo     core     zippy
% ls *
abra.cadabra     baby     bozo     core     zippy
% ls [ac]*
abra.cadabra     core
% ls b???
baby     bozo
% ls ?o*
bozo     core
```

6.4   A Tool is a Command is a Filter is a ...

UNIX has hundreds of programs that can be executed as shell commands. These are sometimes called *tools* to emphasize that they can be put together to build larger things. Many of the tools are very small programs specifically designed to do one simple task. For this reason, there are a great many tools.

While the tool-building concept is extremely powerful, it can be overwhelming to beginners. Some people like to find programs that do exactly what they want. The idea of putting two things together is almost scary. It can certainly be frustrating searching for the right tools to build something when you have no idea what the system has to offer.

In order to experience some degree of comfort with UNIX, you should take the time to become familiar with a fair subset of the tools that UNIX has to offer. Take the time to flip through the man pages for the commands. You may not feel like it is helping you to solve your problem, but it is. You will learn about all the tools. It is not enough to know how to combine tools – you must know which ones are there to be combined.

UNIX is not a system where you can sit down once a month and feel immediately at ease. Imagine going down to your basement right now to make something large, like a sofa. What you want is easy to understand, but you are going to have problems until you learn basic things like measuring, sawing, nailing, upholstery, and Band-Aids.

The rest of this section contains brief descriptions of the most commonly used UNIX commands. All of these are user-level commands – you type them directly to the shell. We have also included the etymology of the command names, since some of them are a little obscure. Most of the commands have optional flags or arguments; however, we mention only the most common use of each command. For a complete explanation, refer to the man page on your system.

While there are hundreds of other commands, the commands presented here are what you will probably use 90 percent of the time. We do not mean to ignore the hundreds of other commands that you will occasionally use from time to time. Those are not important until you understand the basics.

A few commands related to programming are mentioned, but the whole topic is discussed at much greater length in the Programmer's chapter. The Adminstrative chapter discusses some of the commands pertinent to maintaining a UNIX system.

6.4.1   File Manipulation Commands

These commands are the basic file manipulation commands. They include such operations as copying, removing, and listing files. Remember that since directories and devices are files, most of these commands make sense on them as well.

cd   Change the current directory. Stands for "**c**hange **d**irectory."

After the change, all file names are relative to your current directory, including the one in the next **cd**. Compare with **pwd**.

cp   Copy files. Stands for "**c**o**p**y."

cp leaves the original file but makes a duplicate with a new name. **cp** can also copy directory hierarchies. **uucp** (UNIX-to-UNIX **cp**) is a relative of **cp**, allowing copying of files between computers. Other variations on the **cp** theme exist. Compare with **mv**.

df   Show unused space in a file system. Stands for "**d**isk **f**ree."

df actually reports all space and used space as well as unused space. **df** works by keeping track of all free space, rather than by looking at files. Compare to **du**.

du   Show space in use in a directory. Stands for "**d**isk **u**sage."

           du counts the space in use in all files in a directory. If any files are
           directories, **du** will recursively count the space in them. Compare
           to **df**.

find   Act on arbitrary files in a directory. Stands for "**find**."

           find looks for files that match a given description. Once found, a
           given shell command can be executed on the file (such as to print
           out its name). It is hard to appreciate **find** until you actually need
           it. (And the man page is very hard to read but worth the effort.)

ls   List files in a directory. Stands for "**l**i**s**t."

           We have no idea why it is named so peculiarly, but it is short and
           you get used to it quickly.

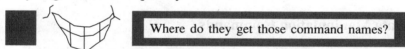

Where do they get those command names?

You may think that **ls** is a peculiar name, but there have been far
worse. **biff**, a command introduced at Berkeley, turned on *asynchronous mail notification*, so that you would get a message at your
terminal immediately if you received mail. Rumor has it that the
programmer who wrote **biff** couldn't think of a short, simple name
for his program, so he used the name of a dog that hung around the
hall where he worked at Berkeley. Why? Because the dog barked
when the mailman arrived!

mkdir   Create a new directory. Stands for "**m**a**k**e **dir**ectory."

           This special command is required to make sure all directories start
           with entries for . and ..

mv   Move files. Stands for "**m**o**v**e."

           Move files to a new place in the file system. Most other operating
           systems call this type of operation "renaming," however, names
           govern where files appear in the UNIX file system as well as what
           they are called. Compare with **cp**.

pwd   Print current directory. Stands for "**p**rint **w**orking **d**irectory."

Compare with **cd**.

rm   Remove files. Stands for "**rem**ove."

Since there can be more than one name to a file, **rm** usually just removes the file name. If the name is the last one for a file, the file is removed as well. There is no way to "unremove" a file that has been **rm**'d if it was the only name for a file.

which   Which program would this command execute? Stands for "**which**."

Prints out the program that would be executed by a given command. When you have a lot of directories in your path, it may not be immediately obvious which one the command is coming from. (BSD only.)

6.4.2   Data Manipulation Commands

These commands perform operations on the data inside files. However, most of these commands are capable of handling files as well as input and output streams. A *filter* is a program that takes its input (usually from **stdin**) and produces output (usually to **stdout**) based on that input. Most of these programs qualify as filters.

cat   Copy input to output. Stands for "con**cat**enate."

This is the archetype of all filters. It does nothing other than copy its **stdin** to its **stdout**. If you give **cat** a file name, it will copy the file to **stdout** – which is its primary use – for listing files at your terminal.

diff   Show differences between two files. Stands for "**diff**erence."

diff also works on directories.

echo   Echo arguments. Stands for "**echo**."

echo is primarily used inside of shell scripts for producing miscellaneous commentary. **echo** is actually useful interactively when typed as a command to display shell variables.

`ed`   Edit file. Stands for "**ed**itor."

          A simple line-oriented editor. Try a screen-oriented editor. Compare to `sed`, `grep`, and `vi`.

`file`   Show type of file. Stands for "**file**."

          `file` guesses at what type of file you have named by looking at the first few bytes of it. It can be fooled, though not easily. Compare to `od` and `strings`.

`grep`   Search for pattern. Stands for the `ed` command, "**g**lobal **r**egular **e**xpression **p**rint."

          `grep` searches its input for a pattern, defined by a regular expression. Any lines that match are printed. Compare to `ed` and `sed`.

`head`   Print first few lines. Stands for "**head**."

          `head` is useful for taking a quick look-see at files. Compare to `cat`, `file`, and `tail`.

`more`   Show data one screenful at a time. Stands for "**more**."

          `more` copies its input to its output like `cat`, but pauses after every screenful. `more` is called `page` on some systems. Compare to `cat`.

`od`   Print uninterpreted data. Stands for "**o**ctal **d**ump."

          Breaks input into bytes or words and prints as hex, octal, or characters. `od` impunes no interpretation on its input, so you can really see what is in the data. Compare to `cat`.

`sed`   Noninteractive editor. Stands for "stream **ed**itor."

          Just like `ed`, but it works on streams rather than files. `sed` is often called from shell scripts when a file has to be edited as if by hand. Compare with `ed`.

`sort`   Sort data. Stands for "**sort**."

`strings` Show printable strings. Stands for "**strings**."

> `strings` is useful for figuring out what a program does without running it. You get the job of guessing based on your seeing the error messages and other printable strings in the program. Think of it as a game. Compare to `file`.

`tail`   Print last few lines. Stands for "**tail**."

> `tail` is useful for looking at log or diagnostic files, where all you care about is the most recent data (at the end). Compare to `head`.

`vi`   Screen editor. Stands for "**vi**sual."

> A much-enhanced screen-oriented version of the editor, `ed`. Compare to `ed`.

6.4.3   Programming Commands

These commands generally take programs as input. Sometimes the output is yet another program. In a way, any of the commands discussed in this chapter can be thought of as programmable, some just more complex than others.

`adb`   Program debugger. Stands for "**a**ssembler **d**e**b**ugger."

> `adb` is used for debugging assembler programs or C programs that you do not have the source for. This is painful.

`a.out`   User program. Stands for "**a**ssembler **out**put."

> The C compiler produces user programs by this name (by default).

`awk`   Pattern processing language `awk`. Stands for the authors, "**A**ho, **W**einberger and **K**ernighan."

> An interpreted programming language, oriented to string processing à la Snobol. Turn to `awk` when your problem is too hard to solve with the shell, and not worth writing a C program.

`cc`   C language compiler. Stands for "**C** **c**ompiler."

Translates C source files into a machine executable program. `cc` is really just a front-end for a large set of programs including `cpp` (the C preprocessor), and `ld` (the linker).

`make`   Construct program from sources. Stands for "**make**."

`make` makes an executable program from sources. `make` uses a program to control the complex task of compiling, `lex`ing, `yacc`ing, and so on.

`sdb`   C program debugger. Stands for "symbolic **d**e**b**ugger."

`sdb` allows you to diagnose and experiment on a running C program or do postmortem analysis on a dead one. `dbx` is another C debugger that is better than `sdb`, but not available on all systems.

`sh`   Bourne shell. Stands for "**sh**ell."

Most shell scripts are written for the Bourne shell. If they are not marked executable, they can be run by hand with this command.

6.4.4   Miscellaneous Commands

`date`   Show the time and date. Stands for "**date**."

`kill`   Send signal to process. Stands for "**kill**."

The primary use of `kill` is to send a *kill signal* to a process, which kills a process. `kill` can actually send any signal.

`mail`   Send and receive electronic mail. Stands for "**mail**."

`man`   Show on-line documentation. Stands for "**man**ual."

`man` displays pages from the "Programmer's Manual" (although this includes all the tools and commands discussed here). Given a keyword, `man -k` prints the names of man pages which have the keyword in the title. Some systems have this as a separate program, called `apropos`.

ps   Show process information. Stands for "**p**rocess status."

Displays information about any or all processes on the system.

who   Show users logged in. Stands for "**who**."

6.5   Putting It All Together

Now that you have read this chapter, we hope you have a reasonable feeling for the philosophy of the UNIX user interface, as well as knowing some of the commands. To drive some points home, and at the same time add some concreteness to the discussion, this section presents a simple tool, composed out of a single shell script, with the commands that were previously mentioned.

Some of the commands have options (or arguments) that we did not mention. (Options are useful in modifying the default behavior of commands.) If you want to learn more about them, consult a UNIX manual.

Our example is a shell script that does an administrative task, not already performed by UNIX – it archives a user. Archiving means that their files are backed up to off-line storage (such as a tape or floppy disk), and they are deleted from the file system. This is typical procedure when a user leaves a company or school. Otherwise the file system would end up with files of users that have long since departed.

Our program is called **remove-user** and is actually quite simple. All it has to do is 1) copy the directory to a backup media, and 2) remove the directory. However, we will also leave mail for the user as a courtesy in case they ever log in again and wonder where their files went.

remove-user is written for the Bourne shell (**sh**). It is good style to have the first line be the special comment **#!/bin/sh**. (The reason for this is discussed in the Programmer's chapter.) Bourne shell comments begin with **#**.

Since we are going to remove files, it is important that we check for errors when archiving or at any other step. A simple way to do that is to set a special flag that will force the shell script to stop if any error is encountered.

```
set -e
```

We also want to make sure that only the system administrator is running this program. While users cannot delete other users' files, it is possible for

users to delete their own files if they mistakenly run **remove-user** on themselves.

```
if test -e $USER = root
        then
        echo "Must be root to run remove-user"
        exit
fi
```

The **if** statement is an example of the shell's high-level language features. **do** loops, **for** loops, switches and other control structures are available.
Most commands return a boolean value that can be tested. Here, we need only
to test a shell variable (**USER**) against a value, so no program is necessary. In
cases like these, **test** can be used to evaluate arbitrary expressions and produce a boolean value.

remove-user takes one argument – the user name. From the user name,
we can figure out the user's directory by finding the corresponding entry in
/etc/passwd. The first argument to the shell is available as **$1**. (The second is
$2 and so on.) We can search through the password file using **grep**.

```
grep "^$1" /etc/passwd
```

grep returns an entire line which contains a lot of other information that
we don't need. What we want is the sixth field. It is easy to select this using
awk. Since we want the output of **grep** to be the input to **awk**, we connect them
by a pipe.

```
grep "^$1" /etc/passwd | awk 'BEGIN {FS=":"} {print $6}'
```

Rather than storing the result in a file, we want to put it in a shell variable. The easiest way to do that is by using the back-quote mechanism. This
replaces the entire previous command with its output.

```
directory=`grep "^$1" /etc/passwd |
        awk 'BEGIN {FS=":"} {print $6}'`
```

The result is that the shell variable, **directory**, contains the user's directory name. Now we can archive the directory using **tar**. See the Administrator's chapter for more on **tar**.

```
tar -c $directory
```

While we are assuming that the user has left the face of the earth, it would be nice to leave a message just in case they log in and wonder where their files are. We can send them mail. Fortunately, mail is not stored in the user's directory but in a directory private to the mail system. Here, we use another type of indirection which allows a command to receive input from immediately following lines in the script.

```
mail $1 << EOF
Your files ($directory) have been archived and
removed from the file system.
Please see an administrator if you need them back.
EOF
```

Once these commands have executed, we know that the user's files are secure and we can safely remove the on-line versions.

```
rm -fr $directory
```

The completed **remove-user** script is as follows:

```
#!/bin/sh
# remove-user username

# exit on any errors
set -e

# check that we are root
if test -e `who am i` = root
        then
        echo "Must be root to run remove-user"
        exit
fi
# get the directory
directory=`grep "^$1" /etc/passwd |
        awk 'BEGIN {FS=":"} {print $6}'`
# archive the directory
tar -c $directory
# send mail to user in case they accidentally reappear
mail $1 << EOF
Your files ($directory) have been archived and
removed from the file system.
Please see an administrator if you need them back.
EOF
# remove the directory
rm -fr $directory
```

There are many things you could do to improve this program. However, our intent was merely to demonstrate some of the things presented in this chapter in an actual shell script.

What is important is the result – we made a shell script out of simple, pre-existing tools with very little effort. It was easy to do, because the tools are easy to use and designed so that they can be hooked together easily.

Much more complex programs can be built out of these same tools. And if you follow the same guidelines in program design, your programs can be used and incorporated as easily into other people's programs.

Many users who use the shell do not feel they are programmers, even when they create long pipelines or write shell scripts. However, programming is an intrinsic part of using the UNIX shell. While shell programming may seem less intimidating than C programming, the results are just as powerful.

This is one of the biggest differences between being a "UNIX user" and a user of any other operating system. It is a daunting task to easily extend or modify the user interface of most other operating systems. But UNIX users are not restricted to the original plans of the designers and find themselves using the tools and commands of the operating system in ways that no one ever dreamed of.

Chapter 7: The Programmer's Environment

"I am a programmer. On my 1040 form, this is what I put down as my occupation." – Ken Thompson in his Turing Award Lecture

Of all the people who use UNIX, programmers have the most favorable impression about it. UNIX is optimized more towards programming than anything else. It was written by programmers for programmers. And it was written by very good programmers.

UNIX programming is not immediately intuitive, and no matter how many good things we say about it, you cannot sit down at a terminal and bang out a magnificent gem of a first program. You must familiarize yourself with the system calls, the libraries, the languages and the tools, and of course, the manual, in order to succeed at this game.

In a way, UNIX is not geared towards helping you get your work done. Rather it is oriented towards helping you understand the UNIX system, so that you fit your solution into a UNIX-style solution. Often this leads to a different solution than you might find on another system.

For example, the use of regular expressions is pervasive throughout UNIX. There are libraries that support their use, and many of the tools understand them. Writing a program that used some other kind of pattern matching would be stupid and painful. You would ignore all the wonderful UNIX tools, spend your time reinventing the wheel, and end up with a program that used a totally different syntax than any other in the system.

It is well worth your time learning a little about the UNIX programming environment and philosophy. By reaching a certain stage of UNIXness, you will feel at home while writing UNIX programs, synergistically directing its power with minimal effort, and producing beautiful and graceful creations.

This chapter will highlight some important concepts of the programmer's environment. If you are interested in learning more after reading this chapter, we recommend the books *Advanced UNIX Programming* by Marc Rochkind, and *The UNIX Programming Environment* by Brian Kernighan and Rob Pike.

7.1   System Concepts

Much of the elegance of UNIX is derived from the design of the functions at the beck and call of a programmer. These functions tend to be simple, efficient routines which do one thing and do it well. For example, `open()` works on files, directories and devices. A subset of these functions are the *system calls*. The system calls are the interface to the UNIX kernel, and are considered the real primitives of a UNIX system. For example, in order to write to a file, the user must use the `write()` system call. There are a number of high-level interfaces to write to files (such as `printf()`). These shield the user from some of the more mundane aspects of programming, but all of them call `write()` at some point to get the work done. (There is no functional reason to differentiate between system calls and library calls. Fortunately, they appear the same syntactically.)

The system calls are defined and implemented in a special program known as the *kernel* (frequently misspelled as "kernal"). The kernel is programmed in C; however, the kernel environment is markedly different than most other C programs. The code has to deal with the possibility of hardware interrupts at any time. Memory is globally shared in what resembles a multi-threaded single process. Hence, each piece of code has to protect its data structures against simultaneous access by another part of the kernel.

Application programs do not often make system calls. While system calls are the most efficient means of controlling the system, they are fairly primitive. Many libraries have been created to save the programmer time in coding and provide robustness. In addition, the libraries are more portable than the UNIX system calls. If you port a program to a non-UNIX operating system, you will more likely find higher-level calls easier to emulate than lower-level ones.

```
creat()
```

Ken Thompson was once asked, "If you were redesigning UNIX, what would you do differently?" He replied, "I'd spell **creat** with an **e**."

7.1.1   I/O

One of the strengths of UNIX is the consistency with which it treats I/O. Files, devices and even processes can be manipulated using I/O primitives. And since the UNIX I/O paradigm is so simple, learning it means that you can access most of what the system has to offer very easily.

One thing that you may initially find confusing is that devices are often referred to as files. In fact, they appear in the file system with normal file names. This is actually an advantage. By treating them as disk files, you do not need special commands or functions to use them. For example, you can set the protection of a device with the exact same command and syntax as for a disk file. Redirection works, too. If you say **who > /dev/tty33**, the output of **who** will appear on terminal 33.

Viewed through I/O-tinted glasses, UNIX looks like the figure below. We refer back to it in the following discussions.

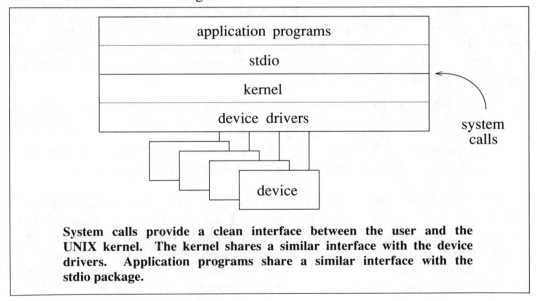

System calls provide a clean interface between the user and the UNIX kernel. The kernel shares a similar interface with the device drivers. Application programs share a similar interface with the stdio package.

7.1.1.1   Ordinary Files and Directories

Ordinary files are a sequence of bytes stored in the file system. There is no structure imposed by the file system upon a file, other than a simple linear ordering of bytes. Files are not explicitly sized by the user. Files are extended simply by writing past the last byte in the file. Attempting to read past the last byte returns an end-of-file. Files may be shrunk explicitly. Users may open a file, move to, read and write arbitrary bytes in the file (if they have the appropriate permission).

The lack of file structure and sizing is a highlight of UNIX. There are no special tools for reading special files with special structures, because there are no such files. All files are simple sequential files. Users may impose working guidelines, of course. For example, files containing source code generally contain only printable ASCII characters, with lines terminated by newlines (ASCII NL). However, the file system does not enforce this through any mechanism.

Each file is tagged by an index (or *i-number*) that corresponds to a field of data internal to the file system. These fields, referred to as *i-nodes*, contain data about each file such as its protection, length, owner, and pointers to other i-nodes containing actual data. The i-node does not include the name of the file.

Directories are files that contain a list of file names. Associated with each file name is an i-number. By retrieving the corresponding i-node, one gets to the file associated with a file name. When presented with a file name, the kernel will automatically perform the mapping to get to the file. In general, programmers do not deal with files at this level; however, there are two important consequences of this representation.

1. Files may have multiple names. Each name is called a *link*.

2. It is impossible to find out the name of a file from just knowing its i-number, other than by exhaustive search. There may be more than one name, or even no names (this is true for pipes).

Each directory appears as a file in the file system. Thus, it may appear in another directory's list of files. This provides the hierarchical structuring characteristic of the UNIX file system. While directories can be read by users, they cannot be written except by a special system call, since references to arbitrary i-nodes could destroy the file system. This is one of the few exceptions to the rule that the file system does not care about the internal structure of files.

7.1.1.2 Devices

Much of what UNIX does is control devices. These include terminals, tape drives, disk drives, and network interfaces. Any peripheral is seen by UNIX as a device. UNIX groups devices into two types – block and character-oriented devices.

Block-oriented devices perform I/O in fixed-size blocks of characters. Disks are typical of block-oriented devices. *Character-oriented* devices are not restricted to fixed-size block I/O. They can transfer any number of characters at a time (including a single character). Keyboards and mice are good examples of character-oriented devices. It is actually possible to treat disks as character-oriented devices, but it is usually inefficient to do so.

You can see which devices are character-oriented or block-oriented on your system by executing the command: `ls -l /dev`. A `b` in the first column indicates it is block-oriented, while a `c` indicates that it is character-oriented. (Directories are indicated by a `d` and ordinary files by a `-`.) For most programmers, the orientation of a device is not important; the higher-level libraries unify them so that they act the same.

It is possible to treat a device as both character-oriented and block-oriented at the same time. For example, disks are normally accessed on a per-block basis. However, when a disk is copied (i.e., for backups), it is more efficient to access it as a character device. This is because character devices can transfer any number of characters at a time, while block devices are limited to the size of a block. Also, block devices are buffered in the kernel while characters devices are not.

Interestingly, memory can be accessed as a device, although this is more of a back door than a sensible idea. There is a tremendous overhead for going through the I/O system (with a system call) to talk to memory, rather than doing it directly (by one machine instruction). However, it is possible to access otherwise protected memory in this fashion. For example, `ps` digs up information about other processes by reading `/dev/kmem` (kernel `memory`) and `/dev/mem` (physical `memory`).

Devices (see previous figure) are considered not as part of UNIX proper, but rather as being underneath it, much as the computer running UNIX is not considered a "UNIX computer." It is possible to incorporate any device into UNIX, however, some devices may be more appropriate than others. For example, devices that power on with interrupts enabled are considered obnoxious and not UNIX-friendly. An amusing reading on the clashes between UNIX and real-world devices is "All the Chips that Fit" by Tom Lyon and Joseph Skudlarek in the *Summer 1985 USENIX Conference Proceedings*.

7.1.1.3   Device Drivers

Each device has a special program designed to present an interface to the UNIX system.   Called a device driver, the interface makes each device "act" alike.   In particular, the driver can either make a device look like a character-oriented device or a block-oriented device.

Each type of device is defined by a small set of functions that can be performed on it. Most of these are directly mapped to system calls. For example, each device has an **open()**, **read()** and **write()** call. Devices appear as files in the file system, usually in the **/dev** directory. When any of these files are accessed, the kernel calls the routine associated with each one. (How the routine is selected is explained further in the Administrator's chapter.)

The result is a unification of access to all objects via the file system. For example, you can read from a disk file as easily as a keyboard, since they both respond to the **read()** system call the same way. Access to a device except through its well-defined interface is prohibited, providing a reliable device subsystem.

Pseudo-devices are theoretical devices that have device drivers but no devices.   You can think of them as simulated devices.   Pseudo-devices are used to implement pipes and many network devices.   A simple example of a pseudo-device is **/dev/null**.

The Null Device – **/dev/null**

/dev/null is the simplest device in the UNIX system. When you write to it, your characters are thrown away. Actually, they are ignored entirely, and **write()** simply returns a successful completion status. This is useful when you don't care what the output of a command is but are just interested in its side effect. (For example, **time grep a /usr/dict/words > /dev/null** will print out the time it took to search for all the words with **a** in them. Without the redirection to **/dev/null**, it will print out the words themselves as well.) **/dev/null** generates an EOF (End-Of-File) condition whenever it is read.

Another major use of **/dev/null** is in messages – as in *"System going down at noon. Complaints to /dev/null."*

Pipes

Another pseudo-device is the UNIX pipe. Just like any device, a pipe can be opened, read and written. However, there is no physical peripheral corresponding to a pipe. When you write to one, your characters are buffered in memory until someone reads it from the other end. Because of this, it is particularly useful as a communications path between two processes.

When the command `who | lpr` is given to the shell, the shell creates two processes with a pipe between them. `who` writes to the pipe and `lpr` reads from the pipe. Notice that `who` doesn't take any special arguments to access the pipe. Neither does `lpr`. Nor does either program make any attempt to detect that it is using a pipe.

The pipe is buffered by the pipe device driver. If the pipe's writer is faster than the pipe's reader, the device driver will stop the writer until the pipe drains a little. Similarly, the reader will wait for the writer when the pipe is empty. When the writer closes the output stream, the reader receives an EOF (just as if it were reading a file from the disk).

This simple device is one of the key mechanisms that provides the shell with the ability to plug programs together without any special prior coding.

One restriction of pipes is that the ends of a pipe can only be inherited through a common ancestor of the executing processes. This is no problem when using pipes in the shell – the shell is the common ancestor which passes each end of the pipe to a different process. However, it prevents unrelated processes from communicating. More recent additions (viz. sockets and streams) to UNIX overcome this limitation.

Named Pipes, or *FIFOs*

Named pipes are an extension to UNIX that first appeared in PWB but did not become generally available until System V. *Named pipes* are just like ordinary pipes except that they have names. Because they appear in the file system, they can be referenced by arbitrary processes, and provide a means of communication between unrelated processes. This overcomes a limitation of ordinary pipes. Named pipes are also called *FIFOs* (for "First *In*, First *Out*").

Unfortunately, named pipes do not provide a simple solution to the client-server model. For example, if a server opens a named pipe and waits for a client, it must have a way of preventing or distinguishing data written into the same pipe by two different processes.

Both sockets and streams provide better mechanisms for communication between unrelated processes than do named pipes.

7.1.1.4 Basic I/O System Calls

All of the devices mentioned so far implement the same set of basic system calls, including `open()`, `read()`, `write()` and `close()`. These are all that most programs ever need. When the shell executes programs, it automatically creates and opens three files for each process. Once a file is open, it is called a *stream*, and referred to by a *file descriptor*. The three streams opened for each process are:

standard in	This stream provides input, such as from a terminal or the previous process in a pipeline. File descriptor 0. File pointer `stdin`.
standard out	This stream is provided for output, such as to a terminal or the next process in the pipeline. File descriptor 1. File pointer `stdout`.
standard error	This stream is provided for errors, just so they will not be accidentally redirected in a pipeline. File descriptor 2. File pointer `stderr`.

In the case of our `who | lpr` example, `who` will automatically have its `stdout` connected to a pipe. The other end of the pipe will be connected to the `stdin` of `lpr`. `who` will ignore its `stdin` since it doesn't read any input. `lpr` will print its results on its `stdout` which is the terminal. The `stderr` of both processes will also be the terminal.

This sounds complicated but is quite simple. The shell has done most of the work. The processes don't even have to call `open()`. All `who` will do is write its results using the file descriptor `1` (see above) and `lpr` will read using file descriptor `0`.

The calls to `read()` and `write()` are straightforward:

```
cc = write(1,buffer,length);      /* in who */
cc = read(0,buffer,length);       /* in lpr */
```

read() reads from **stdin**. At most **length** characters are placed in the **buffer**. When **read()** returns, the number of characters read are stored in **cc**. **write()** works similarly.

While this may seem simple, it is quite primitive. It is also inefficient for most types of processing. The reason is that if a process is calling **write()** for each character (or even each line), a process must context swap with the kernel on each call. Usually, I/O can be buffered. Buffering allows characters to be queued until a high watermark is hit. Then, **write()** is called with a large buffer. This reduces the number of system calls (and corresponding context switches).

7.1.1.5   Standard I/O

Standard I/O is the name of a library. It provides a higher-level interface to the I/O system calls we have just covered (see previous figure). It is even easier to use, and at the same time, much more flexible. Standard I/O is usually abbreviated "stdio" (and pronounced "stud-i-o") because the appropriate definitions for it are set up in a C program with the line **#include <stdio.h>**. Stdio is based on the "portable C library" by Mike Lesk at Bell Labs. The portable C library was designed to allow C programs to remain portable across different operating systems, by providing a common I/O system. Stdio can be implemented on any machine that supports a C compiler.

Like the system calls, stdio is very clean because it works on all objects in the file system whether they are disk files, devices or pseudo-devices. And stdio follows the **stdin**, **stdout**, and **stderr** conventions.

A significant difference between the stdio library and the system calls is that the higher-level stdio functions are buffered. Corresponding to the **open()** system call is **fopen()** from stdio. **fopen()** opens a file and allocates a buffer for I/O in user space. Writing characters to (or reading from) a buffer is very cheap. When the buffer is full, characters are flushed. This is transparent to the programmer, except that programs run very fast. And since the buffering is handled by library calls, programs remain portable even while becoming extremely efficient.

When doing I/O to a terminal, stdio changes its buffering scheme so that the user does not have to wait for an entire buffer to fill up before seeing anything. (The programmer can also explicitly control buffering.) Buffering on input works similarly, and provides more corresponding efficiency over **read()**.

Stdio is even easier to use than the system calls. `write()`, requiring three arguments, can be performed with `fprintf()`, requiring only two. (In addition, `fprintf()` is capable of performing complex high-level formatting.)

```
write(1,"hello, world",12);
fprintf(stdout,"hello, world");
```

stdout is the name of the stdio structure containing the output stream's buffer. Since printing to **stdout** is so common, `printf()` is a shorthand for that.

```
printf("hello, world");
```

7.1.1.6   Some More Device Drivers

Terminals (ttys) – **/dev/tty**

One of the most complex device drivers in any system is that for the terminal (usually written as *tty* and pronounced "titty"). This driver controls terminals and other things that are connected to the system through RS-232 interfaces. There are a surprising number of variations in the way these work.

Various attempts to modernize the terminal interface while still maintaining support for older programs have left the terminal driver incredibly complex. Anthropologists should not find it too hard to uncover the history of the driver by studying its unusual interface. While its complexity may not be justified, it is likely more flexible than any other operating system's terminal interface.

Terminals can be read from and written to just like ordinary files. When the shell is prompting a terminal for commands, it is simply opening a file, reading characters from it, and writing characters to it. When the shell reads an end-of-file, it will stop processing commands and exit. Thus, you can log out of UNIX by sending the shell an end-of-file (usually by pressing control-D). Recent versions of UNIX have added a logout command which effectively does the same thing.

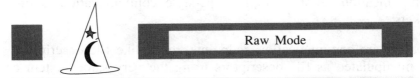

Raw Mode

One of the reasons the terminal driver is so complex is because it has to examine every single keystroke before passing it on to the program. For example, pressing the space bar might cause a space to be sent to the program, but a control-C has to get turned into an interrupt, and a backspace actually has to remove the previous character from the input stream! There are lots of complexities like these that no other drivers have to handle.

Programs may request that the driver do no special interpretation of keystrokes. This is called *raw mode* because the programs see the raw keystrokes from the user. Screen editors often do this.

When the driver is interpreting characters, it is said to be in *cooked mode*. It helps to have a sense of humor about all of this.

Pseudo-ttys – /dev/**pty**

Another pseudo-device is a pty, or pseudo-tty. A pty (pronounced "pity") behaves exactly like a tty, except that there is no I/O occurring on a physical device. It all happens in the pty driver's imagination. A typical use for this is to support logins over a network. The user session appears to have all the characteristics of a serial line controller, but it is all simulated.

Pty's always have a corresponding tty to communicate with. The simulated terminal (the master) is always the pty (for example, **/dev/ptyp2**), while the program (the slave) that we are imagining is connected via a serial line uses the corresponding tty (**/dev/ttyp2**). Put another way, data written on the master is given to the slave as input, as though it had been received from a hardware interface (such as a UART). Correspondingly, data written to the slave can be read from the master, as though it had been sent to a hardware interface.

Sockets

Berkeley UNIX imported the idea of sockets from the Arpanet community to support networking with TCP/IP. Sockets also provide generic interprocess communication. For example, pipe-style communication is implemented with sockets.

Sockets are communication endpoints, much like file descriptors. Indeed, they are manipulated as file descriptors using the very same system calls, such as **read()** and **write()**. However, there are additional system calls defined on sockets to support additional capabilities such as network addressing, and communication between unrelated processes. With minor extensions, existing programs can be rewritten using sockets with the result that they can communicate with processes on other systems.

Besides providing pipe-style communication, sockets can be used for server-client communication, and also message passing or virtual circuits. Sockets can support any kind of networking protocol, including both DoD's TCP/IP and the ISO standards. However, each type of networking requires a different socket protocol interpreter.

Streams

Streams were first implemented in Version 8, as a means of unifying the numerous complex line disciplines used to control terminal handling. Later, they were generalized for interprocess communication. Hence, streams can solve the same problems that Berkeley solved with sockets – namely, communication between unrelated processes and across networks. In this form, streams were introduced first into System V.

Streams are very similar to sockets. They are communications endpoints. They can be manipulated using conventional programs and system calls. Streams appear in the UNIX file system as conventional files just as do UNIX-domain sockets (albeit in the **/dev** directory). Thus, they can be manipulated with conventional programs. When two programs open the same device, they can communicate.

Once processes are communicating, they may pass file descriptors over a stream (between unrelated processes). This makes writing servers very easy.

Network drivers appear not as specialized device drivers, but as kernel or user-level servers waiting on generic stream devices. In order to communicate using a particular protocol, modules are *pushed* onto the stream via library calls. Modules are stacked, allowing multiple levels of protocols.

Berkeley's sockets and System V's streams sound different but are really duals in function. The differences are obvious to the implementor but much less so to the application programmer. Indeed, either system can be emulated by the other with sufficient work. It is likely that both sockets and streams will be available on future UNIX systems. Nonetheless, streams are particularly elegant, and they will probably become the dominant base for interprocess communication in the future.

Other Drivers

It is relatively easy to add new drivers to UNIX. All you need to do is provide a set of calls (`open()`, `read()`, `write()`, etc.) for your driver to execute when accessed. These routines are then linked to the kernel (normally distributed as an object file, exactly for this purpose).

Since the drivers run in the same address space in the kernel, drivers can manipulate any part of the system including any user process or the kernel itself. Thus, device drivers are a simple way of getting UNIX to do things that its designers never allowed for by the system calls. For example, early versions of UNIX only provided timer resolutions down to one second. A common workaround was to build a driver which provided the ability to sleep to a millisecond. If you wanted to sleep for, say, 17 milliseconds, you would code `write(fd,buffer,17)`. The buffer was not actually written anywhere, but the device driver would take 17 milliseconds before returning control to the process.

Drivers have been written to perform file and record-locking and other more imaginative things that UNIX was never designed to handle. Device drivers provide a wonderfully clean interface, but as the previous example shows, they can also be easily abused.

7.1.2   Processes

UNIX supports multiple processes (environments of executing programs). Multiprocessing is transparent to each program. Each process runs without regard to others. While users often take advantage of multiprocessing (e.g., starting several programs in a pipeline), processes need not concern themselves with other processes, since the I/O appears to go to or come from a simple file, whether or not another process is involved. Nevertheless, processes can create or manage other processes explicitly. The shell does this for users, for example.

Prior to execution, programs are built in the usual way. A program is compiled and linked resulting in a file of executable machine instructions. This file can be executed by the kernel with the **exec()** system call. The kernel overlays the calling program with the new program and gives it control of the process. The new program inherits several things from its ancestor, including any open files. The shell takes advantage of this to pass its **stdin**, **stdout** and **stderr** to any new processes. If the user has started programs in a pipeline, the shell creates the pipe and passes one end of the pipe to each program.

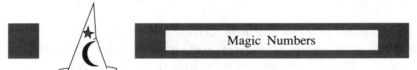

Magic Numbers

When a program is **exec**'d, a few bytes of the file are read and compared against several *magic* numbers. These magic numbers are known constants denoting whether the file is machine code or a shell script. To distinguish between different shells, you can put **#! shellname args** at the beginning of your file. If the kernel sees this, it will run **shellname** with your file as input. If it doesn't recognize any magic numbers, it will assume it is a **/bin/sh** script. Put a line like this at the beginning of all your shell scripts so that it is clear which shell your script is written for.

Executable files are one of the rare instances in UNIX where the kernel looks for a specific internal structure in a file.

There are a number of different forms of **exec()**, although there is only one actual system call (the rest are library versions). The choice of which one you use depends on how you want to pass arguments. (The actual system call is **execve()**, but most people refer to it as **exec()** (the original one) in conversation.)

exec() can run new programs, but it cannot create new processes. New processes are created using **fork()**. **fork()** causes a copy of the current process to be created. The new process is called the *child* of the original. Both child and parent processes continue running.

The shell creates new user processes by forking. Then, the child (still running the shell) overlays itself with the user program by **exec()**. If the shell finds itself running as part of a pipeline, it replaces **stdin** and **stdout** with the appropriate ends of the pipes, before the **exec()**.

The **wait()** system call allows the parent to wait for the child to exit. (There is also an **exit()** system call.) If the user has requested a process to run asynchronously (by placing an **&** at the end of the command), the shell will not execute **wait()**, but will prompt for a new command. Otherwise, the shell will call **wait()**. Hence, asynchronous or synchronous processing is very easy to do.

Each process has a *process id* (or *pid*). The pid is a descriptor which can be used to communicate with the object. For example, you can send a signal to a process if you know its pid. The **wait()** system call mentioned earlier takes a pid as its argument.

Processes may also be grouped by *process group id*s. This is useful for sending signals to a group of related processes. For example, this allows killing any of your miscellaneous processes by logging out.

There have been attempts to unify processes and files (much like the Grand Unification Theory of physics). One of these appeared in UNIX V8 and became available in SVR4. Each process appears in the file system as a file. For example, **/proc/17** is the process with pid **17**. This process can be debugged by opening and modifying bytes in the file itself which represents its image in memory.

Even without this unification of processes and files, UNIX process management is surprisingly easy and straightforward. There are only a few calls, and they take a small number of arguments.

To finish the shell example, it is interesting to point out that each shell eventually exits (when the user logs out or types an EOF). The process that invoked the shell, **init**, receives notification and returns to monitoring the terminal or modem for a new user. If a new user logs in, **init** will once again create a new shell for the user via **fork()** and **exec()**. (The process is explained further in the Administrator's chapter).

7.1.3   Signals

"This manual page is confusing." – BUGS section for **sigvec** from *Berkeley UNIX Manual*
"This manual page is still confusing." – next release of same manual

Signals are software interrupts. Signals may be generated by hardware conditions (e.g., division by zero, addressing exception) or by explicit request (such as another process requesting the process to stop). The complete list of signals can be found in the file **/usr/include/signal.h**.

Programs can declare an action to be taken upon receipt of most signals, such as recovery or clean-up. Signals not caught generally cause processes to terminate. Certain signals, such as **SIGKILL**, are not catchable by a process. Sending **SIGKILL** to a process is a sure way of killing it. **SIGQUIT** (which can be generated by pressing certain keys on the keyboard) kills a process and also generates a "core dump." This is particularly useful for debugging runaway processes.

The term *core dump* is historical. It refers to the use of magnetic cores for main memory. Modern computers do not use core and with technology changing so rapidly, *memory dump* would be more apropos, but people seem not to want to give up the phrase.

Signals may be generated internally, for example, by the alarm clock (**SIGALRM**) or an I/O-ready condition (**SIGIO**). These provide methods of extremely efficient coding for certain types of problems. For example, use of **SIGIO** avoids polling.

Unfortunately, early implementation of signals were difficult to use. For example, signals were not queued, they interrupted system calls (meaning one had to check each system call to see if it was interrupted), etc. An especially grievous problem was that when a signal occurred, the first thing it did was to reset its action to the default behavior. If another signal arrived before the process could set it again, the program would mistakenly terminate.

Berkeley remedied this in its 4.2BSD release of UNIX. Unfortunately, this solution was quite incompatible with previous versions of UNIX signals. So you could either use signals which were standard but not reliable, or signals which were reliable but not standard. System V eventually picked up most of the Berkeley signal properties, thereby reducing major portability issues while gaining reliable signals. Unfortunately, the interface did not get any less complex. The Berkeley manual page describing signals notes under **BUGS** that *"This manual page is still confusing."*

Most signals are generated by the kernel. However, any signal can be sent to any process (if you have permission) using the **kill()** system call. **kill()** is rarely used except to send a signal to kill a process, hence its name. But it is hard to understand why it wasn't named **sendsig()** or something reasonable in the first place.

7.2   C and Other Languages
"The sooner you start to code, the longer the program will take." – Roy Carlson

Research UNIX systems usually come with many languages including all sorts of experimental ones. Commercial UNIX systems usually come with very few languages – some are even unbundled from the C language – but it is possible to buy interpreters, compilers and environments that run under UNIX for just about any language.

A typical UNIX installation will usually acquire dozens of programming languages – many high-level languages such as C and Modula, high-level environments like Ada, Smalltalk and Lisp, the little languages like **yacc** and **lex**, plus the user-oriented languages of the various shells.

Each one has its advantages and disadvantages. Believe it or not, a good UNIX programmer is fluent in all of them. Each time a project is designed and implemented, the experienced programmer chooses the best tools to solve the problem. This is the mark of a good programmer.

It is possible to find interpreters and compilers that run under UNIX for just about any language, including C, Modula-2, Snobol, Forth, BASIC, Pascal, Lisp, Ratfor, Icon, APL, assembler, Ada, PL/I, and Fortran. (See the Applications chapter for vendor information.) Quite a few of these were available in early UNIX systems, although most of them were characterized as "only 90 percent done."

This was quite accurate, and is understandable considering that the work was not done by commercial companies who had to support a product. Rather, these languages were written to compile older applications that no one wanted to recode. Typically, the compiler or interpreter didn't have to support the whole language, just the part that the old applications needed! Several of the languages were derived from class projects and were only used because the sheer demand was so great for anything close to the language that people were satisfied with partial implementations.

Of course, the first languages available were an assembler and then a C compiler. Both of these were complete implementations, although not particularly sophisticated. In particular, the assembler was (and remains) quite primitive. Because people wrote so little code with it (using the C compiler for most tasks), it never even supported macros.

With the availability of **lex** and **yacc**, language development blossomed early on. Many experimental languages were written, including several powerful macropreprocessors including **m3**, **m4** and **m6**. They could be used with any language, such as assembler, but were particularly popular with C and Fortran. Implementations of Fortran 66, BASIC and Snobol existed by Version 7.

Fortran 77 was soon to follow and by then, people at Berkeley made available implementations of Pascal, Lisp, and APL. Numerous other languages have come and gone. Most of these "student" implementations have disappeared as UNIX has become so widespread that vendors produce and support virtually all major languages with complete implementations.

Unlike other systems where Fortran is considered the lingua franca of computers, Fortran is rarely used for new UNIX applications. However, most UNIX systems include a Fortran compiler simply because so much extant Fortran application code is available.

Most operating systems have a single primary implementation language, such as Lisp for the Lisp machines, or assembler for IBM's 370 series. UNIX is no different.

Historically, the C language has been the implementation language of choice on a UNIX system. There are two reasons for this. One is that vendors always had to have an implementation of C – the UNIX system itself is written using it. The second reason is that most C compilers produce assembler, but unlike assembler (which is generally available for all UNIX systems), C was high level, portable, and capable of doing system programming tasks easily.

7.2.1   C and UNIX: A Symbiotic Relationship
"The chicken was the egg's idea for getting more eggs." – Samuel Butler

C and UNIX have a special relationship. UNIX was written in C. C was designed specifically to write UNIX. The original decision to implement UNIX in C was very daring, but it has paid off many times.

Some people do not like C. It has been said that it is a poor language riding its way to glory on the coattails of a good operating system. This is not true. C is a great language. It strikes a balance between necessity and overkill (cf. Ada). C is easy to implement and yet incorporates all the essence of modern high-level languages such as structured control flow, scoping, data structures and modularity. It produces efficient code for most types of computers, without forcing the programmer to write code differently for each one.

Although C was created for UNIX, it has since been transplanted out of the UNIX environment many times. Now, C flourishes in many strange lands, such as mainframes and microprocessors, single-board computers, and even toaster ovens. C has become a particularly popular programming language on microcomputers due to its efficiency and portability. In all, C has proved its worth apart from UNIX.

This is not to say that C does not have flaws. Its lack of type ranges, weak lexical scoping, fall-through in `case` statements, and misuse of `break` are examples of design problems that have induced many people to propose improved C standards. Not surprisingly, most of the so-called "improved" dialects either contain defects of their own, or radically change the intent of the language, resulting in something more like Ada.

While a few other languages (e.g., Euclid, Modula-2) have achieved some popularity for UNIX system programming, C remains the core language for building UNIX tools. There are many tools that primarily support C. For example, both `yacc` and `lex` produce C code as output. It is possible to integrate such output into any project, but it is trivial in C.

Because of these tools, C is often viewed as a reasonable choice for many applications. Unfortunately, this generalization can be somewhat harmful, as C lacks support critical for certain types of programming. For example, C is not apropos for extensive numerical computations (lacking overflow and underflow detection) or list processing (lacking garbage collection). However, just about any application can and has been written in C. Perhaps the only thing that absolutely cannot be done is certain low-level machine operations such as saving registers or popping the stack. But such small fragments of machine code usually only have to be written once – for instance, inside the compiler.

We do not intend to provide a comprehensive look at C. (We have recommended some good books in the Printed Information chapter.) However, we would like to drive home the point that the C language has reached maturity. C compilers are available for more machines than any other high-level language. More new applications are written in C than any other language. *Communications of the ACM*, the most well-known publication for computer science research, regularly presents algorithms in C. Anyone attempting to master the field of computer science, no less UNIX, must become familiar with C.

Design and standards work on C continues to this day. The ANSI C standard, C++ and other C extensions are vehicles that will propel C into the role of a mature, modern language. We expect C to live a long and hearty life.

The decision to implement UNIX in C was either very fortuitous or incredibly insightful. Either way, we have all benefited tremendously, for it is an excellent systems programming language – for UNIX or anything else.

7.2.2   Libraries
"Whenever possible, steal code." – Tom Duff

Libraries of software subroutines allow programmers to make use of other programmers' efforts. For example, you do not have to write a program to clear the screen because a subroutine has already been written to do it (e.g., `clear()` in the `curses` library). All you have to do is find out the correct name and call it.

Most UNIX systems come with a large number of libraries including routines for string handling, math, terminal and window management, and communications. A good programmer should become familiar with all the libraries and subroutines. By doing so, you can dramatically reduce the amount of effort required to implement a project. Further, the library subroutines are usually much more dependable than brand new code.

So before spending time writing a function, you should always check the libraries first. The subroutine you are thinking of writing may already have been written.

Subroutines are kept in object form for efficiency when building programs. Multiple subroutines are organized by type in libraries (also called *archives*, historically) for efficiency and simplicity. The command `ar` (`ar`chive) is used to create and maintain libraries.

When programs are linked (object code is resolved to machine executable code), object files and libraries are passed to the linker. The linker then resolves any external references between the user-supplied object code and the libraries.

BSS

a.out-style files consist of several parts. For example, one is the executable code (known as the *text*). Another is the initialized data. A third is the bss. Everyone always asks what is the "bss" and what does it stand for? Here is the answer.

"bss" stands for Block Started by Symbol. Used by a now obsolete IBM assembler, BSS was an assembler pseudo-opcode that filled an area of memory with zeros. That is exactly the effect of the bss in a.out files. The bss is also called the *uninitialized data*.

UNIX usually stores libraries in predefined directories. **/lib** usually contains the libraries necessary for the C compiler:

libc.a   Standard C library: standard I/O functions, system calls, and other fundamental routines. Included automatically by the C compiler.

The main system-supplied libraries are stored in **/usr/lib**. (The libraries are split between two directories for the same reason that **/tmp** and **/usr/tmp** are – see the Administrator's Environment chapter for an explanation.) Some basic libraries found in **/usr/lib** are:

libF77.a   Fortran library: Fortran run-times.

libcurses.a   Character-graphics library: functions for creating terminal-independent, character-graphics utilities. Depends upon **termcap** or **terminfo** libraries.

libdbm.a   Database library: functions for maintaining a simple keyed database.

libm.a   Math library: functions for trigonometric, logarithmic and other miscellaneous mathematical algorithms.

libplot.a   Plot library: functions for creating device-independent plot utilities. Depends upon per-device plot filters which translate device-independent output to device-dependent output.

libtermcap.a Terminal capability library: functions for accessing and manipulating the terminal description database, **/etc/termcap**. Called "terminfo" on System V.

You may find other libraries on your system as well. Different vendors provide different libraries to support special features. If you find a library that you are curious about and cannot find documentation for it, try the following (assuming the library is called **libxyzzy.a**):

```
% ar tv libxyzzy.a
```

This will list the table of contents of the library. Usually, you can guess what the library is, once you have seen the names of the subroutines in it.

If you examine the directories containing libraries you will also see libraries by the same name but with the addition of the letter **p**, such as **libc.a** and **libc_p.a**. The **p** version indicates that it is to be used when you are profiling code. (See the following explanation of "profiling.") The subroutines have special statements at the beginning and end to count entries and the time spent in each routine.

/usr/local/lib is another directory where users store their own libraries that they wish to share with other users on the same system. The linker automatically searches this directory when looking for libraries.

7.2.3   C Preprocessor
"Include me out." – Sam Goldwyn

Programs written in C often have a lot of lines beginning with **#**. Even if you don't program in C, it is useful to be able to read these lines. Many programs are designed so that likely program changes can be made just by modifying these lines.

Lines beginning with **#** are directives to control compilation. The original C language compilers processed these lines in a separate, precompilation phase called the *C preprocessor*. The preprocessor was implementated as a separate program called **cpp**. Most C compilers still work this way, but there is no requirement in the C language standard that it be implemented as a separate phase, so you should not depend on it. Hence, "C preprocessing phase" would be a better term, but because of history, people continue to call it "the C preprocessor."

The C preprocessor's most important job is code substitution. For example, you can have the preprocessor substitute the string **MAXMEMORY** with the string **2*1024*1024** when the program is compiled. By writing your programs using strings like **MAXMEMORY**, your programs become portable to any system. Writing programs with strings like **2*1024*1024** means your programs will only run on systems with 2Mb of memory.

These substitutions are called *defines* because they appear as directives beginning with the word **#define**. For example:

```
#define MAXMEMORY 2*1024*1024
```

Defines are usually gathered together in *include* files, grouped by their subject. For example, all the appropriate defines having to do with string processing are in the include file called **/usr/include/strings.h**. UNIX systems come with a lot of include files in the directory **/usr/include**. Each such file has a **.h** suffix. The **h** stands for "header file," although most people just call them "include" files. These files often include function definitions and prototypes, typedefs and structure definitions as well as simple defines.

To get one of these files included (hence the name) in your program, put a line like **#include <strings.h>** at the beginning of your C source code. The angle brackets are just a C preprocessor shorthand for the directory **/usr/include**. If you want to see one of these files, you can say **cat /usr/include/strings.h**. Browsing or *grepping* (searching with **grep**) through the include files can often be more informative than reading the manuals. They are certainly the final arbiter, since they are actually used by the C compiler. Much to our dismay, the C compiler does not read the manuals.

The preprocessor does a number of other things including stripping comments and providing rudimentary flow control statements for selectively compiling code. Conditional compilation is another way of producing portable code.

The C preprocessor is limited in some ways. For example, it respects parentheses and literals. It is not a general purpose preprocessor (even though many people use it as one). The UNIX preprocessor, **m4**, is a much more powerful preprocessor that surpasses most of the limitations of **cpp**. When occasion demands, **cpp** can be replaced by **m4**.

7.3 Support Tools

UNIX provides the programmer with a wide assortment of very powerful tools which aid the task of programming. Some of the tools themselves are quite complex and take as much time to master as a programming language. Indeed, Jon Bentley, in his "Programming Pearls" column for the *Communications of the ACM*, has called tools like **yacc** and **lex** *little languages* because they are structured just like a general-purpose programming language including a parser.

However hard they are to learn, they invariably save you development and debugging time. We couldn't live without them.

Fortunately, almost all of the now-classic UNIX tools have made the transition to non-UNIX environments. The Virtual Operating System provided the first release of most of them for non-UNIX machines. But now it is possible to obtain them for just about any machine that has a C compiler. And many system vendors provide these tools as essential parts of the system.

7.3.1 Debuggers
"If we can't fix it, it ain't broke." – Lt. Col. Walt Weir

Debuggers are used to examine working (sic) programs for bugs. Every system has its share of debuggers and UNIX is no different. However, the UNIX debuggers have characteristically been below the level of quality found in all the other UNIX tools.

Early versions of UNIX came with a primitive assembler debugger, **db**, and a primitive C debugger, **cdb**. Version 7 replaced both of these with a somewhat friendlier debugger, **adb**, that understood both assembler and C. **adb** is still supplied with most UNIX versions, although now it is considered only appropriate for patching binaries. Unfortunately, each machine has a somewhat different version of **adb**. This is understandable as assemblers and machines differ from one system to the next.

The same holds true for C compiler interfaces. However, several debuggers have gained popularity. Berkeley releases introduced both **sdb** (symbolic debugger), an improved version of **adb**, and **dbx**, which has a nice user interface. Both of these are source-level debuggers, meaning that the debugger can show you the line of C code being executed. Another debugger that is extremely popular is **gdb** (GNU debugger) from the Free Software Foundation.

Ironically, most of the UNIX debuggers are still somewhat primitive by comparison to debugging environments for microcomputers. Part of the problem is that the UNIX environment gets in the way of debugging. UNIX provides very limited support for controlling a process from another, which is what a debugger needs to do. Mapping a second process's memory into the debugger process is essentially impossible. Debugger implementations end up playing many games to get around these restrictions.

One way to transcend all of these debuggers is by using a C interpreter. These have much more of the compiler embedded in them, so that it is possible to interact at a very high level with the debugger/interpreter. See the Applications chapter for companies that sell C interpreters.

7.3.2   Make

"The structure of a system reflects the structure of the organization that built it." – Richard E. Fairley

make (written by Stu Feldman) is a tool for taking a set of source files and and managing the compilation process to create an executable program. **make** controls the order in which programs are compiled and linked, based on "dependencies" (stored in a *makefile*). Based on these dependencies, **make** can determine which source files need to be recompiled and which don't, saving lots of time and thought.

For example, you can tell **make** that five of your ten C source files depend on a particular include file. If you ever modify that include file, you can be assured that **make** will recompile the five dependent C source files and nothing else.

make has many built-in rules. For example, it knows that if you change **foo.c**, it must recompile **foo.c** before it can link anything to **foo.o**. However, it is completely general, and can be used to keep track of any set of files as long as their dependencies are related by time order. For example, if you are supporting customers and make changes to a product, it is easy to have **make** generate media with only the set of files that have changed since the customer last received an update.

make is useful for all but the most trivial programs. And it extends gracefully to large programs. Indeed, the entire UNIX system is described by a set of **makefile**s which allow **make** to reconstruct the entire system from sources. Without **make**, deciding what steps to take to rebuild a complicated software set (using **cc**, **ld**, **as**, **yacc**, **lex**, **mv**, **cp**, **sed**, and **ln**) would be a nightmare.

The usefulness of `make` cannot be stressed enough. After an editor and a language, `make` is the next tool a programmer should master. Indeed, it is one of the UNIX tools that has been ported to every other computer system. There are even versions in the public domain. There is no excuse for not having and using `make`.

7.3.3   Version Control

"Plan to throw one away, you will anyhow." – Fred Brooks
"If you plan to throw one away, you will throw away two." – Craig Zerouni

Version control enables several people to work simultaneously on a set of files without stepping on one another's toes. It also allows one to administer releases or versions of a product in a manageable fashion.

SCCS (Source Code Control System) was initially distributed with PWB UNIX, and is now an essential part of both System V and Berkeley UNIX. SCCS was written by Marc Rochkind. RCS (Revision Control System) was written by Walter Tichy in an attempt to improve upon some of the features of SCCS. RCS is not in the public domain but can be distributed for free with commercial products as long as you contact the author.

Both RCS and SCCS provide controlled access to files for the purpose of version control. This solves the problem of the lack of high-level file locking in UNIX (discussed in the Real World chapter). Collections of sources may be referred to via a version number.

Access to files is controlled by an automated source code administrator. This administrative software allows, for example, only one person to edit a file for writing at any time, while any number of people may be using the file in other ways. The administrator keeps track of all updates, so that it is possible to go back to an earlier release of a software set by issuing a command naming the desired release. A history is maintained automatically to enable you to track why changes were made.

While the major application of these systems is for source code control, both of them are general enough to manage any kind of files. For example, two authors working on the same book could avoid wiping out each other's changes by using one of these systems.

Most version control systems actually provide much more flexibility than we can explain here. An important point is that version control systems such as RCS and SCCS keep track of changes rather than retaining each version in its entirety. This is less time-efficient but more space-efficient than keeping a complete copy of each version. Such a scheme is desirable when old versions are rarely referenced, as would be expected when maintaining software.

Some other operating systems support file *versioning* directly in the file system, usually by using part of the name as a version number. For example, DEC's VMS file system keeps multiple versions, simply by appending a version number to the file name. It would be nice if UNIX had this kind of versioning; however, it doesn't solve the problem of long-term code control that RCS and SCCS do. Furthermore, built-in versioning restricts you to the set of capabilities originally provided by the file system designer. Code control systems are user-level programs – they can be extended and modified as desired, and even replaced.

7.3.4   Yacc and Lex
"One person's data is another person's program." – Guy Steele, Jr.

yacc (yet another compiler compiler) and **lex** (lexical analyzer) are two powerful tools that aid in the creation of new languages. They are often used together, although that is not necessary.

lex is a *lexical analyzer*. This is a fancy name for a scanner or tokenizer. It reads an input stream, breaking it into tokens. You define the tokens. For example, it is easy to tell **lex** to recognize literals, numbers and operators. This is most of what is necessary when scanning any programming language.

Once you have given your language specification to **lex**, it converts that specification into a C routine that you plug in as the front-end of your compiler. **lex** can do more than just scanning input files for numbers and words. Actually, it is a regular-expression pattern matcher. If you can describe your patterns by *regular expressions* (a theoretical classification beyond the scope of this book), they can be recognized by **lex**. **lex** allows you to specify "actions" or arbitrary C procedures to be executed when it recognizes something. This is powerful enough so that **lex** is often all you need to write an entire language.

yacc is much like **lex** in that it recognizes patterns. Like **lex**, actions (C procedures) may be associated with each pattern. However, **yacc** recognizes a much larger set of patterns than **lex**. The patterns define the class of *LALR(1) grammars* which is powerful enough to define almost all extant programming languages. **yacc** is not powerful enough to describe natural languages such as English.

These definitions are a high-level description. For example, the pattern from a **yacc** grammar describing a C **do** statement is:

do-statement : **do** *statement* **while** (*expression*) ;

where *statement* and *expression* are described elsewhere in the grammar, and the keywords and punctuation are recognized as tokens (by **lex**, perhaps). The action is not shown. The grammar used by **yacc** is very similar to BNF, a theoretical language used by computer scientists to describe context-free languages.

Since UNIX systems come with scant **yacc** and **lex** documentation, we highly recommend the book *Introduction to Compiler Construction with UNIX* by Schreiner and Friedman, Jr. for those intending to make substantial use of the UNIX compiler tools. For instance, the book includes a modification to **yacc** (that you can use even with a binary UNIX license) that dramatically improves error messages from **yacc**-built parsers. Of course, this book is not a replacement for a good compiler theory book.

Like **lex**, **yacc** is applicable to many types of problems besides compilers. For example, **yacc** uses a unique input language of its own, but is not a compiler. Naturally, **yacc** is defined in **yacc**!

yacc was written by Steve Johnson. **lex** was written by Mike Lesk. There are many improved versions of **yacc** and **lex** available now, including several in the public domain. The GNU project, for example, has free versions of each.

The availability of these tools in early versions of UNIX dramatically reduced the effort in building languages for UNIX. Even nowadays, if you need to write your own C compiler, it makes sense to start with a **yacc** description of C. One is in the appendix of *The C Programming Language, Second Edition* by Kernighan and Ritchie.

7.3.5   Profiling

"The fastest algorithm can frequently be replaced by one that is almost as fast and much easier to understand." – Douglas Jones

Program tuning is called *profiling* on UNIX. By profiling a program, a run-time analysis is performed. You can then find out the amount of time spent in each part of the code. The number of times a subroutine is called is also computed. This information is particularly useful when you are trying to make a program run faster.

Profiling is supported through the use of the system call, **profil()**, and the library routine, **monitor()**. However, the programmer does not have to deal with this directly. Most languages automatically generate profiling code on request. For example, the **-p** flag will cause the C compiler to insert special code before and after each subroutine call. In addition, the linker will use profiled libraries.

When the program is run, a file called **mon.out** is produced that has the raw data created by profiling. You can then interpret the raw data file by calling **prof** on System V or **gprof** on Berkeley systems. **prof** can create a graphical display of the data. **gprof** generates a call-graph, displaying the chain of subroutine calls. System V also has **lcomp** which produces a line-by-line profile of the program.

7.3.6   Lint
"Details count." – Peter Weinberger

Early C compilers did not do a lot of error checking. By assuming that compilers only had to do sensible things with sensible programs, the implementors found that compilers were much easier to write.

Unfortunately, there was no guarantee that erroneous programs would be detected. Buggy programs often compiled without complaint, producing equally meaningless results. For example, the C compiler will let you call **sqrt()** without an argument and promptly take the square root of some random junk on the stack, where the argument should have been.

This is an example of an obvious problem that could have been detected at compile-time, rather than waiting for run-time. **lint** is a program which is extremely picky (hence the name) about C programs. It will detect the problem we discussed, along with most other compile-time problems. It will not correct these problems but will notify you of many potential bugs. **lint** has much stricter typechecking than the C compiler and will point out mismatched assignments which will compile fine but may be erroneous, such as pointer assignments of different data types. It will also warn about problems such as unused variables and inconsistent argument usage.

It is possible to communicate with **lint**, by placing comments in your programs. For example, to tell **lint** that a function will be called with varying numbers of arguments, one places the comment **/*VARARGS*/** in front of the function. Unfortunately, getting **lint** to shut up can sometimes be painful. For example, `memcpy()` and `strcpy()` are typical of functions which return values that are almost never used.

In order to check for consistency in the usage of libraries, `lint` requires a file describing each library. The contents of these files are just the stubs of the subroutines with the type definition and declarations of the arguments. If you have created a library, you might also consider creating a `lint` library.

`lint` is not automatically run when you compile a program, but you should get into the habit of using it frequently. It is one of the most helpful tools for C programmers and can quickly point you in the right direction when tracking down bugs. `lint` was written by Steve Johnson.

7.3.7   Curses

UNIX originally grew up on Teletype ASR33s. These were electromechanical beasts that output characters at a stunning 110 baud (ten characters per second). Much of the conciseness of UNIX stemmed from that (as did the term "tty" to describe terminals). Glass-ttys (i.e., dumb CRT terminals) behaved like fast ttys but they were still dumb.

The emphasis in UNIX had always been on programs that produced output that could be used as input to another. Therefore, people generally didn't spend time writing graphic applications. They didn't fit into the UNIX paradigm. However, the one graphic application that stood apart from the others was editing. Editing using a Teletype was not fun, but editing using a CRT was. The Rand editor had proven that.

One of the more annoying drawbacks of the Rand editor was that it had to be customized for each different type of terminal. In the late '70s, there were dozens of CRT manufacturers, producing hundreds of different models. Each worked differently, and it was impossible to write (no less debug) support routines for each terminal quickly enough. The Berkeley solution was `termcap`.

`termcap` (`term`inal `cap`abilities) is a library that supports terminal-independent character-graphics. It uses a simple database that describes each terminal that the system supports. Over 300 different terminals are supported and the number grows constantly. It is relatively easy to add new terminals. `termcap` is described further in the Administrator's chapter.

`curses` is a high-level interface to the `termcap` system. `curses` provides the user with straightforward commands. For example, `box()` draws a box on the screen, and `printw()` prints a formatted string. The basic idea in using `curses` is for the programmer to simply describe the way a screen looks. `curses` takes care of making sure that the physical screen looks the way the description does. It also does this optimally.

For example, suppose you are displaying a page of data, and your program is about to rewrite the screen with a new page of data. But the data is exactly the same except for, say, the page number. Then `curses` will only rewrite the page number. `curses` will also attempt to update by a minimal number of character inserts and deletes – for example, if the data is on the screen but just has to be moved over. It is amusing to watch `curses` on a slow terminal because it works nonintuitively (but fast)!

`curses` also has functions to provide rudimentary windowing. While `curses` is limited to character-graphics applications (including line-drawing characters and color), it has seen much use and has been ported to many other operating systems. The paper "Screen Updating & Cursor Movement Optimization: A Library Package" by Ken Arnold describes `curses` further and is available from Berkeley.

7.3.8   Editors

"The only use I can find for **vi** is editing the **emacs** sources while porting them
to a new machine." – Larry Campbell

Strictly speaking, editors are not programming tools. However, they are what many programmers spend most of their time using while performing programming development. In addition, many of the editors have tool interfaces, allowing them to be called from scripts or in pipelines.

All discussion of UNIX editors must start with `ed` (written by Ken Thompson), the granddaddy of UNIX editors. `ed` is special in so many ways. Even if you never use it (which is unlikely), `ed` is worth learning. It is called for in certain types of emergencies. For example, if you are on a hardcopy terminal or `/etc/termcap` is "broken," you won't be able to use a screen editor. And if you are unable to mount any file system partitions, you won't be able to get to any editor but `ed`.

Another good reason to know `ed` is that you will be able to use `sed`, the stream editor, which allows you to do editing in a pipe or a script. `sed`'s command language is very similar to `ed`'s. Many other tools have borrowed commands from `ed`. For example, the regular-expression pattern matching used by most of the UNIX tools appeared first in `ed`. `ed` pioneered many stylistic conventions such as the "bang" notation to run a command in a subshell. `ed` did so many neat things that the source code for it was originally distributed as one of the UNIX readings. Unfortunately, this is no longer possible due to licensing restrictions.

Most versions of UNIX include a screen editor called `vi`. Written by Bill Joy, `vi` was the first application to use `curses`. `vi` became very popular with early UNIX users because it was based on (you guessed it) `ed`. `vi` went on to become AT&T's standard screen-oriented editor. We recommend you learn it simply because it is the only screen editor available on *all* UNIX systems.

`ex` is a version of `vi`, specifically designed for hardcopy terminals. It is like `ed`, also, but shares all of the extended commands of `vi`. `ex` is also available on all UNIX systems.

Many people intensely dislike `vi` because it is heavily *mode-oriented*. This means that you are either inserting text or executing a command. Since moving the cursor is a command, you have to switch out of *insert-text mode* and into *execute-command mode* to move the cursor. If you move the cursor often while typing text, you will have to type a lot of change-mode sequences. And if you stop to think about something for a moment, you may forget what mode you are in. It is extremely annoying to have your text suddenly being executed as commands.

A general-purpose editor we recommend over `vi` is `emacs`. `emacs` does not have the heavy mode-orientation that `vi` has. `emacs` can also display multiple windows on the screen at once. Unfortunately, it is not distributed with UNIX, so you must obtain it through a third-party source. Despite the inconvenience, many people have turned to `emacs` (or at least away from `vi`). A recent Usenet poll indicated about half of all UNIX users use `vi` and half use `emacs`.

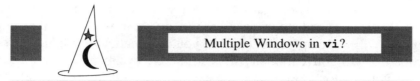

Multiple Windows in **vi**?

Bill Joy actually went so far as to put multiple windows into **vi**. And he was thinking of making it programmable, too. What happened?

While he was adding multiple-window support, the tape drive was broken and there were no backups. Bill continued working anyway, until one day his disk got "scrunched." He didn't have a backup or a complete listing, so he just gave up. Afterwards, he went back to the previous version, finished the manual and that was it with **vi**. On to the next project...

The power of **emacs** (and similar editors such as **mince**) is that it is completely programmable (yet another language to learn). **emacs** is easily configured to be a front-end for news and mail, but we have seen people go so far as to program it to solve first-order predicate logic problems.

A particularly useful feature of **emacs** is that it can edit shell sessions *in progress*! This means you can use all the editor commands while talking to the shell. Plus, you can scroll through your entire session, save it, or do anything else that you can do with a static file.

emacs (which does not stand for "**emacs** **m**akes **a** **c**omputer **s**low" but "**e**ditor **macros**") was originally written at MIT by Richard M. Stallman. It ran as a set of macros on top of another editor (**teco**) which did not run on UNIX. James Gosling at CMU rewrote **emacs** for UNIX. Interestingly, rather than port **teco**, Gosling chose to place **emacs** on top of a small Lisp interpreter.

Several different versions of **emacs** are sold commercially, some of which are not based on Gosling's **emacs** (familiarly called Gosmacs). GNUemacs is a particularly popular version which is available from the Free Software Foundation.

It is important to choose an editor that you will be happy with. Many of the UNIX utilities depend upon an editor to do their work. For example, the mail program will start up the editor for you automatically when you compose mail. Programs will conventionally look in the environment variable **EDITOR** for the name of your editor. **csh** users, for example, would insert the following line in their **.login** file:

```
setenv EDITOR /usr/local/bin/emacs
```

7.4   Other Tools

There are many other important tools that a UNIX programmer will use while constructing programs. We have mentioned only the most important ones.

Many of the commands mentioned in the User's Environment chapter are useful as programming tools, even though we have not classified them that way. For example, the shell is programmable and is often used to build prototypes. If the shell scripts run quickly enough, further development may be unnecessary. There is no reason you have to use the sophisticated development tools mentioned in the chapter if existing commands are sufficient.

We also mention some other tools in the Administrator's Environment chapter. It would be worth your while to read all three of these chapters before setting out to do any serious UNIX programming.

If you work on a UNIX system, it is to your benefit to learn the tools and concepts described in this chapter. UNIX remains a programmer's system and being able to program it is the only way to take full advantage of the capabilities that it has to offer.

Chapter 8: The Administrator's Environment

Overheard at a funeral: "I know this may be an awkward time, but do you recall him ever mentioning source code?" – Charles Addams

This chapter discusses some of the aspects of UNIX administration. Of course, UNIX administrators can make use of many of the same tools that UNIX users and programmers do. UNIX administrators will find their time well spent in becoming versed in the user's and programmer's environment. And of course, UNIX users and programmers might find some so-called administrative tools are equally worthwhile to them.

The UNIX administrator's environment gets short shrift when it comes to quality. The original manuals did not even have a section for administrator's tools. There was no such person as an administrator. The UNIX programmers cared for the system themselves, with the same tools that they used for their regular work. If you stumbled across a bug, you fixed it, recompiled UNIX and continued running.

Things have changed now that UNIX has become a commercial product. Much like any computer system, there are administrative utilities such as backup tools, tuning tools, and even a phone number to call for help. Of course, many programmers continue to ignore so-called useful features such as file quotas and accounting. After all, why do accounting on a personal workstation?

Depending upon whether your UNIX system is shared by many others and has large enough disks, you may find it useful to have a skilled operator take care of it. Good luck finding one. The problem is that most administrative tasks presume great knowledge of UNIX internals. For example, tape backups can fail due to a variety of reasons, but device drivers are notoriously bad at reporting them back to the program. Hence, operators may see anything from `"mt0: sr reg = 5, op failed"` to `"core dumped."`

UNIX is extremely complex, and many things can go wrong. And it is so configurable that it is quite difficult to write administrative manuals that cover any configuration or situation. Because of this extensibility, it is helpful for operators to know some shell programming. But as soon as they start doing this, they are essentially programmers, and quickly become too valuable to "waste" performing tape backups. It's a vicious circle.

The result is that administrative responsibilities are usually handled by skilled UNIX programmers, much to their dismay. There is just no way of avoiding it, short of rewriting most of the UNIX system. Fortunately, there are many vendors attempting to do just that. However, the roots of UNIX are deep, and it will take a long time before the results of such change is felt.

There are many books on the subject of UNIX administration, some of which are mentioned earlier in this book. However, UNIX programming experience goes a long way. Some guts help too, such as when for the first time you get a message asking you to reboot the system without `sync`'ing the disks!

8.1   Managing the System

The effective management of a complex system is nontrivial. Many variables affect the performance and capabilities of a UNIX system, not the least of which is the knowledge and performance of your systems administrator.

8.1.1   Initial Configuration

Before using your system the first time, you will have to *configure* it. This means telling the software what kind of hardware you have. Additionally, you will choose certain software parameters, such as declaring what kind of network protocols you will use. Since UNIX runs in so many environments, configuration can be fairly complex.

The hard part of configuration is putting devices into the kernel. Making any mistakes at this point can crash the system, since you are modifying the kernel without going through any well-defined interface, such as a system call.

Modifying the kernel is typically done by linking the kernel with the appropriate device drivers, along with a small file that makes the associations between the drivers and the device major numbers. Then you reboot using the new kernel. Many systems have automated this process – you just pick all the drivers and it does the rest of the work.

When devices such as **/dev/null** are created, they are assigned a major and minor number. You can see this if you do a **ls -l** of the file. When any operation is performed on the device, the major number is used by the kernel to select the correct driver. The minor number is used by the driver itself, usually to distinguish between multiple devices of the same kind.

Once you have configured your system, you can boot using the new kernel. You can then do some higher-level configuration, such as deciding what background processes to run, setting up spoolers, networks and adding users.

8.1.2 Booting

Booting a UNIX system is a trivial task. Start by turning it on. All computers have hardware that automatically jumps to a ROM monitor. Either the monitor will bootstrap the system into multi-user mode immediately or you will have to press "**b**" and select a "run level" (such as single or multi-user).†

As the system comes up, it goes through several steps, most of which are common to all UNIX systems. All of this is automatic, although prayer doesn't hurt.

1. Checks the integrity and existence of basic hardware, such as a console. Determines how much memory is available.

2. Initializes various parts of the kernel. Bootstraps the root file system into existence.

3. Probes for devices. Each device driver is called to initialize itself.

4. **init** and a process to do swapping are bootstrapped into existence as the first two processes.

5. Runs **/etc/rc**. This is a shell script that usually mounts and checks the integrity of other file systems, initializes networks, starts spoolers, mailers, networks, and terminals.

8.1.3 Halting

It is best not to turn off your UNIX machine by simply flipping the power switch like one does with a PC. Since processes run in the background, they may be in the middle of doing something at any moment. For example, log files are continually being written, even if the system is quiescent (if only to say that

---

† The former is typical of BSD systems, while the latter is typical of System V systems.

the system is quiescent)! If you turn off the system as a file is being written, you will likely corrupt the file system.

Another reason for not flipping the on-off switch is that the UNIX file system is buffered. (This is not the same kind of buffering as the stdio buffering.) As disks are accessed, copies of the disk are brought into kernel memory, and then copied to user memory (or vice versa). When a user writes to a portion of the disk, the kernel memory is updated, and that memory is flagged so that it will later be copied to the disk.

By not immediately writing it to the disk, a large amount of time is saved. It is quite common that disk areas are updated many times in a row. For example, if you delete a lot of files, the directory will be rewritten many times. By only copying the last version to the disk, time is saved. However, it means that the disk does not always represent the reality of the file system.

To keep this unsynchronization between the file system and kernel memory to a minimum, the kernel flushes its buffer every so often. Older UNIX systems actually did this by a background process called **update** which called the kernel **sync()** routine every thirty seconds. There is also a command called **sync**, which does the same thing but only once. If the system is halted between the time a **sync** occurred, and the file system was modified, the file system might be corrupted.

Usually there are system-supplied programs that you run to halt the system such as **/etc/shutdown** or **/etc/halt**. This makes sure that the file system is synchronized, as well as broadcasting messages to users warning them about the impending shutdown.

8.1.4   Debugging After a Crash

UNIX crashes are often accompanied by a *panic* message, such as "**panic: double parity error in memory**." This indicates that the system detected a condition that it recognized as a problem, but it was so severe that it could not be fixed. For example, this might require physically replacing a hardware component.

Some UNIX systems come with backup hardware and software, however without it, the only reasonable thing to do with a severely crippled or corrupted system is to halt it. Letting the system run would undoubtedly corrupt something else.

Once halted, the system should be examined for the cause of the panic. The problem may be evident from the panic message, or it may require debugging.

You may find it useful to do debugging or maintenance work from single-user mode. *Single-user mode* is a way of bringing up UNIX so that no one else can log in and **/etc/rc** is not run. Daemons (see later in this chapter) are not started, and only the root file system is mounted. This is useful, for example, if you need to repair the user file system or perform a backup.

If you cannot even boot to single-user mode, you can boot from a tape or floppy disk. (If you can't boot from either of these, you've got a serious hardware problem!) Once you have booted from tape or floppy, find a spare copy of the root file system which will give you access to the tools you need to debug the kernel. Or restore an older and more robust kernel and reboot the system using that.

Once you have booted, you can then debug UNIX. The UNIX debugger has a special option that allows it to be used when debugging the kernel. By using it, you can tell where the system stopped. For example, it may have stopped in a brand new device driver or a kernel routine. Once you have figured out where it stopped, you can then get out the source code and debug the module.

8.2   Managing Disks

"See a guru." – advice in fsck documentation for receipt of certain errors

While the hierarchical UNIX file system is conceptually clean, its implementation is fairly complex. This is for a number of reasons, one of which is to provide the clean interface on top of a morass of bizarre devices. Another is to provide that file system integrity can be maintained in the event of a crash.

8.2.1   Mounting and Unmounting the File System

Conceptually, the UNIX file system is one tree. What is not apparent is that branches of the tree can reside on physically separate devices. Physical disks may also be logically partitioned, so that they appear as separate devices. Each logical partition is a file system in its own right. However, multiple file systems appear as a single file system to the user.

A logical partition is usually reserved for swap space. *Swapping* means that processes can be moved out of memory and temporarily stored on a disk until such time as they are brought back into memory to continue executing. This is useful when you have several processes that can't fit into physical memory at the same time.

The root file system, "/", is contained in another partition. By putting / and the swap partition on one disk, it is possible to boot a minimal system, independent of the rest of the network or any other disks. This makes the system fairly robust since all it needs is one disk to get running.

Once UNIX has booted, it can then mount other file systems. These are placed in empty directories that merely serve as placeholders. The **mount** command actually does the work. The result of a **mount** is that the placeholding directory now appears exactly like the root of the new partition. The user doesn't see the new root, but views the new file system as just one more directory.

umount undoes the effect of **mount**. Once you have unmounted a file system, it is no longer accessible to users. They will see the original empty directory, and you can remove the disk from the system.

Network file systems (such as NFS and RFS) have extended the semantics of **mount** and **umount**. Using them, you can mount devices that are on remote systems and they appear as part of your local file system. This technique is used with workstations, so that you can sit down at any workstation and gain access to your files by mounting them from a network file server.

8.2.2   Maintaining File System Integrity

Internally, the file system is quite complex. However, as long as it is accessed through its defined interfaces, you needn't be concerned with it. In the event of a system crash, or someone pulling the AC cord out of the wall, the likelihood is high that the file system is "out of sync." For example, if you were in the middle of deleting a file, the file might not appear in a directory, yet the file space hasn't been returned to the pool of empty file space (also called the "freelist").

When the system is booted, each file system is examined for integrity before mounting it. If garbage file systems are mounted without checking them first, the system can go off the deep end while traversing data structures. The integrity of the file system is checked by the program **fsck** (**f**ile **s**ystem **c**heck).

fsck looks through the underlying data structures of the file system and verifies that it is consistent. If it discovers any inconsistencies, it attempts to repair the damage. The file system contains some redundant information, just for this purpose. Because of that, **fsck** can always repair out-of-sync file systems. However, if the problem was caused by a software bug, or a hardware error such as a controller that scribbled garbage on a random sector, it is unlikely that **fsck** can restore your disk to perfect health. When **fsck** finds problems that cannot be restored perfectly, it will notify you. For example, when **fsck** discovers files that have no directories, it will make up names for them and place them in the directory **/lost+found**.

Two excellent articles on **fsck** are (for System V) "Using fsck" by Michael Saxon in *;login:*, vol. 10, no. 3, August 1985, and (for BSD) "Fsck – The File System Check Program" by Marshall Kirk McKusick in the *4.2BSD UNIX System Manager's Manual*.

> What's the name of that file?

Files are not stored with their names. The names are stored in directories, and more than one name may point to the same file.

Internally, the file system identifies a file by an index (or i-node) number, because names are not unique. While it is possible to find out the i-node number of a file (via **ls −i**), it is impossible to find out the name(s) of a file, except by examining all the directories on a file system.

For example, to find the file with i-node number 20899 in the **/usr** file system, you can execute one of the following commands:

```
SystemV % find /usr −xdev  −inum 20899 −print
Berkeley% find /usr −mntpt −inum 20899 −print
```

Early file systems were not as robust as they are now, and **fsck** was not always capable of fixing them. Hand patching was common, either with specialized file system debuggers like **fsdb**, or even **adb**. **clri**, **ncheck**, **icheck** and **dcheck** were part of a suite of programs that performed special operations on the file system, such as zeroing an i-node. Fortunately, these programs are rarely used anymore.

8.2.3   Backups
"Whatever can go wrong, will go wrong." – Murphy's Law

It is impossible to overemphasize the importance of backing up the file system.   If a disk controller goes haywire, or even if you accidentally delete a file, backups are the only way to recover.   Do backups daily!

Backups are usually accomplished by using **dump**.   However, there are several other utilities useful for saving files, including **volcopy**, **dd**, **tar** and **cpio**.   (This list varies from system to system, unfortunately.)   Each of these utilities saves files in a different way.   It may seem strange that each of these are incompatible with each other, but there is a good reason for different types of backups.   Different formats have different purposes.   Each has its own advantages and disadvantages.   For example, **dump** is good for backing up a file system because it saves i-node information.   However, **dump** tapes are an inappropriate format for distributing software – other sites could care less about your i-nodes.   **tar** or **cpio** would be a better choice in this particular case.

Backups usually take a long time to execute because they must record the entire file system.   Since they take so long, it is possible for a user to write files during a backup that are not recorded because the dump program has already dumped that part of the file system which now contains the new file.   For this reason, file systems to be dumped should be quiescent.

Since complete backups require a lot of dedicated time and backup media, most backups are incremental.   Incremental dumps simply copy what has changed since the last time a backup was performed.   This is usually much less than a full backup.   In the User's Environment chapter, we present a utility for using **cpio** to make incremental backups.

After a disk catastrophe, the backups can be restored, either by selected files or in toto.   If incremental dumps have been taken, you will have to restore all of the incrementals until everything looks right.

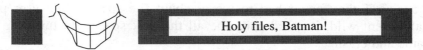

Holy files, Batman!

Files with holes are created by seeking past the end-of-file. Everything between the old end-of-file and the new data is a hole – there is no data there, so no disk space is used. Holes are nice, except that not all utilities understand them.

One day a programmer inadvertently handed a pointer to **fseek**, promptly causing a monster hole. None of the normal file commands such as **du** or **df** were disturbed by this. However, during the next backup, **dump** requested 26 40Mb tapes. It simply wanted to save the 1Gb file from the 146Mb disk partition!

Backups can also be used when a user accidentally deletes a file. If the file has been created before the last dump, the file can be restored. However, users should be cautioned that this is not something to rely on. This is because there is no guarantee that users haven't created their files after the most recent backup.

Backups are a weak point of UNIX, and one of the reasons why UNIX administration is so difficult. They require quiescent systems. They have no tape library system. Few of the tape utilities understand multiple-volume file systems or tapes. The reason tape backup procedures differ from one UNIX to the next is that no one has gotten them right yet.

UNIX tries to straddle a fine line by not requiring operators for managing backups, but yet forcing users to be aware of the decisions, problems and responsibilities of preventative file system maintenance. As disk capacities increase and computer systems grow more complex, UNIX is going to have to develop an integrated and refined solution to managing backups. UNIX is going to have grow up.

8.2.4   Disk Quotas

UNIX has traditionally lived in open environments where users took responsibility for their actions. There was little need for quotas or resource accounting.

Now that UNIX has gone commercial, buyers have asked for these main-frame ideas. Hence UNIX now has quotas. Fortunately, quotas have forced UNIX to clean up some of its problems. In particular, early versions of UNIX liked to act as if they never had to worry about file space. If a user program accidentally went wild, it could consume all the disk space. In turn, the system would panic and crash.

In fact, there are very few places where the system itself depends upon file space being available; however, most programmers have blindly carried foward the practice of ignoring the failure of **write()** due to a lack of disk space. They knew that if their program was out of space, then the system was also, and it hardly mattered that their program was going to dump core if the system was going to crash moments later.

8.2.5   Symbolic Links

Hard links allow one to associate (possibly multiple) names to a single file. These links can only be made to existing files. Their primary shortcoming is that they cannot span file systems. For example, in some particular file system **/usr1** and **/usr2** might be on different file systems and one could not directly access a file in **/usr2** by linking to it with a file which started with a **/usr1** pathname.

One extremely useful Berkeley innovation was symbolic links. Symbolic links overcome the single file system limitation of hard links, allowing one to create a link to a file in **/usr2** which can be made to appear in **/usr1**. This solves a number of longstanding problems. For example, suppose you receive a program (binary only) that insists upon putting a file in a file system partition where you don't have space. You can create a symbolic link from the name the program wants to see to a partition where you can afford the space. Of course, overuse of this can lead to the creation of a spaghetti file system.

Symbolic links have other problems, too. For instance, if you link from one directory to another, you don't have a choice of what .. (the parent directory) is. Symbolic links can link to nonexistent files (although some view this as a feature). And unlike hard links where there is only one set of permissions for the file, there is one for each symbolic link.

8.2.6   Find, Xargs

find is one user command that most administrators overlook – the man page is a little complex, because the syntax is unusual. But it is worth knowing how to use **find**. It can save you much effort.

find lets you perform arbitrary actions on entire directory hierarchies. For example, if you need to change the protection mode of every file in a large directory tree you can either do it by hand, or you can have **find** do it for you. We suggest you do the latter.

find is extensible. You can limit the operation to files with certain characteristics such as ownership, last modification time, and many other parameters. You could have **find** remove all object files which have not been accessed in a week with the following:

```
% find . \( -name '*.o' \) -atime +7 -exec rm {} \;
```

The nice thing about **find** is that you can do things with it that the designer never thought about. For example, it is not restricted to **chmod** or **rm**. It can execute any command, with any level of complexity.

xargs is similar to **find**, except that it is not tuned to traversing file systems. **xargs** accepts file lists from **stdin**, such as generated by **ls**, or even **find**. **xargs** reads **stdin** for files (and more arguments) and applies a given command to the files. For example, the following will prompt the user for a list of files to archive into **arch**.

```
ls | xargs -p -l ar r arch
```

The following command will run **diff** on successive pairs of arguments when run as a shell script:

```
echo $* | xargs -n2 diff
```

8.3   Managing Tapes

UNIX systems come with a somewhat inadequate set of tape handling facilities. What you may find in addition varies from system to system, since everyone has attempted to improve the situation from when they found it.

People often use **tar** (**t**ape **ar**chive) for their own personal backups, as **tar** simply copies directory hierarchies to and from tape, and it is easy to use. Also, **tar** is available on more UNIX systems than any other tape utility. Unfortunately, **tar** can only deal with one tape or floppy and is therefore restricted to dealing with relatively small amounts of data. A few vendors are starting to provide multi-volume versions but these are rare and you may have more portability problems.

Tape access in UNIX provides some classic examples of the 10 percent – 90 percent rule. Support for tapes is simple (10 percent of the work), and quite functional (solves 90 percent of the problems). For example, the lack of utilities that handle multiple volumes can be traced to the belief that this would be a very rare occurrence. (Disks were a lot smaller in the '70s, too.)

Just as there was no file locking facility, and since tapes were treated as files, there was no way to lock the tape drive, or to inform the system that you wanted sole access to the drive. This led to problems, such as one user accidentally archiving a file on another's tape.

A longstanding kludge in tape access is the method of declaring parameters. Since tapes are handled like files, they are opened with the UNIX `open()`. However, `open()` has no place to pass tape information, such as the tape density. This was not a problem for things like disks which remained attached to one system, but tapes were read and written on other systems with different peripherals.

To solve the problem of handling tapes at two different densities, the UNIX designers just created another logical tape device with a different minor device number. While the minor device number is supposed to be used by the driver to differentiate units of the same tape, this is not enforced and the driver can really do whatever it wants with it. For example, `/dev/tape0` and `/dev/tape8` might refer to the same physical drive, but using one in a command selects a different density. A lot of stupid and hard to remember conventions were born from this, such as "*add 8 to the unit number to get the tape to write at 6250bpi.*"

Naturally, people have extended this kludge, so it is quite common to have other conventions like "*add an 'n' to the device name, if you don't want the tape to rewind.*"

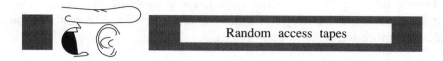

Random access tapes

Since tapes are accessed through the file system just the way disks are, it is possible to mount tapes as if they were disks. Of course, randomly accessing tape blocks is usually quite slow, so don't expect very high performance file systems!

This technique was actually quite popular on PDP-11s which came with DECtape. DECtapes used fixed-block formats which were easy and efficient to access randomly. If your system crashed, you could actually boot from the DECtape and work from it without a disk. (Of course, if the system decided to swap a process out, you might have had to wait a couple minutes!)

8.4   Managing Terminals and Serial Lines

People often claim that the large number of programs to control and define terminals and serial lines in UNIX are confusing. Ports that people log into are controlled differently than other ports. Certain terminal characteristics are defined either in the kernel (with **stty**) or in the shell (with environment parameters) or the user program or library. You're right – it is confusing.

8.4.1   Init and Getty

UNIX manages terminals and serial lines unlike any other operating system. Rather than the system itself waiting for users to log in, the **init** process is given the responsibility of logging users in. This removes some complexity from the kernel itself.

What **init** decides to do is somewhat dependent upon what system you are using, but the basic idea is as follows. Depending upon whether your system is Berkeley or System V based, the file **/etc/ttys** or **/etc/inittab** has a description for each serial line on your system. Each description defines whether people are allowed to log in or not, as well as the characteristics of the line, such as the speed and parity. (Actually, the characteristics are stored in a separate file, but no matter.)

If the serial line is set up to allow people to log in, **init** monitors the RS-232 control lines. If they indicate that a user is there, either by detecting a terminal turning on or a modem being called, `init` forks off a `getty`. (Some versions of `init` fork off a `getty` to monitor each set of RS-232 control lines. This is simpler but more wasteful of resources.)

    `getty` prints out the string: `login`: (or whatever your site has defined), sets up the terminal appropriately and prompts for a username. It then calls `login` which verifies the password and completes the job of logging a user in. The last step performed by `login` is to overlay itself with the shell defined for the user in **/etc/passwd**.

    When the user logs out, the shell returns to the procedure that called it (i.e., `init`). `init` then returns to monitoring the serial line.

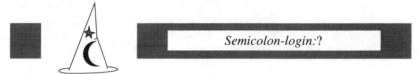

Semicolon-login:?

As you might suspect, the newsletter *;login:* gets its name from the UNIX login prompt. But what about the initial semicolon?

Well, the string that `getty` prompted with actually began with an escape-semicolon sequence. This put Teletype Model 37s into full-duplex. But most people did not use that type of terminal. Other terminals would ignore the escape, and print the semicolon followed by `login:`. Hence, most UNIX users always used to get prompted with `;login:`

    The nice thing about this whole system is that it doesn't have to worry about logging people in. It is all handled by an independent process. And if your local installation has special requirements like having a system-wide password or a special environment variable, it is easy to modify the `login` program.

    Annoyingly, UNIX binary licenses are sold for fixed numbers of users. However, there is nothing inherent in the operating system that prevents more users from logging in. All you have to do is edit the appropriate files. Even if your VAR has rewritten the `login` program to check for multiple users, it is relatively easy to write your own that allows for any number.

    Of course, we cannot condone violating the terms of your licensing agreement like this. But we thought you might be interested in this for technical reasons. For example, `uucp` logins appear as a user, even though there is no human involved. Thus, you might conceivably have two "people" logged in on a single-user system.

8.4.2   Termcap and Terminfo

/etc/termcap is a file that describes the capabilities of terminals. There is an entry for each kind of terminal (e.g., vt100, adm3, hp2621). Each entry describes the characteristics of the terminal. The characteristics are read by a common library (curses) which each character-graphics program uses.

Defining the terminal characteristics only once, and providing a single means of using it, avoids several problems:

- Programmers do not have to code for each terminal, but only for a single "virtual" terminal.

- Programmers do not have to think about optimal screen-drawing procedures, since the system automatically does that.

- Users do not have to wonder if their new terminal is going to run all their old programs correctly.

TERMCAP Environment Variable

When a program such as a screen editor is started, it needs to know the characteristics of the terminal. First it looks in the **TERM** environment variable to find the type of terminal you are using.

Using the terminal type, it retrieves the terminal characteristics from the **termcap** database. If the database is large, this can take quite a while. One way to reduce this time is to place your terminal characteristics in the environment variable called **TERMCAP**. (This is easy to do with **tset**.) If the system finds a terminal description in **TERMCAP**, it will use that. The result is that character-graphic programs start much more quickly.

The sort of information in the termcap database are the character sequences for cursor positioning, insert/delete character/line, and timing information for padding and optimization. It would be nice if terminal manufacturers supplied us with termcap descriptions, but few do. However, it isn't too hard to write them.

termcap was a tour de force in many ways. It worked so well that it has been applied to many parts of the system (as well as many other operating systems). For example, there is a capability file to describe printers

(**/etc/printcap**) and another to describe hosts (**/etc/remotes**) which parallel the style of **/etc/termcap**. The result is an extremely flexible environment.

termcap was originally written at Berkeley. It was very quickly adopted by AT&T for their own systems, however, AT&T redesigned some of it for System V. As well as changing the name to *terminfo* in System V, AT&T reorganized the terminal capability database. Rather than putting all the data into a single file, each terminal's characteristics are in a separate file in one of several directories. This is more efficient than **/etc/termcap**, but the system works essentially the same way. There are several public-domain programs available to convert **termcap** entries to **terminfo** entries and vice versa.

8.4.3   Setting Terminal Options – stty

stty (**set tty**) is used to tell the system certain things about your terminal. For example, you can change your baud rate and flow control with **stty**. **stty** has two major uses. One is to appear in login scripts so that when you log in, your terminal characteristics will be properly set. The second is to fix your terminal after a program has ungracefully exited. For example, if a program left your terminal in raw mode, you can reset the terminal by typing **stty sane** (SV) or **stty -raw echo** (BSD) followed by a control-J.

It is also possible to set characteristics of other terminals, if you have permission. Note that you cannot use **stty** on dialup lines because **init** will promptly set them back according to the descriptions in **/etc/ttys** or **/etc/inittab**.

It is somewhat annoying that **stty** is not integrated with **termcap**. The problem is not that they do two different things. Rather, **stty** does so many things, it is really just the original catch-all for terminal problems. The **termcap** designers did the correct thing by ignoring it.

8.5   Managing Users

UNIX has long straddled the line for user management in staying out of the users way versus providing enough control for a useful system. Early versions of UNIX generated only some files (in **/usr/adm**) which logged connect time and the processes being executed.

New versions of UNIX are beginning to have more and more tools for user management and tracking. Both System V and Berkeley UNIX have comprehensive systems for tracking usage, with breakdowns by user-time versus kernel-time, I/O operations, and so on. Indeed, it's rather frightening.

8.5.1   User Accounts

One of the few really essential management tools is the **/etc/passwd** file. This file contains one line that describes each user allowed to use the system. Talk about being brief!

The **/etc/passwd** file is a text file and can be edited with any editor. The format is certainly trivial enough. However, if there is a danger of multiple people updating the file concurrently, some lockout mechanism should be used. **vipw** is a program designed to do exactly that – it starts up **vi** on the password file and prevents anyone else from editing the file until you are done.

A line from **/etc/passwd** might look like:

```
dmr:tFLKiPzkWavm:29:5:Dennis Ritchie:/usr/dmr:/bin/ksh
```

There are seven fields per line, each separated by a colon. They are:

1. Login name.

2. Encrypted user password.

3. User ID number (called "uid"). This is used by the system internally to distinguish users.

4. Group ID number. (see next section)

5. GCOS field. Typically the user's complete name. It can also contain other things such as a phone number, or silly comment. In other words, it isn't defined. It is called the GCOS field historically because it was originally used to define an accounting ID that was submitted with remote batch jobs to the GCOS system at Bell Labs.

6. Home directory.

7. Shell. Also used to create turn-key systems and login commands.

This simple scheme is enough to provide a very flexible user environment. It is trivial to add users to the system. You just add a line describing the users, and create a home directory for them. (In practice, it is also helpful to give them a couple of prototypical files such as **.cshrc** and **.login** or **.profile**, but that isn't absolutely necessary.)

The shell field is particularly useful. By allowing users to run different shells, it becomes possible to tune the system toward any level of user. Non-technical users can use a simple shell, such as a menu-oriented program. Restricted users can have a restricted shell, which can only access games, for instance. It is also possible to install commands as users. For example, if a user called **who** was created with login shell **/bin/who**, then you could run the **who** command by logging in as **who**. (And when the command finishes, you would be logged out.)

This file is writeable only by the superuser. By limiting the amount of information in this file, the amount of information that the user can't change is limited. Fields that the user might want to change, like the password field, are changed by a special program that limits access to just the right field.

Unlike most other operating systems, the **/etc/passwd** file is readable by everyone. This is feasible because the passwords are stored in encrypted form. As such, they are of no use to anyone, except the system itself. Interestingly, the original implementation used a particularly powerful encryption routine based on the German Enigma cipher machine used in World War II. Though theoretically possible, it was prohibitively expensive to decrypt a password. (And besides, it was easier to guess them.)

8.5.2   Group Accounts

The fourth field of the **/etc/passwd** file defines a group ID (or "gid"). This number is used by the system internally to associate groups of users with common access permissions. Each user in a group can then access any file which permits access according to its group permission.

There is a file called **/etc/group** that looks quite similar to **/etc/passwd**. It simply lists groups by group name, password, numeric group ID and users that are members of the group. The password is optional and allows other people to use the group even if they do not normally have permission to use that group. Here is a typical entry from **/etc/group**:

```
admin:q3gn89:16:carol,henry,joe,tony,gail
```

Like the password file mechanism, the group file mechanism is also easy to use and flexible.

8.5.3   Communication

Since UNIX users and administrators are one and the same, communication between users and administrators is good. Some of the tools to provide communication via the computer are:

- **mail** – sends mail to a user.

- **write** – writes a message to another user's terminal.

- **wall** – writes a message to all active terminals. Good for warning about impending shutdowns.

A particularly important tool is a bulletin board system of some type for news. UNIX comes with a rather simplistic one. There are many better in the public domain that you should acquire immediately. We highly recommend one of the systems that will let you support Usenet (see the Underground chapter). These function well even for communication between users on only a single system.

8.5.4   Uucp

uucp stands for "UNIX-to-UNIX **cp**." Like **cp**, **uucp** copies files. However, **uucp** allows you to copy files from one UNIX machine to another. The syntax of **uucp** is very similar to **cp**. The only difference is that file names can have host prefixes. An exclamation separates the two. For example, the following command would copy **/etc/passwd** from one machine (**lurch**) to another (**kanamit**).

```
uucp lurch!/etc/passwd kanamit!/etc/passwd
```

Originally, **uucp** was designed to run over RS-232 serial lines (at any speed). It has since been enhanced to support many different kinds of communications media.

uucp has error-detection and correction protocols to ensure files are transmitted properly. Since it requires no special hardware, you can form store-and-forward networks of **uucp**-connected computers with virtually no expense other than the wires connecting them. **uucp** also has the capability of using dial-out and dial-in modems. A large part of the Usenet (see the Underground chapter) works using dial-up **uucp** connections.

uux is a cousin of **uucp** which allows remote execution of commands. It uses the same syntax as **uucp** except that arbitrary commands may be specified (again, prefaced with an exclamation). The command is executed on the remote system, after the files have been sent there.

While there are much faster networks available today, **uucp** networks are still quite prevalent on UNIX systems. Part of the reason is that **uucp** is the only computer-to-computer communication system available on every UNIX system shipped. **uucp** networks are slow compared to modern networks, but for many years they were a particularly cheap and effective way of internetworking.

8.6   Managing System Activity

A UNIX system requires maintenance to be performed at regular intervals. The most important of these are backups. Secondly, certain log files should be examined (and truncated) periodically. Lastly, all hardware should have regular preventative maintenance.

Beyond these tasks, there are always things popping up that will keep a system administrator busy. For example, you can expect to keep busy constantly adding users and applications and fixing bugs. Don't ever take a day off.

To start you on your way, it is good to have an idea of what the system looks like, just so that if something goes wrong, you know how far off center the system is.

8.6.1   Miscellaneous Files

There are various log files to keep track of system activity. They are updated and cleaned out automatically. Most of these are in **/usr/adm**, **/usr/spool** and **/etc**. You might look at them occasionally just to see if the system is crashing behind your back.

Programs like **who** reference these log files. If the programs start behaving strangely, you should check the log files themselves.

/tmp and **/usr/tmp** are used as directories to store files temporarily. For example, the C compiler may store temporary files there as it works on your programs. The compiler does this because there is no guarantee it can store files in your current directory (or even your home directory).

The reason there are two "temp" directories is as follows. When the system boots, the first thing it mounts is the root file system with includes **/tmp**. The root file system is usually a small logical disk partition, containing the bare necessities required to run UNIX. This minimizes the number of things UNIX depends on, which is important in the event of a crash. If you can get the system up with only the root partition mounted, at least you can run the basic utilities (which may need a small temp directory).

Once the system is operating correctly, you can bring UNIX up the rest of the way and mount the rest of the file systems. `/usr/tmp` should be on a large partition with a lot of free space. Programs like `troff` (which create large temporary files) can then run, storing their files in `/usr/tmp`.

If you suddenly find your system out of space, you should look in the temp directories for leftover files. In general, anything in the temp directories is subject to removal at a moment's notice. Indeed, a system reboot generally cleans out all temporary files.

The spool directories (`/usr/spool`) can also be combed for excess files, although you should not be as flippant with recently dated files as they may actually be spooled up for service.

8.6.2   Daemons and Other Processes

Daemons (pronounced "demons") are background processes that do useful work on behalf of the user. For example, if you send mail, you might compose the letter and then hand it to a mail daemon for delivery. You go on to something else, while the daemon continues to process the outgoing mail. The mail daemon could as well wake up (without your explicit action) every so often to check for incoming mail.

Users can write daemons as easily as any programs. However, there are some tricky things you should know before starting out. An excellent reference is "How to Write a UNIX Daemon" by Dave Lennart in *;login:*, vol. 12, no. 4, July/August 1987.

Conceptually, the big difference between most programs and daemons is that daemons don't have a `stdin` or `stdout`, and they sleep most of the time. While it may seem wasteful to have a lot of processes that just sleep, it is not inefficient, and the system is easier to manage. It avoids a monolithic program that tries to do everything. UNIX systems usually have a lot of daemons. For example, they almost always come with:

- `update`: Synchronizes the file system with its image in kernel memory every so often. (Not in System V.)

- **cron**: General-purpose background task scheduler. If you want a program such as **uucp** to run every hour, you can ask **cron** to do it.

- **lpd** or **lpsched**: Line Printer Daemon. Picks up files spooled for printing and distributes them to printers.

- **init**: The first process created at system startup time, **init** is in charge of creating all the other necessary processes in the system, as well as creating login processes for each terminal.

- **swapper**: This process handles kernel requests to swap pages of memory to and from the disk.

cron is a general-purpose background task scheduler. It allows you to avoid worrying about the problem of having a task wake up every so often. For example, if you want to automatically run backups every night, you don't have to write a special program – you just tell **cron** to do it. To tell **cron** what to do, just add entries to **/usr/lib/crontab**.†

Try making an entry for **cron** so that something strange will happen on April Fools Day!

Another general-purpose program daemon handler is **inetd** on Berkeley systems. **inetd** monitors network traffic, and when requests for service from remote systems arrive, **inetd** will start up the appropriate server. For example, if mail arrives **inetd** will start up a mail process to handle the incoming mail.

The line printer daemon is an example of a spooler. This type of daemon occasionally gets requests for work faster than it can process them. For example, you might request that the system print out ten files, but obviously all but one can print immediately. The spooler will copy your files into a spool directory (such as **/usr/spool/lp**) and work on the first file. When it is done, it will go back and get the next file.

The **ps** command will give you information about what is running on the system. You should see all the daemons listed above. If you find processes that should not be there, you can kill them by issuing the kill command with the process ID returned from **ps**.

The **kill** command doesn't actually stop processes. Rather, it sends signals to processes. Since most processes die upon receipt of the signals, howev-

---

† This describes BSD **cron**. System V **cron** has a more complicated interface but is functionally equivalent.

er, **kill** is aptly named. The best kind of signal to stop a process for sure is signal 9 which is the signal to kill a process. Thus, to kill process 17, you would say:

```
% kill -9 17
```

In rare circumstances, the process will not go away. This can happen for a number of reasons:

1. The process will become a "zombie" according to **ps**. Zombies are processes that have exited but are kept around in the kernel until the parent process executes a **wait()** to get the status of the process.

2. The process may be waiting on code inside the kernel, such as in a device operation. You should satisfy the device request (e.g., mount the tape, fiddle with the RS-232 lines) to solve this.

8.7   Security & Insecurity

"When it comes to computer security, paranoia is not enough." - Ralph Jones

UNIX security is quite simplistic. Nevertheless, it solves most security problems quite easily. (Another example of the 10 percent – 90 percent rule.) With care, UNIX can be made quite secure, although knowledgeable hackers can probably get into it or any system.

Much work is currently being done on providing more sophisticated security to UNIX, including finer-grain file protections and privilege levels. See the UNIX Meets the Real World chapter.

There are several good books on UNIX security including *UNIX System Administration* by David Fiedler and Bruce Hunter, and *UNIX Survival Guide* by Elizabeth Nichols, Sidney Bailin and Joseph Nichols. In addition, *UNIX REVIEW*, vol. 6, no. 2, February 1988, contains a collection of extremely well-written essays on UNIX security.

8.7.1   File Permissions

File permissions are specified for three sets of users: owner, group and world. The world includes all the users on the system, but the owner and group are determined by each file. Each file gets a default owner and group when it is created. You can also change them with the commands **chown** and **chgrp**.

Permissions for each of these sets of users are further broken down into read, write and execute permission. For example, here are the permissions on a typical file (listed with `ls -l`):

```
-rwxrwxr--  1 don          70270 Nov 11 13:37  AdminEnv.doc
```

The section of the line: **-rwxrwxr--** defines the file permissions. The first – is a placeholder. You will see things like a **d** for directories or a **b** for disks (i.e., Block-oriented devices). The next three characters define read, write and execute permissions for the owner. Since the letters appear in this case, the owner (**don**) has permissions to access the file. The next three letters are for the group. The remaining three are for everyone else. They indicate that everyone else is only allowed to read the file.

You can change the file permissions with **chmod** (**change mode**). It can take octal arguments representing the bits (i.e., **chmod 664** for **-rw-rw-r--**) or a symbolic expression where **u** stands for user, **g** for group and **o** for others.   **+** adds permissions while – removes them. Thus, **chmod o-w** removes write permission for others. See your man page for more details.

The **umask** is a shell variable (in both **csh** and **sh**) which consists of three octal digits that define a default file creation mode. When a file is created, the **umask** is used to determine its file protection (along with the mode value from **open()**). A typical **umask** is **022** – this gives read access to everyone, and write access only to the file owner. Unfortunately, **umask** works backwards from the way you would think it should. The **umask** is X-OR'ed rather than AND'ed with mode supplied during an **open()**.

One of the nice things about file permissions is that they extend to devices, since devices are files in the file system. Most other operating systems have their own special access control techniques for devices that differ greatly from file protection.

8.7.2   Superuser a.k.a. Root
"Keep your eggs in one basket. And watch it carefully!" – Mark Twain

An exception to the previous rules is the *superuser* (who logs in as **root**). Root has access to everything and nothing can be protected from it, although the system still protects its own integrity – for example, root cannot access memory outside its own address space.

The idea of a superuser with a single privilege level is in stark contrast to other multiuser operating systems such as IBM's VM or DEC's VMS which have many levels of privileges. Both approaches have their advantages and disadvantages. The primary disadvantage to multiple levels of privileges is complexity. In fact, they are so complex, that most users ignore them when they are in a hurry, treating them like the single superuser privilege level in UNIX. The primary disadvantage to a single all-powerful privilege level is simply that it is extremely dangerous.

What is clear is that superuser access should only be given to users who absolutely need it, such as the system administrator. The superuser password should be changed often.

8.7.3   Setuid

One of the most well-known parts of UNIX is the setuid mechanism. The idea of the mechanism is that when programs are designated as *setuid*, anyone running them temporarily gains the privileges of the program's owner. A simple use might be to create a game that keeps a file of everyone's high scores. If players had permission to write the file, they could update their scores unfairly (using an editor). By designating the game as setuid, users temporarily get the ability to update the score file, but only as the game allows.

Setuid is simple in concept and solves several otherwise difficult security problems. This was one of the few areas of UNIX that could truly be called innovative. Indeed, the "setuid-bit" mechanism, invented by Dennis Ritchie, is the only patented part of UNIX. Amusingly, the patent describes the mechanism in terms of a piece of hardware because, at the time, they were concerned that software could not be patented!

Setgid is analogous to setuid but for group permission. If a program is *setgid*, than anyone running that program gains the permissions corresponding to the group which owns the file. Programs that are setuid show up with an **s** instead of an **x** in place of the user-execute field from **ls**. Similarly, programs that are setgid have an **s** instead of an **x** in the group-execute field.

Unfortunately, the concepts of setuid and setgid are so simple that people intuit that programs using them are simple to write. That is not true. Setuid and setgid programs that are secure are extremely difficult to write, especially in the face of devious users. Try to avoid writing them if all possible. There are almost always other ways to achieve the same result, without the risk of giving away root access.

United States Patent [19]

Ritchie

[11] **4,135,240**

[45] **Jan. 16, 1979**

[54] PROTECTION OF DATA FILE CONTENTS

[75] Inventor: Dennis M. Ritchie, Summit, N.J.

[73] Assignee: Bell Telephone Laboratories Incorporated, Murray Hill N.J.

[21] Appl. No.: 377,591

[22] Filed: Jul. 9, 1973

[51] Int. Cl. G06F 11/10; G06F 13/00

[52] U.S. Cl. 364/200

[58] Field of Search ....340/172.5; 364/200 MS File, 900 MS File

[56]   References Cited

U.S. PATENT DOCUMENTS

Re. 27,239	11/1971	Ulrich	340/172.5
Re. 27,251	12/1971	Amdahl et al.	340/172.5
3,368,207	2/1968	Beausoleil et al.	340/172.5
3,377,624	4/1968	Nelson et al.	340/172.5
3,469,239	9/1969	Richmond	340/172.5
3,576,544	4/1971	Cordero et al.	340/172.5
3,599,159	8/1971	Creech et al.	340/172.5
3,599,159	8/1971	Hoff	364/200
3,683,418	8/1972	Martin	340/172.5
3,735,364	5/1973	Hatta	340/172.5
3,742,458	6/1973	Inoue et al.	340/172.5
3,761,883	9/1973	Alvarez	364/200

Primary Examiner–James D. Thomas

Attorney, Agent, or Firm–Stephen J. Phillips

[57]   ABSTRACT

An improved arrangement for controlling access to data files by computer users. Access permission bits are used in the prior art to separately indicate permissions for the file owner and nonowners to read, write and execute the file contents. An additional access control bit is added to each executable file. When this bit is set to one, the identification of the current user is changed to that of the owner of the executable file. The program in the executable file then has access to all data files owned by the same owner. This change is temporary, the proper identification being restored when the program is terminated.

4 Claims, 2 Drawing Figures

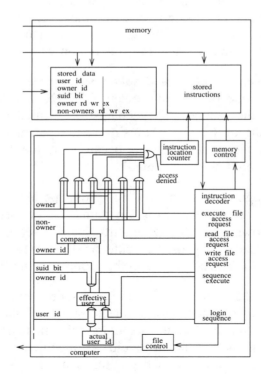

First page of Dennis Ritchie's patent of setuid mechanism

Two good readings on writing setuid programs are "How to Write a Setuid Program" by Matt Bishop in *;login:*, vol. 12, no. 1, January/February 1987, and *UNIX System Security* by Patrick Wood and Stephen Kochan, Hayden Books.

8.7.4   Security in a Distributed Environment

Maintaining security on a network of systems is like dealing with a chain – it is only as strong as its weakest link. In order to have an effective network, file transfers, remote execution, and resource sharing must be allowed among the various systems. Special care must be taken when configuring the network programs and in defining the access for the systems. On the other hand, a friendly environment will make life much easier. This is the dilemma faced by any operating system in a networked environment.

Each network interface (e.g., NFS, RFS, `uucp`, `ftp`) defines its own mechanisms that must somehow integrate with the UNIX file protection mechanism. This is complicated by having UNIX communicate with machines that have different protection mechanisms. An excellent article describing the difficulties of detecting, preventing and tracking an actual computer intruder in a distributed environment is "Stalking the Wily Hacker" by Clifford Stoll, *Communications of the ACM*, vol. 31, no. 5, May 1988.

Section 4

Outside

UNIX

Chapter 9: UNIX Underground

"Congress shall make no law . . . abridging the freedom of speech or of the press." – First Amendment, U.S. Constitution, 1791

UNIX is unusual among computer systems in that it was not developed as a commercial product. For many years, it was simply given away to universities and research institutions – the only cost was for the media and manuals.

During that time, there was a large amount of program and information sharing between UNIX users. There had to be – the system wasn't supported. The documentation was oriented only to a programmer. And there was no way of formally disseminating programs.

Now, there are more formal ways of seeking UNIX help, information and programs, but the underground still exists. Much UNIX development and support still occurs by people who are not interested in commercial gain. These are the people that we call the UNIX underground. Many commercial vendors are surreptitiously involved with the underground as well. In this way, companies can release software that they do not choose to sell or support for some reason.

This chapter discusses the UNIX underground – such as where to find public-domain UNIX programs, where to swap bug reports and fixes, and how to get on Usenet. Our coverage of the underground concludes with a discussion of some games and humor, two areas which never seem to get the support they really deserve.

9.1   Usenet

Usenet (*Users' net*work) is a collection of computers providing integrated network file transfer, archival services, mail, conferencing and news. It is often simply called "netnews," or even just "news."

The way news works is simple. News may be "posted" by anyone from any site (computer) on the network. Each site calls their nearest neighbors and transmits articles to them. The neighbors in turn transmit the articles to their neighbors, ad infinitum, with the effect of propagating articles across the entire network. Since most machines are connected to several neighbors, the network is extremely robust.

Most of the machines are UNIX machines running `uucp` software over dial-up phone lines as the underlying transport service, but there are many other machines as well with gateways to other networks. Most `uucp` links are over dial-up lines. By keeping neighbors geographically local and using off-the-shelf asynchronous modems, costs for transmission are kept very low. There is no administrative charge for using Usenet.

Besides low cost, Usenet is different from other networks in that 1) the largest percentage of users on it are UNIX users, and 2) the largest percentage of any one type of computer system attached to any one type of network are UNIX machines attached to Usenet.

As you can imagine, Usenet is a great place to find information about UNIX. However, such information is distinctly different from that found in manuals, magazines and books. It has many of the characteristics of electronic mail. For example, it is typically informal and opinionated. Much of it is also timely and transient as befits its mode of delivery. Nonetheless, it contains much useful material. It also contains objective material such as benchmarks and source listings that could not possibly appear in any other medium.

Usenet spans the gamut from valuable to trivial to silly, although part of the fun of "the net" is grubbing through all the cruft for the really good gems. (If you are the type who loves digging through your neighbor's trash cans, you'll love Usenet). Usenet covers topics that are of interest to every UNIX user. This not only means UNIX, but computers (hey, UNIX runs on computers), food (hey, all UNIX users have to eat), movies (hey, we all see movies), humor (you'd better have a sense of it to be reading this book), and just about anything that more than ten people want to talk about.

Users may post articles (any text, program source or binaries) to the network by running a program called `postnews` (or any of a number of similar interfaces). `postnews` distributes the article to a small set of geographically local computers that you have made prior arrangements to share articles with. In turn, they redistribute your article to their neighbors. Distribution takes place both ways, so that at the same time your article is transferred, your system also gets any new articles that have been posted at other sites.

You don't have to read them when they are transferred. They are stored as files on your system and you can read them at your leisure. A variety of programs can be used to browse through the articles. Popular programs are **rn** (for **read** news), **vnews** (for **visual news**) and **notes**. Each program has its adherents, and although **rn** seems to be the most sophisticated, **vnews** is the most used because it is bundled with the news software while the others are not. There are also interfaces from programs such as **emacs** (which seems to have interfaces to just about everything).

The articles are stored as files and you could possibly use UNIX commands like **cat** and **ls** to look at them; however, there is so much material that programs like **vnews** are essential. Furthermore, the news readers will help you compose followups, or reply directly back to the original author. Some have the ability to display two articles at once if the second is a reply to the first. Others have extremely sophisticated features such as screening out (or in) articles based on user-defined patterns, or following threads of conversations through different articles.

In a practical sense, Usenet is a piece of software that allows computers to communicate with each other. Unlike packet or circuit networks, Usenet is a logical network – it deals with articles, subjects, followups, etc. Physical networks (such as **uucp** and Arpanet) do the lower-level work of actual communications.

The original network ran on top of **uucp** (see elsewhere in this book) between a handful of computers based at Duke and UNC. As more people started sharing UNIX software (and low-cost modems became more commonplace), this public domain software spread and more sites joined the network.

In the early days of Usenet, typical articles were something like this:

```
From: ucbvax!vax135!allegra!del
Subject: anybody got a hpz29x driver for PDP-11/23?
Newsgroup: net.unix

I am trying to bring up a hpz29x frisbee under V6.  I have
never written a driver before, but I have the source to a
driver for a hpz29q which is pretty similar.

I don't understand the reference to hpregs->zork.
```

```
Any hints?

Reply to allegra!del
---------------------------------------------------------
```

Here we find a user named **del**, at a site called **allegra**, trying to integrate a peripheral which his system has no driver for. He made a good start by finding a driver that was for a very similar device, but eventually needed some expert assistance. So he sent the question out to the net.

Messages like this would typically get a flurry of answers. Not only would people answer **del**'s question about the reference, but invariably someone had already faced the same problem and was sending the source back to **del**. This type of interaction has not changed. It is extremely unlikely to find a bug that has not already been found and fixed. Finding out about it is what the net excels at.

It has become common to distribute drivers, bug fixes for common programs (especially the kernel), symptoms of problems, etc. Many UNIX companies do this, too. People also air general complaints, new software, prototypes of new software, thoughts for prototypes of new software, and bad jokes.

Each type of article is tagged by its *newsgroup*. The newsgroups are a general classification of the material in the article. This allows you to request articles about a particular subject. (You can also request articles much more explicitly, such as by title or keyword.) For example, **comp.unix** is a newsgroup that contains articles on UNIX. There are other **comp.** newsgroups, each having something to do with computers. Jokes, on the other hand, are kept in **rec.humor** ("rec" is for recreation). There are hundreds of active newsgroups. Some of them peter out and die and new ones are created as new topics are born. Some, like **rec.humor** and **comp.unix.bugs**, will undoubtedly be around forever.

Statistics indicate that the ten most active newsgroups (in order of activity) at the beginning of 1987 were:

soc.singles	discussions related to being single
soc.women	discussions of women's issues
rec.humor	jokes, limericks, and other humor
comp.sys.ibm.pc	discussions related to IBM micros and clones
comp.unix.questions	questions related to UNIX

`comp.sources`	program sources
`rec.autos`	discussions about automobiles
`misc.consumers`	discussions of consumer interests
`comp.unix.wizards`	discussion of experienced UNIX users
`comp.lang.c`	discussion of the C programming language

Yes, that's right. The topic of interest to most Usenet readers is single's issues. From our research, we conclude that a UNIX programmer is three times more likely to use Usenet to discuss what to do on a date than how to implement shareable libraries. Just remember to delete the first three newsgroups from the top of this list before trying to use it to justify Usenet to your local management.

Here are some other interesting statistics about Usenet.† Sites receive more than 2Mb of articles every day and an average of 15.4Mb a week. There are 6,760 articles every week (561/day). 2,552 people posted all of that in a month. There were 235 newsgroups. There were 5,300 sites with an estimated 157,000 readers. Wow!

Besides the volume of data that rolls across Usenet, there are several other things about it that make it unique.

No central administration. Not only is there no central administration, there is no one person or body who has absolute power. Consensus and peer pressure seem to be the way things are decided. If enough people send mail or articles in agreement of something (it's never unanimous), something (such as a newsgroup name) will be changed. In actuality there is a small number of people (probably less than 100) who actually discuss the network issues and make the decisions. Changing software and posting the modifications is another way of enforcing or encouraging others to change. Of course, they don't have to listen. (For that reason, there are about 50 different versions of the news software running.)

Access is free. Well, sort of. Unlike commercial networks and funded research networks such as Bitnet and Arpanet, Usenet is not sponsored by anyone. There are no employees, no newsletter, no overhead. The only things that cost are computer time and communications. Most sites run Usenet software at night. Since the machine is unloaded, they figure that the CPU cycles would be wasted anyway. Telephone calls (for **uucp**) are made within the local

---

† These statistics were generated in January, 1987 from Brian Reid's Arbitron system. This suite of programs automatically collects Usenet readership survey data and posts the results to **news.list** every month.

calling area so they are usually free. Some sites actually do pay for international connections in order to establish otherwise impossible connectivity. For this we are eternally grateful.

While there is no central administration to Usenet, it is possible for a small number of sites to privately use Usenet for a selected set of newsgroups. Many companies, for example, use Usenet in this manner. They can set up newsgroups specific to them without forcing the rest of the world to do the same, and the information posted to these newsgroups remains local to the company computers.

In this way, it is also possible to create "forbidden" groups that for any number of reasons cannot be supported by the more public machines. For instance, people love to imagine that some illicit suppliers of drugs could be using Usenet to coordinate their activities and prices. Good luck getting on their distribution.

Most of the newsgroups are *unmoderated*. This means that everyone sees everything that anyone posts. On the other hand, *moderated* groups have a designated person (called the *moderator*) who receives all potential articles as mail, and redistributes them through the newsgroup. The benefit of moderators is that they can cut out all of the useless, repeated, or otherwise inappropriate material. While some people claim that moderation is equivalent to censorship, moderation raises the quality of a newsgroup while cutting down on the volume. However, acting as a moderator takes a lot of time, so not many people do it. Hence, few groups are moderated.

News is documented primarily through its own medium. With the distribution come several documents describing "How to Read News," "How to Install News," and other topics. A document on posting news is called "Usenet Etiquette." It tries to point out how computer conferencing is different from other communication mediums, and why readers in California are not interested in reading about dinette sets for sale in New Jersey.

There are also many groups dedicated to current information about the network. For example, there is a newsgroup where the latest network maps are posted every month, and another which contains an up-to-date list of all the newsgroups and moderators.

Numerous articles have been written about the Usenet both from technical aspects as well as social aspects. An excellent comparison of Usenet to other networks is available in "Notable Computer Networks" by John Quarterman in *Communications of the ACM*, vol. 29, no. 10, October 1986. Other worthwhile articles are "A Perspective on the Usenet" by Erik Fair in *;login:* vol. 11, no. 1, January/February 1986, "News Need Not Be Slow" in the *Winter 1987 USENIX Proceedings* and "Project Stargate" by Lauren Weinstein in the *Summer 1985 USENIX Proceedings*.

9.1.1   How to Get on Usenet

There are several steps to getting on Usenet.

1) Establish communications with a site that is already on Usenet. The first problem here is to find a site close to you that is on the network. The best way is to go to a local UNIX user group meeting and ask. Undoubtedly, there will be many sites represented there that are on Usenet. Ask nicely, if they can *"become your Usenet feed."* If you can establish outgoing connections (e.g., you have a dial-out modem), you should offer to pay the price of the periodic phone calls. Polling other sites is much appreciated and is a sign of good faith and social responsibility. (It also means that you are not making your neighbor pay for the phone calls to you.)

2) Do whatever is necessary to establish a reliable physical connection between your site and your Usenet feed. This usually entails bringing up **uucp**. All the popular UNIX systems come with **uucp**. If you are not on a UNIX system, you should go to your user group meetings (appropriate to your machine) and find out how people communicate between machines. For example, IBM mainframes popularly use RSCS, not **uucp**.

3) Once you have a reliable connection to your Usenet feed, ask your neighbor to send you the latest Usenet sources (they must have them, if they are already on the net). They are in the public domain, so there should not be a problem sending them to you. The most popular source set is available free from UUNET (see following section) and runs on most UNIX machines and many non-UNIX machines (e.g., VMS, MS-DOS).

4) Read the enclosed directions.

5) Read news. Post news. Have fun.

9.1.2   Commercial Usenet and Public-access UNIX Systems

Usenet has historically been a noncommercial service. This has some drawbacks. The primary one is that finding a nearby site willing to feed you news is not necessarily a simple task. Feeding another site means that your computer will be using its own time (and tying up modems) in order to provide service to another site, at no direct benefit to you. Many sites cannot justify the generosity necessary for this. It often leaves sites with the feeling that they are supporting other sites. This is often true. Fortunately, there have been many sites that have enough excess computer power and disk space that it is usually possible to find one, although it often requires some begging and a promise to pay for the phone calls.

UUNET

To solve this problem, USENIX began a communication service in 1987 called UUNET. UUNET is available to anyone on a pay-for-usage basis. In 1988, it owned a large (Sequent) UNIX machine dedicated towards Usenet, mail gatewaying and UNIX archives, and was accessed nightly by 250 subscribers. Usenet does not offer login service.

Rates are established only to recoup costs. The prices compare very favorably with other electronic networks (due to its nonprofit nature), and the quality of the service is exceptionally high. UUNET provides high-speed modems, 800 numbers, off-peak rates, access through and to other private networks (e.g., Arpanet, Tymnet), and the subscriber's choice of newsgroups. In addition, UUNET provides `pathalias` service, allowing people to mail to other `uucp` sites without specifying routing.

Public-access UNIX

Alternatives to UUNET are *public-access* UNIX systems. These systems provide login service to all comers. Some are for-profit and charge a usage fee, while many are free. While it is possible to log into them with the intent of learning about UNIX, the predominant use is for communication with other users. Some of them also have substantial disk storage devoted to public-domain UNIX and C programs which you can copy. Many of the systems are part of Usenet, and quite a few are also on other networks.

One representative (and particularly well-known) public-access system is WELL. WELL is owned by Network Technologies Inc. and the Point Foundation (who brought us the Whole Earth Catalog). WELL (**W**hole **E**arth 'lectronic **L**ink) provides access to Usenet and other networks. Unlike UUNET where you download material to your own computer, you actually log in to WELL and run `postnews`, `readnews` or any of the other communications tools interactively. Indeed, it is possible to use this service with just a terminal (although a personal computer will provide you with the option of recording sessions, and uploading or downloading files). The rates and phone number of WELL are listed in the following table.

The WELL provides other services which make it unique. Several magazines are electronically "published" through the WELL. The magazines accept and provide to users news, art, classifieds, fiction, and so on. A high percentage of WELL users are professional editors, writers and artists. WELL is located in Sausalito, California and is connected to many other local computers and networks in that area. Thus, much of the information that passes through it is of local interest. This is the case with most public-access systems.

Many, many other public-access UNIX systems exist. Unfortunately, we cannot possibly list and describe them all. Furthermore, many of these systems (especially the nonprofit ones) can shut down and disappear without any warning. Therefore, we will list just a few of these systems. Hopefully, they will still be running by the time this book is published. No guarantees, however.

Phone #	Name	Location		Baud	System Type
201-752-2820	`unirot`	NJ	NJ	12	Heurikon Unisoft
201-753-9758	`acgnj`	NJ	Plainfield	12/24	286 SCO XENIX
no fee, 60 min. limit					
206-367-3837	`eskimo`	WA	Seattle	3/12	Tandy 6K XENIX
fee $1/mo. 1st 2 weeks free					
206-863-0453-6		WA	Sumner	12	Tandy 6K XENIX
Micro Magic BBS, $30/yr. $5 shell access					
212-420-0527	`magpie`	NY	NYC	3/12/24	UNIX SVR2
Magpie BBS, no fee					
212-675-7059	`marob`	NY	NYC	12/24	286 UNIX SV
AKCS/ERACS BBS, donation requested					
212-879-9031	`dasys1`	NY	NYC	12	Unistride SV
$5/mo.					
213-376-5714	`pnet02`	CA	Redondo Beach	3/12/24	XENIX
Usenet, mail, conferencing					
213-459-7231	`stb`	CA	Santa Monica	3/12/24	Tandy 16
Serial Tree BBS, no fee, shell access					
214-250-1764	`warble`	TX	Plano	12/24	286 SCO XENIX
XBBS, no fee, don't call between 5AM-5PM					

214-824-7811   **killer**   TX   Dallas   3/12/24   3B2/400 UNIX
    no fee

215-275-2429   **prapc-1** PA   Norristown   12   286 Coherent Sys7
    UNaXcess BBS, no fee, 60 min.limit, shell access, login: **fhbbs**

216-781-6201   **ncoast**   OH   Cleveland   3/12/24   PLEXSUS
    Usenet, no fee, donation requested, $2/hr. prime, $1/hr. non-prime

217-529-3223   **pallas**   IL   Springfield   3/12/24   Convrgnt Minifr SV
    Minnie BBS, $25 donation reqested

301-540-3656-9 **netsys**   MD   Germantown   12   Altos 986 XENIX
    $5/mo.

303-632-4111   **chariot** CO   Colo Sprgs   3/12   Convrgnt Minifr SV
    Picospan BBS, $12/mo.

305-584-4440   **pinn**   FL   Ft. Lauderdale 3/12/24   AT Microport SV
    MAGIC BBS, $12/yr.

313-994-6333   **m-net**   MI   Ann Arbor   3/12   Altos 68020 SV
    Picospan BBS, fee for extended service

312-272-5912   **igloo**   IL   12   PC7300
    Picospan BBS

312-283-0559   **chinet**   IL   Chicago   3/12/24   3B2/300 SV
    Picospan BBS, fee $50/yr. for Usenet access

312-833-8126   **vpnet**   IL   Villa Park   3/12   3B1 UNIX
    AKCS/ERACS BBS, no fee, shell access

312-566-8909   **ddsw1**   IL   Mundelein   3/12   286 Microport
    ERACS/UX BBS, 1 hr./day free

312-566-8911,2 **ddsw1**   IL   Mundelein   24   286 Microport
    ERACS/UX BBS, 1 hr./day free, contribution requested

313-623-6309   **nucleus** MI   Clarkston   12/24   286 UNIX SV
    AKCS/ERACS BBS, donation requested

314-947-0895   **slacbbs** MO   St. Louis   3/12   286 SCO XENIX
    XBBS, no fee, 60 min. limit, shell access, login: **bbs**

403-295-2541   **xenlink** AB   Calgary   3/12/24   286 SCO XENIX
    Term BBS, no fee, shell access, login: **bbs**

408-725-0561   **portal**   CA   Cupertino   3/12/24   Sun SunOS
    Usenet, $10/mo. plus any Telenet charges, conferencing

415-332-6106 **well**   CA Sausalito   3/12   VAX 750 4.2BSD
    Picospan BBS, $8/mo., $3/hr., Telenet $20/hr peak, $4/hr off-peak

618-277-6417 **herky**   IL   3/12/24   386 SCO XENIX
    XBBS, no fee, 60 min. limit

619-444-7006 **pnet01** CA El Cajon   3/12/24   BSD UNIX
    Usenet, login: **pnet**, id: **new**, contributions requested, mail, conferencing

714-635-2863 **dhw68k** CA Anaheim   3/12/24   Unistride 2.1
    don't call between 2-7AM

714-662-7450 **turnkey** CA Southern   12/24   286 XENIX SV
    XBBS

714-842-5851 **conexch** CA Santa Anna   3/12/24   XENIX
    XBBS, $25 quarterly, 714-842-6348 for BBS

714-828-0288 **alphacm** CA Southern   12/24   286 SCO XENIX
    XBBS, no fee, 60 min. limit

714-894-2246 **stanton** CA Irvine   12/24   286 SCO XENIX
    XBBS, donation requested, 240 min. limit

812-334-8453,5 **cguild** IN Bloomington   12   286 SCO XENIX
    XBBS

812-334-1204 **nuchat** TX Houston   3/12/24   286 Microport
    Usenet, mail, shell access

814-333-6728 **sir-alan** PA Meadville   3/12/24   Tandy XENIX/68K
    UNaXcess BBS, anonymous **ftp**

9.1.3   Accessing Other Networks

Most other noncommercial networks (e.g., Arpanet, Bitnet) can be accessed from Usenet, although the addressing can be difficult to figure out. The article "Notable Computers Networks" (as previously mentioned) provides a table that allows you to correctly address mail between any two (indirectly) connected networks, given that you know the gateways (connections between them).

Commerical networks (e.g., the Source, GEnie) can also be accessed through Usenet, though such gateways have not and cannot be published. The primary problem is that the commerical companies want to be paid for their services, but it is not clear how to charge customers interacting with a noncommercial network. Another problem is one of liability. For example, if a Usenet user posted an offensive message on Compuserve, it would be extremely difficult for Compuserve management to punish that user. Some systems (e.g., BIX) copyright all public correspondence they carry. If they were to disseminate such material over the network, they would be losing much of the benefit of their copyright.

9.1.4   Usenet History

V7 UNIX with **uucp** was released in 1978. Within a year, the ideas that formed the foundation of news were thought of by Tom Truscott and Jim Ellis, graduate students at Duke University. The first version of Usenet was written by Steve Bellovin, a graduate student at the University of North Carolina. Written entirely with shell scripts, it serviced two sites: **unc** and **duke**. A third site, **phs** (also at Duke) was added in 1980. This system was described at the following Usenix conference in January.

Early Usenet Logical Map (June 1, 1981)

```
        !-      Uucp links
        :       Berknet links
        @       Arpanet links


                          pdp
            (Misc)         ! (NC)           (Misc)
      decvax sii  reed  phs--unc--grumpy  duke34  utzoo  cincy teklabs
        ! !  !     !      !   !            !       !      !      !
        ! +--+----+-----+-+--+--------------+-------+------+      !
        !                  !                                     !
        !                 duke                                   !
        !                  !                                     !
        !          +------+---+----------------------+--------+ !
        !          !          !                      !        ! !
    ucbopt  !  hocsr--mhtsa----research  allegra     harpo-----chico
       :    !       ! !                 !
    ucbcory !       ! eagle   ihnss    vax135  (Bell Labs)
    (UCB) : !       ! !        !        !
    ucbvax--++---------+--+--+-----+--+------+--------+
       :    @                !        !              ! (Silicon Valley)
    ucbarpa @    (UCSD) sdcsvax       !        menlo70--hao
       :    @    sdcattb-----+        !          !    !
    ucbonyx @           +-----ucsfcgl          sytek sri-unix
            @    phonlab-----+
         cca-unix       sdcarl
```

Steve Daniel and Tom Truscott produced a version of news (the "A" release) written in C, which was distributed to the public. In April 1981, there were 35 sites in the US and Canada running news. Since access required a minimum of hardware (a UNIX machine and a modem), and the cost of joining was free, participation grew explosively. Intended for less than 100 sites and a handful of articles per day per newsgroup, the news system quickly reached a point where the performance was unacceptable.

Mark Horton, a graduate student at Berkeley, and Matt Glickman, then in high school, revised the software substantially, adding features and optimizations. In 1982, this became the "B" release, also known as 2.1. It is difficult to keep track of changes to the software after this as many people have fixed bugs and contributed enhancements along the way. The list of names scattered throughout the news source is staggering. Some of the major contributions are from Kenneth Almquist (**vnews**), Larry Wall (**rn**), Ray Essick and Rob Kolstad (**notes**), Rick Adams (2.11), Geoff Collyer and Henry Spencer (C news), Brian Kantor, Phil Lapsley, Erik Fair, Steven Grady and Mike Meyer (NNTP), Lauren Weinstein (Stargate).

The news software is like UNIX in that so many people have had their hand in it, adding features and bugs, and making it grow ever larger. As you might have already guessed, numerous versions of news now exist. Nonetheless, some standards exist (such as the format of articles). Several are published through the Network Information Center at SRI International in Stanford, CA, while most are defined in the news distribution releases.

9.1.5   April Fools Day on Usenet

There is clearly a sense of humor behind many of the postings on Usenet. Humorous remarks are often tagged with a *smiley* such as :-) which looks like a little smiling face if you turn your head sideways. This ensures that the reader understands the text is not entirely serious.

One posting (reproduced as follows) that made its way around the world has become rather famous for fooling so many people into taking it seriously. It didn't have a smiley, but it was a hoax nonetheless. (Notice the many references to April 1st. Surprisingly, many people didn't.)

```
From: kremvax!chernenko
Newsgroup: net.general
Subject: New site - kremvax
Message-Id: <17@kremvax>
Date: 1 Apr 84 16:39:01 GMT
Organization: Moscow Institute for International Affairs

Well, today, 840401, this is at last the Socialist Union of Soviet
Republics joining the Usenet network and saying hallo to everybody.

One reason for us to join this network has been to have a means of
having an open discussion forum with the American and European people
```

and making clear to them our strong efforts towards attaining peacful
coexistence between the people of the Soviet Union and those of the
United States and Europe.

We have been informed that on this network many people have given strong
anti-Russian opinions, but we believe they have been misguided by their
leaders, especially the American administration, who is seeking for war
and domination of the world.
By well informing those people from our side we hope to have a possibility
to make clear to them our intentions and ideas.

Some of those in the Western world, who believe in the truth of what we
say have made possible our entry on this network; to them we are very
grateful. We hereby invite you to freely give your comments and opinions.

Here are the data for our backbone site:

Name: moskvax
Organization: Moscow Institute for International Affairs
Contact: K. Chernenko
Phone: +7 095 840401
Postal-Address: Moscow, Soviet Union
Electronic-Address: mcvax!moskvax!kremvax!chernenko
News: mcvax kremvax kgbvax
Mail: mcvax kremvax kgbvax

And now, let's open a flask of Vodka and have a drink on our entry on
this network. So:

                    NA ZDAROVJE!
--
        K. Chernenko, Moscow, USSR
        ...{decvax,philabs}!mcvax!moskvax!kremvax!chernenko

9.1.6   The Future of Usenet

Usenet has long faced the problem of overload. There has never been
any totally effective way of controlling the massive numbers of voices in
Usenet. Typical of the problem is that someone posts a question that many people know the answer to, such as *"How do I change the speed of my terminal?"*
Almost everyone on the net is capable of answering this question correctly, and
it is difficult for many people to resist showing off their knowledge and personal
wit. Other people write nasty messages to the original person, suggesting they
need not use such a powerful medium as Usenet for questions as simple as
that. Sometimes others will write back suggesting that the network is no place
for nasty messages. And so on.

Of particular worry to Usenet is the availability of low-cost workstations,
such as TRS-80s and PCs running UNIX. Since every UNIX system includes

`uucp`, they all can potentially become part of the net. However, this would probably substantially increase the amount of traffic on the net and the propagation delays. Further, it would be even harder to control these individuals, except by threatening them with removal from the net.

Many people continue to work on optimizing Usenet for more and more computers and traffic. Stargate is just one such project. It transmits Usenet news on subcarrier frequencies of television broadcasts. This unused bandwidth in existing television transmission systems costs nothing, avoiding the growing charges for dial-up and leased data lines. (Unfortunately, TV stations are discovering other uses for unused frequencies and will probably begin charging for this soon.)

At the human interface, many projects exist that attempt to use AI to sift through massive amounts of text looking for articles of interest. This can be used by each individual user when reading news. Alternatively, such a system could substantially cut traffic by replacing the human moderator in already moderated groups. More and more newsgroups are being moderated, but it will probably be many years before we trust a computer program to do the job.

Usenet is also feeling pressure to become more commercial. Many organizations have come to depend on it as part of their daily business. And due to its ever growing size, it needs management and authority. For example, gateways to other networks often require that there be a contact point for the network (e.g., for routing purposes). In order to support such an administrator, costs will be levied against Usenet members.

While it will probably always retain the flavor of being a highly informal, technical medium, we predict a much more structured and pay-as-you-go attitude towards Usenet, such as through UUNET. Naturally, some sites may object to this and fragment themselves from the commercial side of the network. This will lead to two or more networks, with the others remaining totally fee-free and anarchistic, much like Usenet began.

9.2   Public-domain or Otherwise Free Software

Quite a lot of UNIX software is in the public domain. Why? The early years of UNIX did not even have profitable distribution channels, only nonprofit ones. Even now, many people have no interest in the software business or in making a profit. A lot of programs are not even appropriate for the marketplace and would not sell enough to pay the overhead in running a business.

Another source of free software is from students, who rarely have expectations of getting paid. Some software written at universities cannot be marketed commercially depending on who funded it. It can, however, be given away for free. Some college programming projects have become very popular computing standards (e.g., **emacs**). Many universities offer distribution sets of UNIX software.

There are now many profitable distribution channels for UNIX software; however, many of the original reasons for public-domain UNIX software still exist. Furthermore, more people than ever before are writing UNIX software, and lots of software written for other computer systems is easier than ever to port to UNIX systems.

Of course, there is a trade-off here. For instance, getting any reasonable level of support is usually rare with public-domain software. Usually, such software is provided "as is." Of course, the good side of the story is that you invariably get the software in source form so you can remove any remaining bugs and add the features that are of interest to you. If you are a reasonably competent programmer, it may actually make sense to pass up a vendor-supported product if you can get the entire source and maintain it yourself.

Please note that while the majority of free software is public domain, this is not always the case. In particular, some software is copyrighted (e.g., MINIX, Mach) preventing you from selling it commercially without prior permission of the author. Copyright allows you to make a "reasonable" number of copies of the software. Ideally, the result benefits you. For example, the Mach authors want people to send modifications and bug fixes back to them, so that they will be able to coordinate all changes and redistribute a single version. (Mach is discussed in the Future chapter. MINIX is discussed later in this chapter.)

9.2.1   Archives

Many sites maintain immense archives of public-domain software. Some of it is kept on-line and is directly accessible via **uucp** or **ftp**. Some is too large to be kept on-line and can be received by request from the specific archive maintainer. Avoid making requests like *"Please mail me all the March 1985 sources."* Archive access is provided on a volunteer basis. Expect to supply a tape and return postage, if you ask for off-line sources.

Since archives are usually kept without help from the local administrator and budget, it is impossible to document them here. Similarly, they occasionally go out of business with little or no notice. The best place to learn about which sites have current archives and what they contain is in the Usenet newsgroup `comp.sources.d` and `net.sources`.

In July 1988, the following sites were acknowledged archives:

Allegheny College, Dept. of Political Science
> Archives: `net.sources comp.sources.unix comp.sources.misc`
> Service: anonymous `uucp`
> > 814-333-6728, 300/1200/2400 baud, `login: pdsrc`
> Contact: `sir-alan!mikes` (Michael Squires)

AT&T
> Archives: `comp.sources.unix`
> Service: anonymous `uucp`
> Contact: `killer!billw` (Bill Wisner)

CSNET CIC
> Archives: `mod.sources`
> Contact: `postmaster@sh.cs.net`
> Info: mail the following message to `Info-Server@sh.cs.net`
> > ```
> > topic: help
> > topic: index
> > ```

DKUUG - Danish UNIX User Group
> Archives: `comp.sources.unix comp.sources.games GNU emacs`
> Service: anonymous `uucp`
> Restriction: limited to EUnet users in Denmark
> Info: mail the following message to `diku!archive`
> > ```
> > Subject: help
> > ```

Motorola, Inc.
> Service: anonymous `uucp`
> > 312-576-7902, 1200 baud, `login: pduucp password: public`
> Restriction: limited hours: avoid weekdays 8am-6pm Chicago time.
> Contact: Ron Heiby
> Info: `uucp mcdch1!~/howto.snarf !~/MYNAME/`
> Info: `uucp mcdch1!~/directory !~/MYNAME/`

Perdue University
>	Archives: `comp.sources.unix kermit news rn nntp`
>	Contact: `rsk@j.cc.purdue.edu` (Rich Kulawiec)
>	Info: `~ftp/news/comp/sources/unix/volumeX`

Pyramid Technology
>	Archives: `comp.sources.unix comp.sources.games`
>	Contact: `usenet@pyramid.com` (Rick Preston)

University of Australia
>	Contact: `kre@munnari.OZ` (Robert Elz)

University of California at San Francisco
>	Contact: `thos@ucbvax!ucsfcgl!cca.UCSF` or `cca.ucsf.edu`

University of Kent
>	Service: anonymous `ftp`
>	Restriction: limited to users in United Kingdom
>	Contact: Peter Collinson
>	Info: mail the following message to `info-server@ukc`

```
        request: comp.sources.unix
              topic: help
              topic: index
```

UUNET
>	Archives: `comp.unix.sources`
>	Service: anonymous `ftp/uucp`
>	Contact: `rick@uunet.uu.net` (Rick Adams)
>	Info: `~ftp/comp.sources.unix/volumeN`

9.2.2   Usenet Source Newsgroups

One frequent source of sources are the Usenet source newsgroups. These newsgroups are for posting various types of sources. For example, `comp.sources.games` contains games, `comp.sources.amiga` is specific to Amiga microcomputers, and `comp.sources.bugs` carries bug reports and fixes for sources that have been posted in the source newsgroups.

There are many source newsgroups for other operating systems and the level of quality is unusually high. (If it isn't, the authors will get deluged with bug reports.) Often, software is posted here that would not otherwise become available. For example, many thesis projects, utility programs, or education code fragments appear in this group. For this kind of resource, Usenet is price-less.

9.2.3   User Group Software

Most user groups offer user-contributed software for nominal distribution costs. For instance, both /usr/group and Usenix have regular software distributions to their members. Since the amount of software they have is substantial, you must request specific software rather than having it sent to you automatically just because you are a member. They have a variety of releases available depending on the type of system you own. You may need to show a UNIX license in order to receive certain software.

Many manufacturers also have user groups that provide software strictly (i.e. nonportable) for their computers and users. In fact, many of the demos that are regularly shown at computer conferences were not written by manufacturers but by their users. Contact your computer's manufacturer for more information.

There is also a heavy base of C software that is coming out of the PC/MS-DOS world. While not specific to UNIX, much of this software can be run on any UNIX machine with little or no changes. One of the best places to keep up with this is in the C magazines, such as the *C Users Journal*.

9.2.4   GNU and the Free Software Foundation

In response to the strict UNIX software licensing enforced by AT&T and many other computer companies, the Free Software Foundation was formed and is "dedicated to eliminating restrictions on copying, redistribution, understanding and modification of software."

Originally created by Richard Stallman (who wrote the first version of `emacs`), the FSF has set about recreating the best of UNIX, all of which is available for the cost of copying the software. The software is not public domain but can be freely copied, modified, and given away. The collection of software from FSF is amusingly called GNU, which stands for "GNU is Not UNIX." It is pronounced "gä-new'."

A large amount of UNIX software has been rewritten and contributed to the GNU system. It is important to note that none of the software uses any copyrighted UNIX software. GNU expects to be able to provide most of the utilities and kernel (possibly based on CMU's Mach) of UNIX in the near future. GNU also maintains a directory of people who can be contacted for service on GNU software, including bug reports, porting, and so on.

As of June 1987, GNU includes GNU Emacs (an extremely sophisticated general purpose extensible editor), GDB (a source-level C debugger), GCC (a C compiler), BISON (yet another `yacc`), X Windows (a portable, network transparent window system), MIT Scheme (a lexically-scoped dialect of Lisp), GNU Chess (a class-C player which can use several machines in parallel for increased playing speed) and Hack (a game of adventure, similar to Rogue). All of this software is distributed in *source* form!

The easiest way to get any GNU software is to find someone who already has it and copy it. There is no one to pay, or license agreement to sign! GNU software is also available in various archives. The most up-to-date on-line archive is via Arpanet host `prep.ai.mit.edu`. For more information, read the file `/u2/emacs/GETTING.GNU.SOFTWARE` on that host.

GNU software can also be ordered directly from FSF. There is a nominal charge to cover the cost of tapes, handling and shipping. FSF accepts tax-deductible donations of money, as well as software and hardware. FSF is also interested in reducing unnecessary restrictions on copying in other domains besides software. For example, they are fighting the proposal to prevent copying of digital audio signals.

More information about GNU and FSF can be found in *Byte*, October 1983, where "The GNU Manifesto" was first published. The manifesto, license, warrantee and other philosophical writings (such as "Some Easily Rebutted Objections to GNU's Goals") can also be found in every GNU manual.

9.2.5   MINIX

MINIX (Mini-UNIX) is a V7-compatible UNIX written by Andrew Tanenbaum at Vrije Universiteit in Amsterdam. ("Mini" refers to the small size with respect to modern UNIX systems such as Berkeley and System V.)

The software copyright is held by Tanenbaum; however, the system can be purchased with a book describing the entire system, and the complete sources very cheaply ($80 in 1988) from Prentice-Hall. The source contains no AT&T code, so it is entirely free from its licensing restrictions.

MINIX runs on IBM PCs, XTs, ATs and clones. It supports a hard disk but can be run with only floppies (and it can read and write MS-DOS floppies). Like UNIX V7, MINIX is multitasking, and comes with a V7-compatible shell, K&R C compiler, `emacs`-like editor, a large set of utilities and libraries. The complete source is included, except for the C compiler which is available separately. Due to its low cost, implementation on a PC, and distribution with complete source, MINIX is an ideal system for someone who wants to learn more about UNIX and operating systems in general.

MINIX is structured quite differently from V7 internally, although to the naive user, the two systems function exactly the same. (There are actually four rarely used V7 system calls that are not supported in MINIX.) The system was designed for teaching and is completely described by the MINIX text. Permission is available for students to copy the software for study and porting to other CPU's. The Usenet newsgroup `comp.os.minix` carries discussion of MINIX.

The C compiler included with MINIX is based upon the Amsterdam Compiler Kit. The kit was a very ambitious project to produce compilers with many common components and a small number of separate front-ends for different languages, and separate back-ends for machine code production on different machines.

The kit is available from UniPress Software, or Transmediair Utrecht BV. It is described in "A Practical Tool Kit for Making Portable Compilers" by Tanenbaum et al. in *Communications of the ACM*, vol. 26, no. 9, September 1983.

9.3   Public-domain Hardware

We're all familiar with public-domain software, but public-domain hardware? Yes. Several people have designed a system to run UNIX with the specific goal of having the hardware design in the public domain. The system is called the PD32. "32" refers to the 32-bit hardware it is based on.

The original desire was a UNIX system with good performance costing less than $1,000. This includes the price of System V UNIX from AT&T. The system is built around the NSC32016 processor. The complete hardware design has been released to the public, including schematics, PAL equations, interface software and the PCB artwork.

It is important to note that homebrewed hardware systems were much more popular in the '70s. This was partially because there was less of an investment in software designed to run on specific hardware, and also because personal computers were still not commodity items. But now, the price of boards and whole systems is low. If you don't have the desire to muck with the hardware, it will be cheaper for you to buy a complete system than to build one from scratch. It's sad to have to admit this, but the age of building your own computer system has been over ever since the Asian clone makers entered the computer market.

Definicon sells the PD32 in kit form (a single board computer for a PC), or you can simply buy the design and construct it from the bare chips and software yourself. For more information about the PD32, refer to Micro C #32, or contact the PD32 Users Group or Definicon Systems.

9.4   Games

UNIX has always had an enthusiastic attitude towards games. It is arguable that the first UNIX application (Ken's Space Travel) was a game. (And some day, we may even win at **cc**.)

The original UNIX programmers provided a nice assortment of games with each distribution, perhaps to attract potential users. These were actually documented in the manual, just like any system software. In the V6 manuals, they appeared in section VI (User-maintained Programs). As well as such semi-useful programs as **azel** (compute satellite predictions) and **factor** (prime numbers), there were such classics as **bj** (blackjack), **chess**, **cubic** (3-D tic-tac-toe), **quiz** and **wump** (hunt-the-wumpus). Certain programs (notably **tbl**, the table formatting program) began life here and eventually earned enough respect to be moved to section I (User Commands).

Some of the games are more amusing simply for the manual pages. For instance, under the section header **BUGS**, **wump** simply says "*It will never replace Space War.*" **cal** (print calendar) says "*The year is always considered to start in January even though this is historically naive.*" **graph** says "*A limit of 1000 points is enforced silently.*" **chess** has the unique section header **WARNING**, "*Over-use of this program will cause it to go away.*" The complete documentation about diagnostics of **chess** takes one line, "*The most cryptic diagnostic is 'eh?' which means that the input was syntactically incorrect.*"

These kinds of astute, concise remarks are exactly on par with the rest of UNIX. Much of the rest of the manual tended to try to live up to this style.

Fortunately, most of the games did not go away and are always provided with the UNIX system. Interestingly, **chess** doesn't always appear. This is because large chunks of it were written in PDP-11 assembler, and that is the way it is supplied on the AT&T source distributions. UNIX resellers must either translate the assembler into C, or not offer it at all. (Forget about it and get GNU chess, which is a much stronger program.)

Those earlier versions of **chess** eventually evolved into extremely strong chess-playing programs. Ken Thompson was the primary author of Belle, which won the title of World Computer Chess Champion. Based on the original UNIX chess, Belle also used special "chess hardware," which was a PDP-11 with special purpose hardware (built by Joe Condon) dedicated to certain move calculations.

While no longer the title holder chess program, Belle will probably remain famous because of a run-in with the U.S. State Department. Belle had been invited to a chess championship, which happened to be in Moscow that year. Unfortunately, the PDP-11 was on the State Department's list of high-technology items that were not allowed to pass behind the Iron Curtain. The idea is that modern computers would give the Soviets the same speed in creating warfare and worldwide catastrophe that the U.S. has. Belle and the PDP-11 were seized at the airport by the State Department, which led to Ken remarking, "...*the only way you could make a weapon out of it is if you dropped it out of a plane and it fell on somebody.*"

Version 7 of UNIX saw the introduction of even more games, again, with exemplary manual pages. Under **DESCRIPTION** on **backgammon**, it says, "*This program does what you would expect.*" At the other extreme are the rather inexplicable **BUGS** of **ching**.

Once UNIX reached Berkeley, games flourished. We will only suggest that several kernel additions occurred in order to support certain games. Some of the most addictive games that you are likely to find on every UNIX system today are:

adventure – The original adventure game. You invariably give up in a twisty little maze of passages, all alike.

rogue – a screen-oriented game based on Dungeons & Dragons.

trek – cruise around the universe and protect your files from the Klingons.

fortune – prints out something likely to be found in a fortune cookie in a restaurant owned by George Carlin. Many people like to put this in their **.login** or **.profile**. Try the undocumented **-o** (obscene) option.

Games are often distributed for free, since they are hard to justify to management. See the previous section on public-domain software.

9.5   Obfuscated C

Many C programmers take their religion quite seriously. To these C dogmatics, the goal of reaching nirvana can only be achieved by studying the *K&R*, turning out programs that are portable between PCs and Crays, and never, ever writing lines like **#define BEGIN {**.

While this can make C programmers seem like a dull class of people, there is humor to be found. Your everyday C humor is stuff like **char broiled;** and **double trouble;**. If you start seeing your coworkers wincing whenever they read your programs, you might think of entering the International Obfuscated C Code Contest. Run annually by Landon Noll and Larry Bassel, the IOCCC provides a forum for code that is so awful to read, it is actually funny. Viewed in the right light, you might even call it educational. Landon says:

> *The contest was motivated by reading some UNIX source code (in /etc/config from 4.2BSD). I was shocked at how much simple algorithms could be made cryptic, and therefore useless, by a poor choice of code style. "Could someone be proud of this code?"*

It is not possible to reproduce all the winners, but a few should be just enough to give you the general idea, and perhaps encourage you to go look up all of them. Each one is guaranteed good for hours of study. Not only do they show you what *not* to do, but they teach you how to deal with very strange code. And you can actually learn some of the finer points of C by studying these very unusual programs. Unlike the rest of this book, we will follow the spirit of the contest by not providing any explanation of each program. You are on your own. The envelope, please...

In 1985, the *Award for Best One-Liner* was given to Jack Applin (with help from Robert Heckendorn) of Hewlett-Packard for the following program:

```
main(v,c)char**c;{for(v[c++]="Hello, world!\n)";(!!c)[*c]&&(v--||--
c&&execlp(*c,*c,c[!!c]+!!c,!c));**c=!c)write(!!*c,*c,!!**c);}
```

In 1987, the *Award for Worst Style* was given to Spencer Hines of Online Computer Systems for the following program:

```
#include <stdio.h>
char *malloc();
main(togo,toog)
int togo;
char *toog[];
{char *ogto,    tgoo[80];FILE  *ogot;   int     oogt=0, ootg,   otog=79,
ottg=1;if (    togo==  ottg)   goto    gogo;   goto    goog;   ggot:
if (    fgets(  tgoo,   otog,   ogot))  goto    gtgo;   goto    gott;
gtot:   exit(); ogtg: ++oogt;   goto    ogoo;   togg:   if (    ootg > 0)
goto    oggt;   goto    ggot;   ogog:   if (    !ogot)  goto    gogo;
goto    ggto;   gtto:   printf( "%d     goto    \'s\n", oogt); goto
gtot;   oggt:   if (    !memcmp( ogto,  "goto", 4))     goto    otgg;
goto    gooo;   gogo:   exit(   ottg); tggo:   ootg=   strlen(tgoo);
goto    tgog;   oogo: --ootg;   goto    togg;   gooo: ++ogto;   goto
oogo;   gott:   fclose( ogot);  goto    gtto;   otgg:   ogto=   ogto +3;
goto    ogtg;   tgog:   ootg-=4;goto    togg;   gtgo:   ogto=   tgoo;
goto    tggo;   ogoo:   ootg-=3;goto    gooo;   goog:   ogot=   fopen(
toog[   ottg],  "r");   goto    ogog;   ggto:   ogto=   tgoo;   goto
ggot;}
```

In 1985, the *Award for Worst Abuse of the C Preprocessor* was given to Col. G. L. Sicherman of the State University of New York at Buffalo for the following program:

```
#define C_C_(_)~' '&_
#define _C_C(_)('\b'b'\b'>=C_C>'\t'b'\n')
#define C_C _|_
#define b *
#define C /b/
#define V _C_C(
main(C,V)
char **V;
/*      C program. (If you don't
 *      understand it look it
 */     up.) (In the C Manual)
{
        char _,__;
        while (read(0,&__,1) & write((_=(_=C_C_(__),C)),
        _C_,1)) _=C-V+subr(&V);
}
subr(C)
char *C;
{
        C="Lint says "argument Manual isn't used."  What's that
        mean?"; while (write((read(C_C('"'-'/*"'/*"*/))?__:__-_+
        '\b'b'\b'|((_-52)%('\b'b'\b'+C_C_('\t'b'\n'))+1),1),&_,1));
}
```

And in 1984, the *Grand Prize* (for all-around obfuscation) was given to Sjoerd Mullender and Robbert van Renesse of Vrije Universiteit for the following program:

```c
/* Portable between VAX11 && PDP11 */

short main[] = {
        277, 04735, -4129, 25, 0, 477, 1019, 0xbef, 0, 12800,
        -113, 21119, 0x52d7, -1006, -7151, 0, 0x4bc, 020004,
        14880, 10541, 2056, 04010, 4548, 3044, -6716, 0x9,
        4407, 6, 5568, 1, -30460, 0, 0x9, 5570, 512, -30419,
        0x7e82, 0760, 6, 0, 4, 02400, 15, 0, 4, 1280, 4, 0,
        4, 0, 0, 0, 0x8, 0, 4, 0, ',', 0, 12, 0, 4, 0, '#',
        0, 020, 0, 4, 0, 30, 0, 026, 0, 0x6176, 120, 25712,
        'p', 072163, 'r', 29303, 29801, 'e'
};
```

Results of the IOCCC are posted every year to the Usenet newsgroup **comp.lang.c**. The contest is also given a special presentation at the annual USENIX Conference, and has been published formally in *Micro/Systems Journal*.

Chapter 10: UNIX Services

> "Less than 10 percent of the code has to do with the ostensible purpose of the system; the rest deals with input-output, data validation, data structure maintenance, and other housekeeping." – Mary Shaw

This chapter discusses UNIX services, such as consulting and timesharing. The Nonprinted Information chapter covers more services related to education and training.

As with the chapter on UNIX Applications, commercial UNIX services can also be found listed in /usr/group's product directory. Besides these listings and advertisements in the back of, say, *UNIXWORLD* and *UNIX REVIEW*, there is a clear lack of published information about such services. In particular, we are unaware of a single magazine review of any of the services listed here. Of course, it is rather difficult to do a scientific comparison of, for example, two consulting services.

While we cannot give you hard, cold facts about these topics, we can give some general guidelines, as well as things that we have heard via word of mouth.

10.1   Benchmarking

> "There are lies, there are damn lies and then there are benchmarks." – Anon.

Benchmarking is used to judge the quality of different programs (or machines, operating systems, etc.) by comparing the length of time (or space, price, etc.) it takes to get the job done. Benchmarks are often ridiculed because they are usually used for the basis of an invalid extrapolation, leading to wildly misleading conclusions. However, it is possible to make intelligent use of benchmarks for, say, system tuning.

It is said that there are systems which recognize they are running benchmarks and print out an answer which is precalculated. While this is hard to believe, good optimizers are capable enough to remove the usually substantial portions of dead code in most benchmarks, thereby voiding the benchmark designer's intent. Whatever the case, be extremely wary of benchmarks. A much more realistic test of system throughput is to sit down at the system and try running a sample of your own applications. Don't forget to make sure it has a comparable amount of memory and the same speed, disks and network as the system that you are interested in. (Typical showroom systems are fully loaded with memory and fast disks.)

Should you choose to ignore our warnings, there are plenty of companies that sell benchmarks. Some well-known companies include: Aim Technology, Neal Nelson & Associates and Performance Awareness. It goes without saying that you should especially beware of benchmarks from UNIX vendors themselves.

Some good readings on UNIX benchmarking are: "The Evolution of UNIX System Performance" by J. Feder, in the *AT&T Bell Laboratories Technical Journal*, vol. 63, no. 8, October 1984; "Benchmark Confessions" by P. Marvit and M. Nair in *The UNIX System – Encyclopaedia*, Yates Ventures, 1984; and "Benchmarking UNIX Systems" by D. Hinnant in *BYTE Magazine*, vol. 9, no. 8, August 1984.

10.2   Consulting

While UNIX is a wonderful system, there will come a day when you need something done that has never been done before, and you are not capable of doing it. Perhaps you just need some customization. Or you need some information so that you can continue your work. Consulting is the answer.

Consultants come from everywhere. UNIX vendors very often have a team for hire, specifically designed to work on problems about their system. This is not an escape hatch. Rather, it is more convenient to have people reserved to work on problems after a system is designed than to try and guess everything that customers will want in advance.

Consultants also come from independent companies with staffs ranging from hundreds to a staff of one. The larger companies often provide similar solutions again and again, such as porting a product. They can be cheaper to work with than in-house staff on certain types of problems. We have known many consultants to work for a year or more based at one location, alongside full-time employees.

When contracting out for consulting services, it is important that you precisely spell out your needs. The more you can pin it down, the easier it is for the company to find a person matching your requirements.

Some well-known independent companies offering UNIX consulting are: Abmind Corporation, Acorn Systems, Ltd., Daniel Farkas and Associates, Datix Systems, D.L. Buck & Associates, Lachman Associates Inc., Parkridge Computer Systems Inc., Sobell Associates, Specialized Systems Consultants Inc., Unidot Inc., and Unisolutions Associates.

There are many small consulting firms, some with only one person. It is hard to generalize on these. They can be students, needy programmers moonlighting on the side, or they can be the very best UNIX wizards. Some of the more competent UNIX programmers need no full-time staff behind them to line up jobs. They are so good that word-of-mouth is enough to keep them well-employed for as long as they want.

Your best bet in finding qualified independents is by making inquiries with other sites using similar systems.

10.3   Emergency!!

Sometimes you just need a quick, short answer to a problem. Consultants aren't what you need. The time cost in finding the right one is prohibitive when you just need the answer to one question fast.

Fortunately, many companies offer support services over the phone. Most UNIX vendors provide technical support via the phone, specifically to solve problems and answer questions about their system. You should contact your vendor to see if they can provide this service. Don't expect this service to be free, however. Having UNIX gurus answer phones is just as expensive as having them do whatever UNIX gurus normally do.

Fewer independent consultants offer this kind of service, since it requires people to sit by the phone all day. Ideally, there should be several people at the phones. If you contract with an independent vendor, make sure they have experience with your system. Also, you should inquire what kind of hours they keep. Even if you don't plan on working during the evening, it is nice to be able to ask them a question on Friday evening and get the answer on Monday morning. One such service is Dial-A-Guru (Specialized Systems Consultants, Inc.).

An alternative to these is the electronic guru. Many UNIX companies have **uucp** or some electronic mail address where you can send bugs or questions. For problems of a more general nature, you can try Usenet (see the Underground chapter). We have gotten answers to highly technical questions from halfway 'round the world in less than two days. The only drawback is that people will send you nasty letters if you ask something too simple. You have no excuse for not looking it up in the manual first.

When your disk is *munged* (i.e. trashed, scorched, zapped) you turn to **fsck** to repair the damage, and your backup tapes to restore the files. However, there are times when neither of these is good enough. For example, you may have not done a backup recently enough and inadvertently removed a file.

One company that offers a hope (99.5 percent effectiveness claimed) is the Gawain Group with a product called Data Rescue Service. Simply send your disk to them and they will salvage whatever they can from it, including the superblock, i-nodes and data blocks if possible. And cross your fingers.

10.4   Jobs

The UNIX job market is a seller's market. There are many more job openings than qualified UNIX people. This will always be the case. (Has there ever been a glut of any type of computer programmer?)

As in any job or personnel hunt, contacts are important. Knowing the people can be just as important as knowing the subject matter. Companies will try known people before resorting to the unfocused employee search through a personnel department or classified ad. It is quicker, cheaper and more likely to yield results.

10.4.1   Looking For New Employees

If you have any contacts at all, even if they aren't suitable, call them and ask if they know anyone who is. If you are willing to take new college graduates, you should call up local computer science professors.

A good place to find technical people is at the UNIX conferences. The technical conferences have a job bulletin board where you can post advertisements, and you can open your suite to prospective employees with the lure of food and drink, while you get a quick look-see. (You can also find out about the state of your competition by observing their employee-hunting strategies.)

Many people come to the conferences looking for jobs, or at least with an eye open for anything that might make them think about changing jobs. Look for people wearing brand new suits. More experienced technical people will be wearing jeans.

Another good way to find an employee is to post a job opening on Usenet in the newsgroup `misc.jobs.offered`. Many UNIX programmers looking for employment read this newsgroup! And for some reason, Usenet articles will hold people's attention longer than classified ads. Unlike a typical job announcement, these are usually much more informal, possibly humorous, more personable and quite a bit longer. This is what people would like to see in the first place, but most personnel departments can't seem to fathom the idea.

Resumes are regularly posted to the newsgroup `misc.jobs.resumes`. You can also get or send resumes or other information privately through electronic mail. It is also possible to get an idea of any other attributes of a candidate by reading other Usenet postings they may have made. If you are an equal-opportunity employer, you should properly only look in the technical newsgroups, but you might find an off-the-record peek in the other newsgroups quite educational as well.

10.4.2   Looking For New Jobs

Before you graduate, it is helpful to get job experience. Take on some consulting. Work for professors or the computer science department or computer center. Try to write and market your own software. At the very least, you can go to work for AT&T (although they hire mostly M.S.s). They seem to have an inexhaustible thirst for UNIX programmers, and there are few UNIX programmers that they have not employed at one time or another.

A good place for job hunting technical people is at the UNIX conferences. The technical conferences have a job bulletin board where you can read job advertisements, and you can visit various suites of prospective employers while they feed you with munchies and booze.

Many companies come to the conferences looking for employees. They know that this is where the highest concentration of UNIX hackers are and that this is their best chance at getting one. Go to the talks and exhibits so that you can at least begin to make contacts. This is all important!

Another good way to find a job is to read the job openings on Usenet in the newsgroup `misc.jobs.offered`. Employers post job openings there. You can also post your resume to `misc.jobs.resumes`. A lot of companies watch this newsgroup for resumes. There are drawbacks to posting resumes, but they should be obvious. For example, your own boss may be reading this newsgroup. Another problem is that if you don't make your job interests precise enough, you may get too many companies responding.

A nice advantage of Usenet is that you will be talking directly to a technical person without going through personnel. You can send them resumes (directly), programs you have written, and followup by electronic mail before visiting in person.

There are several headhunters (companies that simply find employment for people) that specialize in UNIX employment. Quite a few of them attend the UNIX conferences and read and post to Usenet.

Some of the better-known employment services in the UNIX field are: Nayland Associates, Scientific Placement, Inc., and Software Alliance Inc.

10.5   Mailing Lists

Mailing lists are useful if you want to advertise a new product. With computerized mailing lists, it is possible to cross-match and more effectively target likely consumers for your product. This allows you to waste a minimum of money on your advertising.

Since most user groups and magazines do periodic surveys of their readership, their mailing lists are excellent places to start. Some of these are Uni-Ops Books, /usr/group, Usenix, *UNIXWORLD*, and *UNIX REVIEW*. See the Information chapters for others.

Another medium for advertisement is Usenet, which has a newsgroup devoted to announcements of new computer products called `comp.newprod`. Note that market-oriented hype is discouraged. Try to write such postings from a scientific and objective point of view.

10.6   Porting, Integration and Installation

10.6.1   Porting

Since one of the advantages of UNIX is that it is portable, you should not hesitate to take advantage of this ability. However, porting is not unlike any other computer problem – it takes some experience to do it well. The problems are different than in user-level programming but similar between ports.

Unskilled but competent programmers can port the entire UNIX system in a year, while an experienced porter can usually complete it in four to five months, for, say, $60,000. If the hardware is very similar to a previous port, it might take less. And vice versa. A complete job of porting to "reasonable" hardware including packaging the rest of the system can take one to two years. In contrast, most other operating systems cost ten times as much money and involve much longer development times.

Major porting companies include Interactive, Unisoft (Uniplus+), SCO (XENIX), Microsoft (XENIX) and AT&T (System V). See the first two chapters for more information on porting houses.

Most of the major CPU manufacturers have a port of UNIX generic to their hardware that you can start from. Plus, there are many smaller companies that specialize in porting entire UNIX systems or just an individual application. Some of these are BOSS Systems Inc., Genus Systems Ltd., Glockenspiel Ltd., HCR Corp., Lachman Associates Inc., Microport Systems Inc., Palomino Computer Systems Inc., Root Computers Ltd., and Technical Solutions Inc.

10.6.2   Integration and Installation

Integration is the act of taking a port and bringing it up in the customer's desired configuration. This is especially useful if you have a nonstandard system configuration.

For example, you may already have a copy of XENIX configured for a PC, but you might have a PC clone with extended memory, five disks and a network device. Figuring out which device drivers to load, the jumpers and switch settings on each board, and what other support software you might need is the job of the systems integrator.

Additionally, integrators can configure in a weird piece of hardware, supplying a new device driver if necessary. Like porting, device driver construction takes experience to do well. It is quite unlike user-level application programming.

The last step in getting UNIX up on your system is installation. Complete installation includes deciding a lot of low-level but necessary information – such as deciding what background processes run, what the names of machines are, network configurations, and so on.

Actually, installation doesn't stop when UNIX finally runs. Few people run UNIX "as is" out of the box. You will probably want to tune your system, set up various administrative procedures, install third-party software, and so on.

"I said *UNIX*, you damn fool. Not *eunuchs!*"

® 1984, Ziff Communications

Many companies were created to provide UNIX support, integration, and installation because originally neither AT&T nor Berkeley provided these services. Berkeley still doesn't. Mt. Xinu supports Berkeley UNIX. They will supply you with a version of Berkeley UNIX, to which all known bug fixes have been applied. In addition, they will provide you with real support, such as notifying you about new bugs or answering questions. Cambridge Digital is a company which will take Mt. Xinu's Berkeley UNIX and configure it for whatever set of devices and hardware you have on your system.

AT&T left many customers behind when it dropped support for UNIX on DEC's line of computers. One company supporting such customers is Uniq Digital Technologies. Many other companies exist – most for BSD, System V and XENIX integration and installation. Some of them also do complete portings. A sampling of these companies are: Abmind Corp., Conner Scelza Associates, Eakins Associates, Inc., The Instruction Set, Lachman Associates, Inc., and SHL Systemhouse, Inc, and of course, DEC.

10.7   Security

Traditionally, UNIX systems have offered relatively little in the way of security measures. While modern versions offer better protection measures, they are more complicated than before. Users and system administrators may not appreciate the subtleties of computer-directed attacks, or they may simply not have the time to constantly scrutinize computer usage for possible intruders and misuse.

Here is a brief list of common security problems (some of which are not unique to UNIX):

- Problems with user environments: trojan horses, odd permissions in home directories, unprotected files, unauthorized copies of games, vulnerable or readable temporary files, liberal **PATH**s.

- Problems with password file: phony logins, easily guessable passwords, users with duplicate or root user IDs.

- Problems with other system files: unprotected files, unauthorized setuid files, hidden trojan horses.

- Vulnerable **uucp**, **mail** and other spool files: improper file or command access via network.

- Known security bugs.

- Physical disasters: fire, earthquake, flooding, power fluctuations, head crashes.

- Inadequate backups.

Several companies offer security analysis. Such analysis may involve running programs that try known UNIX loopholes. Alternatively, you can arrange for your system to be professionally attacked. This is a common test by the Department of Defense when trying to verify secure systems. Some companies that offer security analysis are: Lachman Associates, Inc., and Spectrum Technology Group, Inc.

10.8   Validation

It is easy to claim that a system is "UNIX compatible" or "meets System V Interface Definition" or "is ANSI C." However, these are meaningless unless they have been tested by the tests laid down by a standards body. For example, AT&T has specified that the SVVS (System V Verification Suite) programs be used to test for conformance with SVID.

Getting a system or compiler validated or certified is an important step in light of UNIX standards. Some companies who provide verification or validation services for UNIX and/or C are: AT&T Information Systems, COS (Corporation for Open Systems), Human Computing Resources, MindCraft, Inc., Plum Hall, Software Research, Inc., Unisoft Corp., and various national standards agencies such as the U.S. National Bureau of Standards.

10.9   Timesharing

It is occasionally useful to buy UNIX time. For example, consultants working on short-term projects may buy UNIX time at other UNIX sites, if they do not have access to the specific type of machine required by the problem. One company offering such a service is Practical Computing, Inc.

10.10   Typesetting and Publishing

UNIX users have long had the ability to produce high-quality output from `troff`. There are many companies who will take that `troff` output and produce commercial publications from it.

Many companies also accept other popular UNIX output formats including `ditroff`, TeX and PostScript. Large publishers such as Prentice-Hall accept all these formats. Smaller publishers that specialize in UNIX texts are also capable of doing the same work. These include: Ace Microsystems Ltd., August Mohr Consulting and Publishing, CBM Type, Textset, Inc., Textware International, and Unicomp.

Chapter 11: UNIX Applications

"I do not fear computers. I fear the lack of them." – Isaac Asimov

UNIX has finally grown up and guess what? If you've got an application, somebody has probably written a UNIX-based solution to your problem. Yes, everything from office automation or robot control systems to restaurant information and swine management systems have been implemented on UNIX-based systems.

In this chapter, we will survey UNIX third-party software and discuss some particularly notable products and applications. *Notable* may mean excellent, first-to-market or just plain popular. We will not attempt to provide an encyclopedic view of what is on the market. We can't hope to keep up to date in this fast-changing market. Our intent is more to try and give you a feeling for the state of UNIX applications in general.

For up-to-date market reviews and product listings we refer you back to the chapters on UNIX Information. In particular, /usr/group's product directory is a good starting point for listings of virtually all UNIX products. The UNIX magazines are a good next step for finding in-depth product reviews. And UNIX conferences give you a chance at hands-on use of products. Also, there are many public-domain noncommercial implementations that are as good as anything in the commercial domain. See the Underground chapter for more on this.

11.1   Vertical Software

Software applications marketed to a narrow slice of consumers are called *vertical software*. For example, a "real estate portfolio manager" is of use to a small fraction of UNIX users. On the other hand, compilers are of interest to most UNIX users and are therefore considered "horizontal software." The rest of this chapter will primarily discuss horizontal software. However, we will briefly list some categories of vertical software, just to let you know they exist.

/usr/group has divided UNIX software into the following major vertical software markets: construction, employment and recruiting, engineering, financial analysis, government and school administration, insurance, inventory control, legal, manufacturing/distribution, medical and dental, membership organizations, nonprofit groups, project management, real estate, retail/point-of-sale, sales and marketing, typesetting and publications, vehicle management, and Zen Martian discography. (Just kidding on that last one.)

The point is that there is software to support virtually any application you need for your UNIX system.

11.2   Accounting and Finance

"What's the best way to balance a checkbook using a computer?   Sell the computer and deposit the money." – Jon Bentley

The early history of UNIX has absolutely nothing to do with financial applications. And this is entirely understandable. Would you trust your accounts to an unsupported operating system that was still under research? UNIX did not support transaction processing, file or record locking, checkpointing and many other features that were necessary for financial processing. Furthermore, the system was inherently tuned for interactive use, while banks and other companies did primarily batch-oriented processing.

Times have changed. UNIX has changed. UNIX now supports file and record locking, sophisticated databases, and everything one needs for a modern accounting system. (UNIX even supports COBOL!) UNIX mainframes are supplanting many IBM systems in established banks. UNIX workstations are becoming quite popular on Wall Street for forecasting and analysis. These UNIX systems are just as reliable as any other systems, and they are cheaper.

The trends in accounting systems are to incorporate many techniques that require interactive use, like spreadsheets, and analysis from other dynamic sources such as the stock exchange. UNIX tools and multiprocessing provides just the flexibility that is needed for these problems. We expect that the next generation of accounting systems will be heavily integrated with databases, and incorporate expert systems using AI techniques. Along with sophisticated user interfaces, these systems will demand systems with superior performance. We think people will find UNIX a good fit.

While we expect a significant amount of future development in this area to occur on UNIX systems, most older accounting packages designed on other systems have been ported to UNIX. Their heritage will be evident by examining a number of things – in particular, the implementation language. Packages written in COBOL will have come from the mainframe environment, while BASIC products will have come from the micro world.

The *1987 UNIX Products Directory* lists approximately 300 accounting packages. Good luck finding out which one is best.

11.3   Artificial Intelligence

"Dave, I know that you and Frank were planning to disconnect me. And that's something I cannot allow." – Hal 9000

Like UNIX, AI (**a**rtificial **i**ntelligence) is a product of universities and research institutions. AI programmers are likely to be familiar with UNIX concepts even if they don't develop their applications on UNIX systems.

Early AI research was done on large mainframes or crude timesharing systems running Lisp. Lisp used a distinctly simple hardware interface, and had a ferocious demand for memory. Because of these attributes, AI applications written in Lisp did not make the transition to smaller computers easily. Instead, a heavy emphasis was placed on designing machines dedicated to Lisp. These *Lisp machines* had special Lisp hardware and substantial memory. They were more expensive then general-purpose computers, but ran Lisp very efficiently.

One of the main objectives of Berkeley UNIX was to provide the necessary operating system support for AI systems. This meant large virtual memory systems. And it meant Lisp. Berkeley was successful. It added both virtual memory, and Franz Lisp to UNIX. Many large AI systems were built on this work.

It is now common to run large AI programs on UNIX systems. Furthermore, UNIX workstations have become so cheap and powerful that it is often more cost effective to buy them than a dedicated Lisp machine. In some cases, the speed of the proprietary hardware of Lisp machines is being surpassed by garden-variety 32-bit processors readily available in UNIX boxes.

Yet another reason we find AI applications migrating to UNIX boxes is that it has long been common to recode Lisp applications in another language for speed once development is complete. And C is proving to be universal and efficient enough to be the target language. Many of the expert system tools on the market have been recoded in C. Naturally, they are quite at home on UNIX.

It is likely that UNIX workstations will remain the system of choice for AI applications rather than migrating even further into the PC world. CP/M and DOS do not support large enough amounts of memory, and even OS-2 lacks support of demand-paged virtual memory. Almost all UNIX workstations support virtual memory and can be equipped with third-party AI tools and languages.

Some popular AI systems include Duck (Smart Systems Technology), KEE (Intellicorp), Knowledge Engineering System (Software A & E), OPS5+ (Artelligence, Inc.), Poplog (Systems Designers Software, Inc.), RuleMaster (Radian Corporation), and S.1 (Teknowledge, Inc.). In addition, there are many Lisp and Prolog implementations available. These are listed in the section on languages elsewhere in this chapter.

11.4   CAD, CAE, CAM

Computer-aided design (CAD), engineering (CAE) and manufacturing (CAM) are finding very comfortable homes on UNIX workstations. Inexpensive UNIX workstations provide the networking, sufficient file system and computer power as well as peripherals (such as color displays and funky keyboard) necessary for doing design work. This includes architecture, drafting, circuit layout and simulation, process planning, finite element modeling and analysis, geometric modeling, and so on.

Only a few years ago, this type of work was either done on expensive, proprietary workstations, or it was done in a very limited way, since the cost of such computations was simply too expensive.

Some well-known CAD products are AutoCAD (Autodesk, Inc.), DD/1 (Unicad, Inc.), N.2 (ENDOT Inc.), CADDS 4X (Computervision), Pro-Series (CAETEC Systems, Inc.), SDS (Silvar-Lisco), SILOS (SimulCad) and VersaCad (T&W Systems).

11.5   Character Graphics, Form and Menu Systems

`termcap`, `terminfo` and `curses` provide character-based graphics capabilities. Quite often, that is all that is necessary for an application's user interface. However, if you need something more sophisticated, like a menu or forms system, you will probably want to buy one from a third-party vendor. You might also be interested in "improved" versions (such as color `curses`) or ports to other operating systems of these basic UNIX utilities.

There are many companies (as well as public-domain versions) providing such systems. Some companies are Information Concepts, Inc. (FSP), Micro Applications and Hardware (C-Form), Parkridge Computer Systems Inc. (TIC/TOC) and Vermont Creative Software (Windows for Data).

11.6 Communications

There was nothing in the original design of UNIX to support communications with other systems. Everything has been added on. Nonetheless, people think of `uucp` and `tip` (and its predecessor, `cu`) as the original communications software because they come with every copy of UNIX.

If you remember, AT&T was actually in the communications business a while back. Many researchers explored the problems of letting UNIX communicate with the world. Indeed, Bell Labs had a network between its UNIX systems as soon as they had two of them. This innovative communications work included building RJE interfaces, networks (e.g., Datakit) and distributed file systems (e.g., Spider). Many of these supported heterogenous environments with non-UNIX machines. AT&T's latest efforts include streams and RFS, both included with System VR3.

`uucp` lives (see the Administrator's chapter). While originating on UNIX systems, `uucp` has since been ported to many other systems including IBM PC compatibles and DEC's VAX/VMS. Honey DanBer `uucp` (or simply "HDB") is a totally rewritten modernized implementation of the original `uucp` functions. HDB `uucp` is available from AT&T as BNU (Basic Networking Utilities).

Many additional communications packages have been created by other companies, too. Some of these have been transported from the micro world, such as the extremely popular Kermit, which is in the public domain. Others are designed to support communication with mainframe systems using Digital's DECnet or IBM's SNA. There are programs to support communications over serial lines, Ethernet, broadband links using SNA, CCITT, OSI and DoD and many other protocols. Often these are bundled with applications such as file transfer, electronic mail or network file systems.

Communications is an extremely vast field, and the science of networking is changing year to year. We recommend that you study the needs of your applications to see what kind of communications they require, rather than vice versa.

11.7   Databases and Database Management Systems

"We promise 2000 transactions a second, and a free Isuzu for every customer."
– Joe Isuzu (Judith Love).

Early UNIX systems did not come with databases – at least by modern standards. Indeed, the UNIX designers went out of their way to point out how inadequate the system was for that. (This is discussed at length in the Real World chapter.)

As a backlash, or maybe because of that (it's hard to tell), many tools were created that were able to manipulate text files as databases. And very well, indeed. It was possible to create database systems without doing anything but writing shell scripts. And it still is, for that matter. This remains a valuable prototyping technique.

Many small databases exist on UNIX. Some, like **/etc/passwd**, are manipulated with simple text tools. Another example is the **refer** database which accepts bibliographic references for later automatic referencing by **troff**. Larger databases use **dbm** or a commercial database.

The **dbm** library (a rewrite of which is available in the public domain) is a simple database management system that continues to be distributed with most versions of UNIX. **dbm** provides a simple keyed-record system, suitable for many small applications.

Around 1979, the Ingres Project (a relational database system, now marketed by Relational Technology Inc.) was distributed with Berkeley UNIX, leading to the acceptance of large database systems on UNIX. At the same time, commercial companies began studying the problems of porting existing DBMS's into the UNIX environment. Soon after that, several file locking implementations were commonly available. One was standardized by /usr/group in 1985. (This was the first identifiable UNIX standard.)

While UNIX now supports many database systems quite successfully, the database story is by no means over. For example, distributed databases, heterogenous databases, and knowledge representation databases for AI are some of the problems that are still quite open. UNIX machines are supporting much of this research, and we can expect many new database implementations to appear on UNIX systems first. Two examples of this are the Camelot distributed transaction research at Carnegie Mellon University and the IMDAS project for distributed automated manufacturing at the U.S. National Bureau of Standards.

Of course, many databases that were implemented on micros have also been ported to UNIX, which is no great feat since their file and operating systems are typically even cruder than that of UNIX. The result is that UNIX can share databases with both micros and mainframes.

Other popular UNIX database systems include Boeing Rim (Boeing Computer Service Company), Focus (Information Builders, Inc.), Informix (Informix Software), Mistress (HCR), Oracle (Oracle Corp.), /rdb (Robinson, Schaffer & Wright), Unify (Unify Corporation), Zebu (Specialized Systems Consultants, Inc.)

11.8　Desktop Publishing
"Why isn't troff more like my Mac, and vice versa?" – John Mashey

UNIX has always come with `troff` and friends. The programmers at Bell Labs had access to a phototypesetter, a device that can produce camera-ready copy directly. (Phototypesetters commonly have resolutions of 1,000 dpi (dots per inch) and higher.) Thus, UNIX has always included such an interface. Unfortunately, phototypesetters are prohibitively expensive for the majority of UNIX sites, costing upwards of $100,000.

Around 1975, the only alternatives to phototypesetter were electrostatic printers. These were not as high quality, but could still do graphics, and were much cheaper. Unfortunately, they had a number of other drawbacks (required special paper, output had to be cut apart, and so on). However, they were quite common at UNIX sites that could not afford a phototypesetter and yet wished to use the lovely text processing tools that UNIX had.

By 1980, laser printers had become available for a fraction of the price of a phototypesetter. These were soon interfaced to programs like `troff`. Four years later, the price of a 300 dpi laser printer was less than $10,000, making them more popular than daisy-wheel printers. (Daisy-wheel printers were inexpensive – about $3,000 – and produced high-quality output, but lacked software font control and graphics.)

While laser printers do not equal the quality of phototypesetters, they are able to handle the majority of tasks that most people need (e.g., reports, papers, letters). (This is another example of the UNIX rule that 10 percent of the effort (uh...price) solves 90 percent of the problems.)

With the introduction of the Macintosh (not running UNIX!), Apple brought a different kind of desktop publishing to the world. Apple's vision was an easy to use, what-you-see-is-what-you-get (WYSIWYG) interface. `troff`, is neither of these. The Apple products were also much cheaper than anything comparable.

Many companies have since moved this technology and style of desktop publishing from Macs to UNIX machines. With it, `troff` has been displaced by a number of very user-friendly systems. Some of the more popular UNIX desktop publishing systems are Interleaf (Interleaf Inc.) and Frame Maker (Frame Technology). (This book was created using Frame Maker.) Unfortunately, `troff` continues to be the only publishing system distributed with bare UNIX, hence it is still used by the unsuspecting.

Admittedly, `troff` is extremely flexible, and experts can do amazing things with it. However, the real reason `troff` is so ingrained is that it did not have any serious competition for many years. This has had unfortunate effects as some publishers (e.g., USENIX) only accept manuscripts in `troff` format. Some publishers (e.g., Prentice-Hall) convert all other electronic forms to `troff`.

`ditroff` is a rewrite of `troff`. (It stands for "device-independent **troff**" but is pronounced "dit-roff.") Oddly, `troff` produces output for a specific typesetter (C/A/T now sold by Wang) which few people have. To use any other output device, you must pipe the output of `troff` through a filter which translates it to a device-independent form. Then another filter translates it to whatever form you really need. `ditroff` produces device-independent output directly, as well as supporting many other things that `troff` never did very well (such as supporting more than four fonts in one document). `ditroff` is sold by AT&T and others.

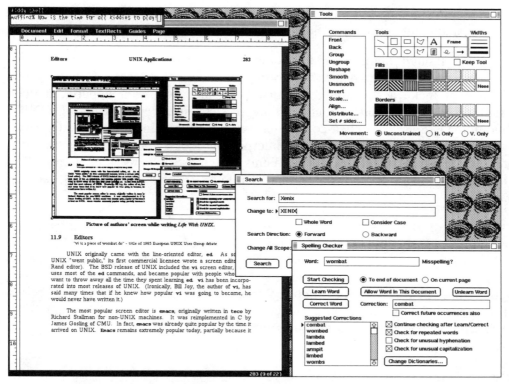

Picture of authors' screen while writing *Life With UNIX*.

11.9   Editors

"vi is a piece of wombat do" - title of 1985 European UNIX User Group debate

UNIX originally came with the line-oriented editor, `ed`. As soon as UNIX "went public," its first commercial licensee wrote a screen editor (the Rand editor). The BSD release of UNIX included the `vi` screen editor, which uses most of the `ed` commands, and became popular with people who didn't want to throw away all the time they spent learning `ed`. `vi` has been incorporated into most releases of UNIX. (Ironically, Bill Joy, the author of `vi`, has said many times that if he knew how popular `vi` was going to become, he would never have written it.)

The most popular screen editor is `emacs`, originally written in `teco` by Richard Stallman for non-UNIX machines. It was reimplemented in C by James Gosling of CMU. In fact, `emacs` was already quite popular by the time it arrived on UNIX. `Emacs` remains extremely popular today, partially because it has been implemented for just about every computer and operating system in existence, and many implementations are in the public domain.

Even though there are public-domain versions of both `vi` and `emacs`, there are now many companies supporting commercial releases of both. You will have to make a decision for yourself whether you want a public-domain version or a commercial product, although we think very highly of GNU's public-domain `emacs`. Other companies selling editors include CCA (Emacs), Custom Software Systems (PC/VI), Enterprising Ideas, Inc. (ae), Lugaru Software Ltd. (Epsilon), Fenix Software (Fenix), Grand Software, Inc. (Grand Editor), Marc Software (WordMarc), and UniPress Software (vi-PLUS, emacs, cmacs).

Many of these editors support much more than character manipulation. Most will check spelling and many support a thesaurus. Surprisingly, few compare favorably to the tools known as the Writer's Workbench (still sold by AT&T). These programs help writers by identifying grammatical problems ranging from spelling errors to more complex structural problems such as punctuation, split infinitives, run-on sentences and sexist phrases. The programs suggest alternatives according to the rules built in to the programs as an aid to the writer.

11.10　Fourth Generation Languages

"The limits of my language stand for the limits of my world." – Ludwig Wittgenstein

Fourth-generation languages (4GLs) are high-level interfaces to high-level languages (3GLs). Theoretically, the programmer uses the problem specification as input to the 4GL. The system automatically converts the specification to code.

In reality, most 4GLs are still procedural. Rather, 4GLs have simply become a buzzword for languages that allow one to code using English-like sentences along with a good set of libraries for database manipulation, screen formatting and user interfaces.

While not obsoleting programmers, a 4GL can immensely speed up certain types of programming tasks and are especially good at prototyping. The reason we say this is because they can also be slow. This is analogous to using a shell script for an application.

Some 4GLs are ABF (Relational Technology), Accell (Unify Corp.), DataFlex (Data Access Corp.), Empress/32, Informix-4GL (Informix Software

Inc.), M-Builder (Rhodnius Inc.), Oracle (Oracle Systems Corp.), Progress (Data Language Corp.), Today (bbj Computers International) and System Z (Zortec, Inc.).

11.11   Graphics

UNIX has a couple of rudimentary tools for drawing lines, circles and splines. This system (known as "plot") is implemented very cleverly using a number of filters that can be joined together using pipes. While we can't recommend a specific replacement, we do suggest that you ignore this software. It is quite inflexible, unfriendly and pales by comparison to third-party graphics software.

There are many excellent end-user products for creating graphics in an application requiring graphics. Simple uses include presentation graphics (e.g., bar charts, pie charts) for business and scientific presentations. Some companies selling presentation graphics tools include AT&T Information Systems, Precision Visuals, Inc., Data Business Vision, Inc., Graphic Software Systems, Arens Applied Electromagnetics, and Quality Software Products Co. Probably the most well known of these is DWB (Documenter's Workbench) from AT&T. This includes `grap` (graphs), `pic` (pictures), and some other programs which allow you to set up graphics in `troff` very easily.

More sophisticated demands occur in applications such as VLSI design or image processing. Since graphics is a fairly mature field, most systems come with implementations for at least one of the Core, GKS or PHIGS graphic libraries. They are also available from third-party suppliers such as Advanced Technology Center, ISSCO, Omnicomp Graphics Corporation, Peregrine Computer Systems, Precision Visuals, Inc. and Template Graphics Software Inc. Their products can easily support a variety of sophisticated applications.

More complex and demanding graphics work can be done on UNIX, though generally on a one-shot basis. The reason such state-of-the-art work is more feasible on UNIX systems should be understood. As new display systems are spawned each year, UNIX stands out as being the first to have its software ported to them. Another reason is that efficiency is often an important consideration for many graphics applications and writing in C is a good way to go. (To a large extent, C is replacing Fortran as the vehicle of choice for graphics work.)

Graphics Trends

Research at Berkeley and Bell Labs illustrates both the UNIX programming philosophy and its relationship to graphics. Carlo Sequin (from Berkeley) has designed a set of tools, called UNI-GRAFIX, which can create 3D and 4D objects, and manipulate their geometry by using pipes and filters. (See "The Berkeley UNI-GRAFIX Tools," *Tech. Report UCB/CSD 86/278*). In a similar style, Tom Duff (from Bell Labs) has produced a number of programs which work with a common data structure to produce high-quality computer graphics. (See "Compositing 3-D Rendered Images" in *SigGraph 1985 Proceedings*). And Potmesil and Hoffert (also of Bell Labs) have created FRAMES using some of the same ideas. (See "Frames: Software Tools for Modeling, Rendering and Animation of 3D Scenes" in *SigGraph 1987 Proceedings*).

The implications of this are quite elegant. Rather than having a single monolithic program which can do all things for all people (in a confusingly complex way), a number of small utilities can be joined together as needs demand. For example, one utility generates a 3D object, the next shades them, another adds a synthetic camera view, and so on. Plugging in different algorithms for shading or ray tracing becomes as easy as typing in a UNIX command line.

11.12   Mail, Messaging

"How to process 200 messages a day and still get some real work done" – title of talk by Marshall Rose and John Romine on Rand's Message Handling System.

Modern electronic mail systems are usually implemented in three parts. The top part is the user interface (or user agent). Like shells, users like to write their own mail user interfaces, and thus, many of them exist. You are likely to find more than one on your system (although **/bin/mail** is always there).

The bottom part is the transport mechanism. This performs the actual delivery of mail, and is necessarily different for different networks and computers. For example, SMTP is used for Arpa/Internet mail, and **uucp** is used for mail between hosts that are connected by serial lines. Mail transport mechanisms are usually closed related to file transport mechanisms.

The leftover part is the glue that holds the top and bottom halves together. It is really just a router, but it gets left doing all the hard work that no one else wants to solve. The problem is that most mail systems use completely different formats for addresses, so something is needed to do the conversion.

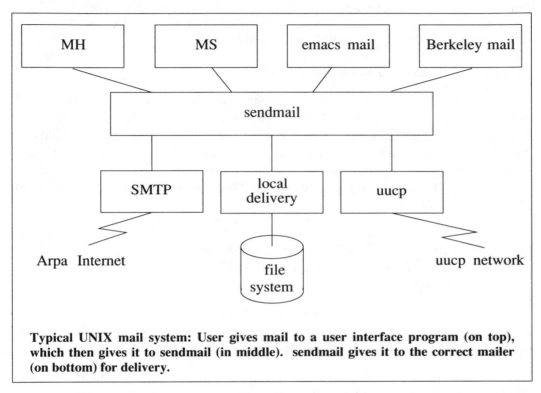

Typical UNIX mail system: User gives mail to a user interface program (on top), which then gives it to sendmail (in middle). sendmail gives it to the correct mailer (on bottom) for delivery.

Examples of popular mail routers are `sendmail` and MMDF. Good presentations on the subject of electronic mail are "An Internetwork Memo Distribution Facility – MMDF" by D. Crocker et al. in the *6th Data Communication Symposium*, Asilomar, November 1979, and "Sendmail – An Internetwork Mail Router" by Eric Allman, *4.2BSD UNIX Programmer's Manual*, vol. 2C, University of California, Berkeley, July 1983.

While many mail systems are available from early versions of UNIX, newer ones are undeniably much better. They understand multiple networks, interface to heterogenous mail systems and are often graphical or menu-oriented. Many are bundled and heavily integrated with office automation software.

Some mail systems are Calem (AT&T IS), EuroText (Asicom, S.A.), Handshake Colt Computer Linked Telex (SST Data Inc.), INmail (Interactive

Systems Corp.), IDesk (Intel), Infolink (Clever Connections Ltd.), Office Telesystem (AT&T IS), Q-Mail (Quadratron Systems, Inc.), R Desk (R Systems, Inc.), RootMail (Root Computers Ltd.), Take Notice (V-Systems, Inc.), Teletex (TITN, Inc.), Twice MHS X.400 (TITN, Inc.), UNIX PC Electronic Mail (AT&T IS), VoiceServer (Digital Sound Corporation).

11.13   Mathematical Modeling

Mathematical models start in capability where spreadsheets leave off. Some of them have a front-end that looks like a spreadsheet but are far more sophisticated.   Packages are available to solve simultaneous linear equations, calculus, sorting, correlation and regression analysis, Poisson series, as well as image processing, mechanical design and electrical engineering problems. Many of the packages include subroutine libraries so that you can call them from your own programs.

Many of these packages are not new, having been developed and used on supercomputers in the '60s. They were all written in Fortran, with highly optimized code. Examples of these are NAG (Numerical Algorithms Group) and SPSS (SPSS Inc.)

More recently developed packages include symbolic systems, originally written in Lisp for the most part, but now often recoded for speed. Examples of symbolic systems include Macsyma (Symbolics, Inc.), SMP (Inference Corp.).

Other popular mathematical libraries and programs include GPSS (Simulation Software Ltd.), Linear Optimizer (Acme Computer Co.), LP/Protran (IMSL Inc.), Math Advantage (Quantitative Technology Corp.), Simtec (Terotech), S (AT&T), SORITEC (Sorites Group, Inc.), and SunTrend (Systems Union Ltd.).

Each type of system is appropriate for particular classes of problems. However, you will find that almost all of them are supported on UNIX systems. And with supercomputers (such as the Cray) running UNIX, there are no mathematical modeling applications out of reach of a UNIX system.

Negative Zero?

After finding differences when solving systems of equations on two different machines running the same version of UNIX, Eugene Spafford and John Flaspohler (*;login:*, vol. 11, no. 2, March/April 1986) decided to find out if there were any other differences. They ran accuracy tests for various mathematical functions on 11 different commercially available computers.

Their results were startling. The quality of the mathematical subroutines varied widely. Some machines produced quite inaccurate results for several tests. Some showed complete loss of significance on one of the tests. One machine raised errors on values that were within a function's domain. Another machine computed measurably less accurate answers when its floating point accelerator was turned off. And one machine produced values of minus zero that were not equal to positive zero.

Some errors were determined as software, some as firmware and hardware, but the results were clear. There was little standardization on mathematic computation. While some of the problems they noted have been now fixed, it is still the case that people depending on mathematical accuracy should perform their own testing or demand well-documented test results.

11.14   Office Automation

While UNIX is a general-purpose operating system, it is admirably suited to office automation tasks. Indeed, one of the original applications of UNIX was for word processing. Remnants of this can be seen in tools such as `spell`, `refer` and `typo` as well as the dictionary that can be found in `/usr/dict/words`.

The first public release of the UNIX system was not particularly user-friendly. Now, however, many companies have seized upon making UNIX accessible to people without a degree in Computer Hackery. There is a wide diversity of offerings. Some integrate the whole of office applications such as spreadsheets, word processing and communications, while others key in on specific areas like publishing and typesetting.

There are some disadvantages to this route for office automation. One is that since UNIX is a general-purpose system, it is necessarily less efficient adapting to applications such as word processing than other systems designed for this purpose. Lower-priced dedicated systems can adequately do much of the simpler office automation tasks at much lower cost than a complete UNIX system.

On the other hand, as office-automation processing demands get more complex, the slower processors of these cheaper machines become a hindrance. Further, in a distributed environment, PC-class machines are much more limited at sharing files, electronic mail, and so on than a UNIX system.

Some of the more popular office automation systems are Alis (Applix, Inc.), Uniplex-II Plus (Uniplex Integration Systems, Inc.), XED Integrated Office System (Computer Methods, Ltd.) and systems by Quadratron Systems, Inc. and R Systems Inc.

"UNIX Muscles into the OA Market" by Vanessa Schnatmeier in *UNIX-WORLD*, vol. 4, no. 6, June 1987, is an extended discussion of this topic. Patricia Seybold's *UNIX in the Office* is a periodical dedicated to such coverage.

11.15   Programming Languages
"If you want PL/I, you know where to find it." – Dennis Ritchie

While UNIX comes with a healthy complement of languages, there are many reasons for buying one from a third-party vendor. For one thing, there are new languages (and new versions, thanks to the standards committees) being born every day. There are new machines to support, possibly by cross-compilers. And there are vendors that are more capable of creating languages than your original hardware vendor. Since it is now possible to buy UNIX "unbundled" or piecemeal, shopping for a language is not unlike shopping for a component to go into your stereo system.

Here are some language vendors you can pursue.

ADA: ALSYS S.A., AT&T Federal Systems, Intermetrics, TeleSoft, Verdix Corp.

APL: Dyadic Systems, Ltd., I. P. Sharp Associates, Oregon State University, STSC, Inc.

Basic: ABC Development Systems, Inc., AT&T, Basis Inc., Basmark Corp., Concept Omega Corp., Control-C Software, Cromemco, Inc., Databoard Inc., HCR Corp., Microsoft Corp., Microware Systems Corp., NKR Research,

Philon, Inc., Silicon Valley Software, Software Innovations Inc., Tektronix, Inc., UX Software, Inc., UniPress Software, Inc.

C: Alcyon Corp., AT&T, Flexible Computer Corp., Free Software Foundation, Interactive Systems Corp., MetaWare Inc., Microsoft, Microware Systems Corp., Microtec Research, Oasys, Oregon Software, Silicon Valley Software, Inc., Software Development Systems, Southwest Technical Products Corp., Systems & Software, Inc., UniPress Software, Inc., Whitesmiths, Ltd.

While virtually every UNIX system comes with a manufacturer-provided C compiler, there are valid reasons for buying a third-party version. A typical reason is for cross-compilation – when you need to generate code for another machine. Such a feature is rarely provided by the default C compiler.

Another reason is that some companies specialize in producing high-performance compilers. While these are certainly attractive, most customers feel more comfortable using the C compiler that comes with their system. Rather than end users buying these third-party C compilers, we more often see the UNIX system manufacturers themselves investing in the third-party compiler products and embedding them in their final product.

C interpreters: Impacc Associates, Informatix, Lattice, Rational Systems, Saber Software, Inc.

C++: AT&T, Lifeboat Associates, Inc., Glockenspiel Ltd., Oasys, Oregon Software

COBOL: Austec, Cromemco, Inc., IBM Corp., Micro Focus, Philon, Inc.

Dibol: Digital Information Systems Corp., IBM, Omtool Corp., Software Ireland Ltd.

Forth: Adaptive Optics Associates, Laboratory Microsystems, Inc., Specialized Systems Consultants, Inc., Interactive Systems Corp., Ubiquitous Systems

Fortran: Absoft Corp., AT&T, Interactive Systems Corp., Microware Systems Corp., Philon, Inc., Ryan-McFarland Corp., Silicon Valley Software

Lisp: CRIL, Digital Equipment Corp., Franz, Inc., Lucid, Inc., University of Utah, The r/l group, Systems Designers Software, Inc.

Modula-2: Ana-systems, Djavaheri Bros., Sun Microsystems

Mumps: Plus Five Computer Services

Pascal: AT&T, HCR Corp., MetaWare Inc., Microtec Research, Microware Systems Corp., Oregon Software, Silicon Valley Software, UniPress Software, Inc., Whitesmiths, Ltd.

PL/M: Systems & Software, Inc.

Prolog: ALMA, BIM, CRIL, Logic Programming Associates, Ltd., Logicware Inc., Quintus Computer Systems, Inc., Scientia Computer Applications Pte Ltd., Systems Designers Software, Inc., University of New South Wales

RPG: International Computers Ltd.

Smalltalk: ParcPlace Systems, University of Calif. at Berkeley, Xerox

Snobol: University of Leeds

And here are some vendors selling products that will do language-to-language conversion.

Basic-to-C: JMI Software Consultants, Inc.

Cobol-to-C: Rapitech Systems, Inc.

Fortran-to-C: Intrinsic OY, Rapitech Systems, Inc.

Pascal-to-C: Holistic Technology

11.16   Shell Compilers

The UNIX shell is an interpreter. This means that it spends a lot of time interpreting the instructions in shell scripts before it gets around to executing them. Unlike interpreters, compilers look at a program only once but can execute them many times. The resulting programs are much faster.

Shell scripts were originally envisioned as prototyping tools, where efficiency didn't matter. But shell programming turned out to be so easy (and C programming so hard), that many valuable shell programs have never been converted into compiled programs.

Several companies have introduced shell compilers. These take shell scripts as input and produce executable programs. Depending upon the original shell script, incredible speedups are possible. Reducing the run-time of a shell program by 90 percent would be quite believable.

Three shell compilers are CCsh (Comeau Computing), QuickShell (UniPress Software) and Shacc (Concentric Associates, Inc.). All of these compile Bourne shell scripts only.

11.17   Spreadsheets

Spreadsheets are yet another tool, that while not developed on UNIX systems, have made the migration easily. Virtually all of the popular microcomputer spreadsheets are available for UNIX. UNIX also runs many of the public-domain versions. Most of them look exactly like their cousins (or Lotus 1-2-3) on the smaller machines, and many can even read and write floppies written on micros, allowing you to transfer spreadsheets back and forth. Some of the spreadsheets are only part of larger office automation systems.

Of course, running a spreadsheet on UNIX has many advantages. For instance, UNIX systems typically have much more memory and compute power than a micro. Thus, you will find your spreadsheets can be larger and more complex. And if you need more complex capabilities than a spreadsheet can provide, you can move up to one of the many mathematical modeling systems that are available for UNIX.

Some popular spreadsheets are 20/20 (Access Technology Inc.), C-Calc (DSD Corp.), Handle Calc (Handle Technologies, Inc.), iPlan (Intel Corp.), Impact (Integrated Micro Products), Multiplan (Microsoft Corp.), Prelude (VenturCom), PubliCalc (Specialized Systems Consultants Inc.), Q-Calc (Quality Software Products), Q-Plan (Quadratron Systems Inc.), Tactician (Southwind Software Inc.), Twin (Mosaic Software Inc.), UltraCalc (Olympus Software Inc.), Unicalq (uniq Digital Technologies), SCO Professional (The Santa Cruz Operation Inc.), VC (Software Innovations Inc.), ViewComp (Unicorp Software, Inc.). A good review of some of these spreadsheets is "Getting the Most From Spreadsheets" in *UNIXWORLD*, vol. 4, no. 9, September 1987. There are also several good UNIX spreadsheets in the public domain, including VC (Mark Weiser) and SC (James Gosling). See the Underground chapter for information on how to obtain public-domain software.

11.18   System Administration

UNIX has traditionally provided inadequate tools for system administration. The old saying that *"UNIX was designed for programmers, not for users"* should be amended with *"nor for system managers."* For example, UNIX lacks quality backup mechanisms, flexible security systems, and a resource quota system. The Administrator's Environment chapter goes into great detail about this, describing the many areas of system administration for which UNIX has rather shabby solutions.

Many companies have attempted to remedy this. Products are now available to do automated backups, comprehensive security and full-featured spooling which put the original ones to shame. If you want to implement load control across multiple systems, or manage a tape library, you should investigate these applications.

Some companies specializing in this area are AIM Technology, COSI, Flexible Solutions, Intermetrics, Throwaway Software and UNITECH.

11.19   The Toolchest

While not an application, AT&T's UNIX System Toolchest is appropriately covered here. The Toolchest is an automated software store.

Using the Toolchest, you can browse through an electronic stockroom of software, decide what you want, and order it. The software is delivered to your computer electronically.

The way it works in reality is surprisingly easy. You dial up the Toolchest from an intelligent terminal. You can log in as `guest` the first time, and order a contract for billing purposes. Next, you can browse through a large collection of software. For example, you can get the latest releases of `awk`, Honey-Danber `uucp` and the Korn shell this way. Several public-domain programs are available for free. Finally, the software is delivered that night via `uucp`.

The Toolchest was started as a means of solving the distribution problems at AT&T internally. With thousands of UNIX systems in-house and hundreds of programmers modifying UNIX programs constantly, how could they possibly keep all the machines up to date with the latest programs? The answer was: Don't try to keep all the machines up to date. Rather, let users request the latest copies of programs as they need them. This made sense since most people didn't need the latest copies of every program, but if they stumbled across a bug in one program, they wanted it fixed pronto.

Many other companies have begun to support their own dial-up toolchests, although AT&T's is by far the most well known, having several technical papers about it published in UNIX periodicals. A more comprehensive description of the Toolchest is "Experiences with Electronic Software Distribution" by Catherine Brooks in the *Summer 1985 USENIX Conference Proceedings*. The Toolchest phone number is 201-522-6900 in the U.S., 44-1-567-7711 in London, and 81-3-431-3670 in Tokyo.

11.20 Windows

The first bitmapped workstation was the Xerox Alto.† While the Alto did not run UNIX, its ability to provide a windowing system to remote hosts made it a jewel of a terminal.

Many people seized upon this idea and attempted to abstract out the essential parts of the Alto that would allow them to provide a terminal with multiple windows (at a much lower cost – each Alto cost approximately $30,000 including a mouse, Ethernet, 256Kb and a small disk).

Several systems stand out. The AT&T Blit was extremely similar to the Alto, although the Blit used 1981 technology and was quite a bit cheaper.‡ The Blit could provide windows to a remote host, and like the Alto, could also run programs locally, although it did not itself run UNIX. Unlike the Alto, the Blit communicated over RS-232 connections and did not have a disk. Its operating system was downloaded from the host computer. The Blit was never commercially sold, but the technology was picked up by ATT/Teletype Corp., and marketed as the 5620 DMD (Dot-Mapped Display).

At the same time, the SUN (Stanford University Network) computer was being developed at Stanford. This machine was similar to the Blit and Alto, except that it ran UNIX locally. This was especially attractive, since it relieved the user of reliance upon a remote host computer. The SUN design was quickly picked up and marketed by dozens of startup companies.

---

† C. P. Thacker et al., "Alto: A Personal Computer," CSL-79-11, August 1979, Xerox Corp.

‡ The Blit's creators claim that "Blit" stands for the Bacon, Lettuce and Interactive Tomato. However, it is easier to stomach the belief that "Blit" comes from the `bitblt` (BIT-BLock Transfer) opcode popularized by the Alto.

In 1983, Hewlett-Packard began selling the HP Integral PC, the first portable UNIX machine. Using a ROM'ed UNIX operating system, it included a windowed bitmapped display and sold for $5,000.

The price of windowing hardware has dropped dramatically since originally introduced, and most UNIX workstation vendors offer window systems as an option. While there are many window systems for sale, there seems to be movement towards settling on two basic "strains" of window systems. Both have their advantages and disadvantages.

X Windows was developed jointly by DEC and MIT at Project Athena. X is based on the W window system, written at Stanford for the V operating system. X has become extremely popular for several reasons. The source code has been placed into the public domain. X has been ported to virtually every computer that runs UNIX, and many that do not. It is distributed and supported by many vendors. Technically, X is not particularly outstanding although it was the first window system to allow an application to display a window on an internetworked host's screen without any change to the software. X is also being considered as a windowing standard within the Graphics/Windows Working Group of the IEEE P1003 POSIX Standard.

An alternative to X, is Sun's NeWS (Network/extensible Window System). Yet another system is Display PostScript. Both NeWS and Display PostScript use the PostScript language internally.

PostScript is a page-description language originally developed to drive laser printers. It contains a powerful image model which allows for arbitrarily-shaped windows. More importantly, all of these PostScript-based window systems are completely programmable, and can be made to mimic other window systems such as X. NeWS and Display PostScript are proprietary products, although many vendors support PostScript itself. PostScript was created by Adobe Systems.

It is likely that future window systems will be able to support any of a number of other window systems. For example, AT&T's System VR4 includes a windowing system that supports both X and NeWS concurrently.

Chapter 12: UNIX Meets The Real World

"The world is moving so fast these days that the man who says it can't be done is generally interrupted by someone doing it." – Elbert Hubbard

During the mid-'70s, many of the students who had been using UNIX at school, began to graduate. It was a great shock to many of them to find that real work was being done on inflexible computers and operating systems put out by IBM, DEC and others. You had no choice in what could be configured in the operating system. If the vendor supplied source, you could bet it was in assembler. Code wasn't portable. Some systems weren't even interactive. It seemed as though computing in the real world was back in the dark ages.

These recent graduates were somewhat spoiled by UNIX. However, some of them managed to bring many of the good concepts of UNIX to other operating systems, although certain systems did not allow anything remotely resembling pipes. Some systems did not have hierarchical file systems, interprocess communication, and so on. The epitome of this was work discussed in Chapter 4 on the Virtual Operating System.

VOS and other UNIX emulators did not appease the masses. UNIX was available for licensing and prices for hardware were dropping. Several problems had to be remedied on the way before UNIX was acceptable for commercial use.

Some of these were vague critiques like *"UNIX isn't user-friendly."* Others were more specific, *"We need the ability to lock files."* The other primary complaints were that UNIX wasn't robust, UNIX wasn't real-time, and UNIX wasn't supported. Some of these issues have turned out to be red-herrings. For instance, many studies have shown that it doesn't matter what command names are – it takes the same amount of time to learn them. Some of these problems no longer exist (i.e., UNIX is now well supported). Other factors have turned out to be more critical. For example, a system monitoring a nuclear power plant really does need to be reliable.

This chapter will discuss some of the ordeals that UNIX had to overcome, either in rumor or substance, on the road to maturity.

12.1   Databases and Database Management Systems

"The kernel needs to provide record locking about as much as it needs to provide trigonometric functions." – Marc Rochkind

It used to be common knowledge that UNIX did not support databases. It did not have record locking or job checkpointing, the file system did not support fancy file access techniques, and there was no way to tell if a file had *really* been written to the disk. It was lunacy to even begin to contemplate keeping a database on a UNIX system!

Interestingly, the following comment appears in the seminal article "The UNIX Time-Sharing System" by Dennis Ritchie and Ken Thompson which appeared in the *Communications of the ACM*, vol. 17, no. 7, July 1974, p. 368:

> There are no user-visible locks in the file system, nor is there any restriction on the number of users who may have a file open for reading or writing. Although it is possible for the contents of a file to become scrambled when two users write on it simultaneously, in practice difficulties do not arise. We take the view that locks are neither necessary nor sufficient, in our environment, to prevent interference between users of the same file. They are unnecessary because we are not faced with large, single-file data bases maintained by independent processes. They are insufficient because locks in the ordinary sense, whereby one user is prevented from writing on a file which another user is reading, cannot prevent confusion when, for example, both users are editing a file with an editor which makes a copy of the file being edited.

The view of the UNIX designers was clear. And yet at the same time, people always needed to keep data whether it be organized in a traditional database or otherwise. The many tools and filters on UNIX systems were more than adept at one form of data: text.

The password file was text. The log files were text. And so on. While there were exceptions, they really were rare, and programs like **cat**, **ed** and **grep** didn't demand any special format file, just text. People began to find that it was relatively easy to keep textual databases since UNIX already had a fabulous collection of tools for doing exactly that.

Text files and UNIX tools continue to be the choice for small databases such as the on-line manual pages and word dictionary. However, such an approach does not scale up to large applications with real-time demands.

The real answer is to do what is generally done on other operating systems. Building a database requires a centralized DBMS, so that only one module has access to the file system. All users then go through the DBMS. This solution obviates the need for a kernel modification and puts the decisions and power where it belongs – in the lap of the database designer. This solution extends gracefully to distributed database systems, each with multiple data repositories per computer. In such a system, data is accessed by going through the per-computer, per-database DBMS.

Most modern UNIX systems provide sufficient support for record locking, synchronization, semaphores and other database management tools. Additionally, it is not difficult to build your own device driver on top of a raw UNIX file system (and you may wish to do this for top speed). Nonetheless, it is not the case that lack of such support makes sophisticated transaction-oriented database systems unachievable.

An alternative solution which bypasses the whole question of building databases in UNIX is to use UNIX systems as front-ends to specifically-designed high-performance database machines (e.g., Britton Lee). However, our conclusion should not be that DBMSs and UNIX don't mix – clearly UNIX can be and has been extended to handle DBMSs by database companies (mentioned in the previous chapter). The large amount of work required for a professional-quality DBMS is not any more so on UNIX than it is on other operating systems.

12.2   Distributed UNIX

Distributed processing refers to a job (a set of cooperating processes) running on multiple computers. Distributed processing is a kind of parallel-processing, but usually implying different instructions are being executed at different processors which are loosely coupled (do not share memory in a common backplane).

This field is extremely difficult, yet even nonoptimal solutions are worthwhile. For example, if you are compiling a program and `troff`'ing a paper on your local computer, the job manager can search out a computer on the network that is idle. If it finds one, it will borrow it by performing the `troff` there.

These can more than halve compute time if paging and swapping can be avoided.

With the advent of personal workstations, it is quite likely that there will be networks of idle computers available. Many UNIX jobs are made up of a set of processes that are easily decomposable and farmed out to separate computers. There are already systems (e.g., Apollo's Domain system, Berkeley's Maitre d') which do exactly this. Such a system makes sense, simply because of the UNIX-process-oriented style of computation, and the easy accessibility of workstations connected to local area networks. Alternative approaches (e.g., DUNIX) join together multiple computers under the aegis of a single operating system, providing transparent distributed processing by fiat.

Distributed processing, however, is not a solved problem. Achieving good results can be extremely difficult, depending on the application itself. For example, a single process can be distributed but careful analysis must be made to be sure that the communication and setup costs do not overwhelm the savings in time gained by processing the parts at other computers.

Optimal use of every processor's capabilities is impossible in the general case. A classic result of computer science is that it is impossible to tell if any computation may halt without running it first. Given our inability to answer such basic questions, determining more complicated ones, such as how long a computation may execute, is out of the question. Thus, heuristics and programmer estimates are used for such distributed systems which attempt more sophisticated solutions of load balancing.

Some systems incorporating distributed processing are Domain (Apollo), DUNIX (Bell Communications Research), DYNIX (Sequent), Locus (Locus Computing Corp.), Mach (CMU), Maitre d' (Berkeley), Multimax (Encore Computer Corp.), M Series (MIPS), and Sprite (Berkeley). Some worthwhile articles on this subject include "The DUNIX Distributed Operating System" by Ami Litman in *Operating Systems Review*, January 1988, "Load Balancing with Maitre d'" by Brian Bershad in *;login:*, vol. 11, no. 1, January/February 1986, and *The Yates Perspective*, p. 21, August 1984.

12.3   Emulators and Coexistence
"I'm O.K...You're O.K." – Thomas Harris
"I'm O.K...You're a Pain in the Neck" – Albert Vorspan

O.K., we confess – UNIX is not the only operating system in the world. And we admit it – there are more versions of UNIX than we care to think about. The question that remains is, what happens when you need to run two different operating systems on the same machine?

This situation may occur for a variety of reasons – political, economic or technical. For example, suppose you can only afford one computer but you want to run both UNIX and something else.

It can be done. Obviously the solutions vary depending on the situation. And some are less graceful than others. Melding two operating systems that both want to have complete control of the hardware can be a sticky problem. Sometimes, it is not really necessary to run both operating systems rather than *provide the functionality* of both operating systems.

The simplest case is running two different versions of UNIX at the same time. Most commands are identical from one UNIX to another, but there are cases where program, system calls, or library names conflict (i.e., have the same names but different parameters and functions). To ameliorate this, the user typically specifies a default version to use. Some systems allow this on a command-by-command basis; others on a session-by-session basis.

Examples of such systems are Altos (Xenix and System V), and Pyramid and Wollongong (System V and 4.3BSD). A public-domain implementation of System V under 4.2BSD is available from the U.S. Army's Ballistic Research Laboratory (BRL).

More difficult than getting two versions of UNIX on the same machine is getting UNIX to live with a non-UNIX operating system. Operating systems that are complex can emulate enough of the UNIX systems calls so that UNIX applications can run without change. Since UNIX is so portable, it is not impossible to rip out the machine-dependent parts of the kernel and provide an efficient emulation of the UNIX system calls on top of the native operating system. Examples of this are UTS on top of VM (Amdahl Corp.), and Eunice on top of VMS (The Wollongong Group).

However, while UNIX itself is portable and doesn't demand a particular hardware environment, the UNIX-style of programming can cause peculiar hardships on native operating systems. For example, it is not untypical for a UNIX process to fork many child processes while executing. On operating systems where process creation is an expensive operation (e.g., VMS), such a UNIX application can bring the native operating system to its knees.

On the other hand, since many proprietary operating systems are specifically designed around the single type of hardware that they run on, they are often faster than UNIX, which does not take advantage of specialized hardware. It is even possible (and we have actually seen such cases) for emulated UNIX to be faster than native UNIX!

While UNIX emulations are never seamless, they can be quite livable. Consider that UNIX was designed for programmers, with the system administrator getting the short end of the stick. On many other systems, the priorities seem to be reversed. Hence, UNIX running on top of another operating system allows the programmers to use UNIX, while the system administrator uses a completely different (and better) set of tools for system management.

Some companies providing UNIX on top of other systems are: Data General (AOS/VS), Convex, Interactive, HCR & Wollongong (DEC VMS), IBM (VM), Apollo (Domain).

Just as UNIX can be placed on top of more complex operating systems, there are systems that are simple enough that can be run on top of UNIX. A good example is MS-DOS. Since DOS is a relatively simple system (compared to UNIX), it is easy to provide support for it on top of UNIX itself. Early DOS/UNIX systems worked by emulating Intel 8088 assembler as well as BIOS and DOS system calls. Nowadays, prices for PC-compatible boards are so low that most vendors support DOS by plugging a PC board in the UNIX backplane and using it as a coprocessor. The result is a flawless DOS environment running as fast as a real DOS system.

Some vendors that support an MS-DOS environment under UNIX are AT&T, ICON International, Inc., Interactive Systems Corp., Locus Computing Corp., Microport Systems, Inc., Prime Computer Inc., The Santa Cruz Operation, Inc, Sritek, Sun Microsystems, Inc., and TeleVideo Systems, Inc.

12.4   Fault Tolerance, Transaction Processing

"We don't go down on our customers" – Parallel Computers advertisement

While fault tolerance and transaction processing are different subjects, they tend to be demanded by the same set of customers. They have also gotten the mutual reputation of being difficult to achieve in UNIX systems.

Early versions of UNIX were notorious for requiring arcane knowledge in order to restore the file system to its former state in the event of a power failure. Modern versions of UNIX have excellent file system recovery procedures which make losing a file extremely rare. (But there isn't much it can do about a tornado or lightning).

While program developers are willing to wait a couple of minutes as the computer is rebooted and the file system restored after a crash, UNIX is no longer just a developer's toy, and many applications cannot wait at all (see "Real-Time Processing" in this chapter). Some applications (e.g., controlling a space shuttle) cannot afford any loss of the processor, while others (e.g., banking) can stand some delays but at loss of revenue, sometimes thousands of dollars per minute.

Fault tolerant systems attempt to continue providing service in the face of partial failure. The typical approach is to provide redundant components, invariably at a high price. The original approach of buying two complete computers has been refined in many ways by the many vendors of fault-tolerant UNIX systems.

Systems can fail in many ways. Failure may occur in power supplies, memory, disks, CPU's, communications paths, and so on. Providing multiple access to each of these is more expensive but provides better ability to recover from redundancy. In order to do any of these things, the result is usually a heavily modified or completely rewritten UNIX kernel. Extra system calls may be added to provide checkpoints.

Transaction processing is usually carried out on fault-tolerant systems. For example, a bank transaction may involve a transfer of money from one account to another. Not only should the computer system be reliable, but the transfer must be completed in a given amount of time.

Systems are good for transaction processing only if they are reliable and can guarantee response time. This requires atomic transactions, fast database systems, deterministic communications, and recovery facilities in the event of a crash. High-level demands such as these were impossible in early UNIX systems because kernels lacked primitives like semaphores, real-time schedulers, record-oriented databases and efficient support for hundreds of terminals.

Several companies now offer fault-tolerant UNIX systems for transaction-based processing. It is safe to say that such systems are built on top of kernels that are drastically different from earlier UNIX kernels. Most of these systems provide redundant hardware components as well. Achieving fault tolerance and transaction processing is a difficult goal for any computer system, no less for a UNIX system.

Some of the leaders in this type of processing are: Origin Corporation, Parallel Computers, Stratus, Sequoia Systems, Tandem Computers, and Tolerant Systems. For more information about fault tolerant UNIX computers, see the article "Many Roads to Fault Tolerance" by Vanessa Schnatmeier in *CommUNIXations*, vol. 5, no. 3, April/May 1985.

"Interview with Richard Searle" by Bill Freiboth in *UNIX REVIEW*, vol. 4, no. 7, July 1986, is an interesting interview with Citicorp/TTI on its use of UNIX in banking. Discussed is why the company chose UNIX over "bank-standard" IBM, the modifications that were made to UNIX to support reliable transaction processing, and how satisfied it was with the results.

12.5   International UNIX

% grep 唐李贝斯 /etc/passwd

UNIX was developed in the U.S. by English-speaking natives. The origin shows as the use of ASCII is deeply embedded in the system. For example, the UNIX programs have English phrases (e.g., `No such file or directory`) and the character set hard-coded into them.

People often joke about the non-English UNIX command names (e.g., `grep`, `ls`) as showing no bias towards English speaking, but this is misdirected, since the result is only that everyone feels equally uncomfortable with them! As UNIX becomes more user-friendly, we shall see not just English speakers but all users finding UNIX easier to use. Translating English error messages to other languages is just one small part of it.

Before solving the problem of using other languages, UNIX faces the difficulty of representing the character sets of other countries. Most UNIX text utilities manipulate characters using seven bits (to support ASCII) out of every byte. Trying to use all eight bits often causes unexpected failures in many utilities (e.g., shells, mailers) which use the extra bit for their own purposes. So just adding a few characters is difficult. But what about languages like Chinese? It has over 25,000 characters. Such characters cannot be conveniently represented by single bytes. Multibyte representations are necessary but require rewriting of support routines (e.g., `ctype` macros, string subroutines) and often the applications, also.

Some languages print in different directions. Depending on context, characters may be capitalized, and multiple characters may be mapped to one (e.g., German). Sorting is no longer the simple task of comparing character representations, since alphabets may not be ordered by the machine's representation of them. And some alphabets require sorting from the opposite end of a string, while others require context of the surrounding word. Regular expression parsing may no longer be powerful enough to match certain patterns in other alphabets, as in English.

Date, times and currency have to be printed in the local conventions. For example, UNIX has always understood the concept of a time zone, but there are time zones where multiple designations are used depending upon which country you are in. Some countries adjust their clock by smaller fractions than one hour.

The internationalization of UNIX requires extensive research and development, but much has been already been done by large, international vendors on other computer systems. Members of the X/OPEN consortium and other international organizations are making great headway towards solutions of these problems. Currently, several vendors sell versions of their product oriented towards other languages, such as the System V Japanese Language Version. Eventually, UNIX systems may come with extremely flexible language support allowing, for example, any message to be changed by the user.

For more information on the use and capability of UNIX in non-U.S. territory, see the December 1985 issue of *UNIX REVIEW* which has several articles on this topic. Another worthwhile article is "Parlez-Vous L'UNIX? The European Perspective, Past and Future" by Jean Wood & Hans-Joachim Brede in the *Summer 1985 USENIX Conference Proceedings*.

12.6   Mainframes and Supercomputers

One of UNIX's unexpected successes is its popularity on large computers. While UNIX was originally designed with a small machine in mind, it is admirably suited towards a wide range of computers. Remember that the designers of UNIX rejected the "kitchen-in-a-sink" philosophy of MULTICS in order to support "simple" computing on a minicomputer. This makes it especially ironic to find UNIX on some of the largest computers in the world.

For a variety of reasons, UNIX is a very suitable choice on many large computers:

1) UNIX is easy to port to new hardware, having been written in a portable manner and making relatively few demands for special purpose hardware.

2) While a "small" operating system, UNIX is still rich enough in function that it makes a good operating system for any machine.

3) Being able to run UNIX means you automatically have a large collection of other software immediately available.

It is almost rare for a large machine not to have an implementation of UNIX available for it. In general, UNIX porting is so easy (requiring two to six man-months depending on how novel the architecture is), many of the ports have been done as "midnight" projects either by students or disgruntled users of the machine's native operating system. Often, the manufacturer has taken over the support for a port, and offers its native operating system and a UNIX port depending on the customer's preferences.

Some operating systems have the ability to simulate multiple machines (e.g., IBM's VM). In such systems, it is possible to support multiple users each choosing for themselves whether they want to run UNIX or another operating system (on the same machine at the same time). In any case, the differences between UNIX on a minicomputer and a mainframe are minimal. Most notable is the terminal handling, as the UNIX style of character handling requires tight interaction with the CPU, which is inefficient on a processor with hundreds of terminals. Many vendors have obviated this problem by offloading I/O to specialized I/O processors.

Large computers include understandable improvements and extensions to UNIX, such as supporting multiple processors and files that span multiple volumes. Schedulers are typically rewritten to support the large number of processes and unusual processing requirements.

An interesting article describing the management of a large UNIX site is "A Strategy of Accommodation" by Alan Fernquist in *UNIX REVIEW*, vol. 4, no. 7, July 1986, discussing the NASA Ames Research Center. At the time the article was written, the center had a network of computers including a Cray-2 running UNICOS, two Amdahl mainframes running UTS, twenty-five Silicon Graphics IRIS workstations and four DEC VAXen running different versions of UNIX. Management (i.e., allocation, backup, placement of home directories) of disk storage alone was a staggering problem. The Cray had 20Gb while the Amdahl was heading towards 1Tb!

Other worthwhile readings on this subject include "Meeting Mainframe Expectations" by Hal Jespersen in *UNIX REVIEW*, vol. 4, no. 7, July 1986, and the *USENIX Winter Conference Proceedings*, January 1986, which included a dozen papers in the "UNIX on Big Iron" technical session.

Other manufacturers of UNIX mainframes and supercomputers include Alliant Computer Systems Corp., Ardent Computer Products Inc., Concurrent Computer Corp., Convex Computer Corp., Elxsi, and Stellar Systems.

12.7 Micros

UNIX on a micro is an attractive idea. Micros are cheap. You don't have to share one with anyone else. They are simple enough to master. It is easy to see why micros caught on even without a real operating system (e.g., CP/M). But the idea of having your favorite operating system, UNIX, which you have probably gotten used to on larger machines is tantalizing.

Several versions of UNIX are now available for microcomputers. Indeed, the number of Xenix systems far outnumbers the number of other UNIX systems of all other types. Based on System V, SCO's port of Microsoft's Xenix runs on IBM PC/XT/ATs and compatibles, as well as other microcomputer systems. Other implementations of UNIX on PC-class machines include Venix V/86 by VenturCom, PC/IX written by Interactive Systems Corp. and sold by IBM, and System V/386 by Microport Systems, Inc. Several UNIX look-alikes exist for PC-class machines. These include Coherent by Mark Williams Co., and Co-Idris by Whitesmiths, Ltd. All of these UNIX and UNIX-like products range from about $300 to $1,000, depending upon how complete a system you get. Don't forget to check out Minix (in the Underground chapter), a V7 rewrite which includes source and sells for the cost of the books and media.

Interestingly, the first versions of UNIX ran on 16-bit machines, which, in some ways, were superior to the microcomputers of today. Two useful things they did have that are not common among all microcomputers are memory management hardware and a generous amount of disk space.

Memory management hardware allows processes to be moved in memory without their knowledge. It also protects processes from references outside of their allocated space. While memory management is not necessary for UNIX, it is very helpful. Certainly, for developers, protected memory is almost certainly a prerequisite. If memory is not protected, user programmers can crash the entire system and scribble on the disks. We do not recommend running UNIX on any system without memory management hardware (e.g., PCs, XTs) unless it is a fully debugged and dedicated application (like a toaster oven).

Unlike MS-DOS, UNIX comes with a large amount of utilities, libraries, languages and other baggage. Estimating 10Mb to hold UNIX alone, you need a 20Mb disk to be able to store this, plus whatever applications and personal files you need. In practice, an even larger disk is desirable. Some versions of microcomputer UNIX swap. This means that processes are temporarily copied out of memory on to the disk. In such systems, it is useful to set aside several megabytes of disk space for this purpose. If possible, this swapping disk or partition should be on a fast disk drive.

Microcomputer systems which do not have enough disk space can still run UNIX, however. If you are only doing word processing, you don't need the software development tools (e.g., C compiler, `yacc`, `lex`). Similarly, you may not need the word processing utilities if you are only doing development. Some versions of UNIX are sold *unbundled* (in pieces) so that you can buy only what you need. Most systems come complete, however, and during installation you can decide which floppies to read in to your system.

It is also possible to stick with MS-DOS or PC-DOS and add software that gives you many of the functions of UNIX. For example, most of the utilities (development tools, Writer's Workbench tools, and so on) have been ported to the DOS environment. It is even possible to get `csh` and `uucp` for the PC. There are public-domain versions of almost all of these. Many companies offer special versions of their UNIX products that will run on DOS, plus there are companies such as Mortice Kern Systems which specialize in porting UNIX tools to DOS.

The result of all this is that it is possible (in 1988) to get a reasonable UNIX box for $2,500. This would include an AT compatible, 20Mb disk and one of the UNIX ports. That's not bad, considering it would have cost you about $25,000 for the same thing only six years ago. Of course, for a little more money ($5,000), it is possible to buy a preconfigured UNIX box, such as an AT&T 7300, or an HP portable.

Alternatively, you can buy a coprocessor board with a real 32-bit microprocessor and add it to your existing microcomputer or replacement motherboard. This way you can still run all the existing software that you ran before UNIX arrived. Such systems range from $600 to $2,000 and are available from a variety of vendors including AST, Intel, Opus Systems and others.

It is also possible to go the other way. For example, many vendors sell IBM PC-compatible coprocessor boards that fit into their 32-bit bus. This would allow you to be able to run existing UNIX software and also begin to run DOS. See the section on Emulators and Coexistence elsewhere in this chapter for more on this.

The Future chapter discusses the future of UNIX on a PC. Another source of related material is "The UNIX System on the IBM PC" by Phil Hughes in *UNIXWORLD*, vol. 3, no. 3, March 1986.

12.8   Network File Systems

By using a personal workstation you have complete control of your own machine's processing power, but what about its files? You may have some files that are your own, but it is likely that most files you access are shared. For example, there is no reason to have your own copy of the C compiler.

Network file systems allow everyone to share files. This allows more convenient information sharing and provides better disk space usage. Furthermore, it is more cost effective to buy a single large disk rather than provide small cheap disks at each workstation. The small disks are typically so much slower that even access over a network makes communication with the large disk faster. Other advantages are that backups are easier, management is easier, and since UNIX treats devices like files, printers and others peripherals are just as easily shared.

Shared file systems reduce the need for multiple copies of the same information. Expensive resources such as printers, tape drives and special computing hardware can be shared. Two very popular (but incompatible) systems are NFS (developed by Sun) and RFS (developed by AT&T).

RFS is designed to provide UNIX file system semantics across a network of computers. The result is a file system that is quite transparent as to where your files reside. One drawback of this is that non-UNIX file systems cannot easily be integrated into RFS, since they do not support UNIX semantics. RFS is called *stateful*, because it maintains the state of open files at the file server where the file resides. This approach is very efficient but can cause difficulties when a remote file server crashes causing you to lose state. RFS is supplied as part of System V.

In contrast to RFS, NFS is *stateless*. This means that no state is maintained for open files at the remote server. In theory, this is less efficient since the remote file server may have to reopen a file for each network I/O transaction. However, caching helps dramatically. More importantly, when a remote file server crashes, recovery is transparent to the client since the server has no state to lose. Unfortunately, some UNIX semantics are impossible to support if the remote server does not save state. Thus, NFS does not support all extant UNIX programs. At the same time, the set of semantics supported is relatively primitive enough that most non-UNIX file systems can be accessed under NFS.

Both RFS and NFS are well supported and have a large set of adherents. Interestingly, we have seen implementations of NFS on top of RFS and vice versa for people who just have to have it all. Unfortunately, there is no clear choice – each system has its advantages and disadvantages. One thing that is clear is that they are the dominant network file systems at this time and probably will remain so.

The particular problem of accessing file systems from other operating systems may turn out to be an unsolvable problem for arbitrary systems. While NFS can do it, access is limited. For example, it is impossible for a UNIX system to understand some other operating system's protection mechanism. MS-DOS has no protection system to speak of. VAX/VMS on the other hand, has access control lists, which cannot possibly be mapped on to the UNIX file system. Other problems include mapping user IDs, file names, record formats, and so on. A paper which discusses the problem faced by a generic file system is "GFS Revisited – or – How I lived with Four Different Local File Systems" by Matt Koehler, *Summer 1987 USENIX Conference Proceedings*.

While not as popular, there are some other file systems that are worth mentioning. Peter Weinberger's Version 8 Network File System (described in the *Summer 1984 USENIX Conference Proceedings*) served as an example for many of the other UNIX network file systems, including the Extended File System (EFS) of Masscomp and Todd Brunhoff's RFS (not to be confused with AT&T's RFS) from Tektronix. Especially noteworthy about Brunhoff's RFS is that it is available for the cost of the media and postage, and it comes with complete sources. While you may not be interested in running it, the price makes it worthwhile for simply being able to study the code.

The Newcastle Connection was one of the first popular distributed UNIX file systems. Unlike the other systems mentioned here, the Newcastle Connection provided support for distributed files by providing a modified `open()` routine in the standard C library. The advantage of this over all the other approaches was that no change was necessary to the kernel to support it. While it had obvious disadvantages (such as nontransparent file names), it is often mentioned in research, as many people still use this approach for other distributed problems. You can read more about it in "The Newcastle Connection or UNIXes of the World Unite!" by D. Brownbridge et al. in *Software – Practice and Experience*, vol. 12, 1982.

CMU's Andrew has a file system called VICE. VICE was specifically designed to support a distributed file system of 5,000 workstations. Because of this, it works differently than the other file systems mentioned here. For example, `open()` normally causes transfer of the entire file to the workstation. This avoids any network transmission for `read()` and `write()`. Given reasonably sized disks, caching on a per file basis reduces loading on the network and servers substantially. VICE is further described in "The ITC Distributed File System" by M. Satyanarayanan, et al., *Proceedings of the 10th ACM Symposium on Operating System Principles*, December 1985.

Two other systems that are occasionally found on UNIX class machines are DEC's DECnet and Apollo's DOMAIN network. While both predate NFS and RFS, they were originally designed for each company's proprietary operating system, inhibiting distribution. This is unfortunate as each has interesting features. Apollo's network is the most unified of all the networks mentioned here in that it provides for transparent load sharing on CPUs distributed across the network.

12.9   Networking

Networking includes the topic of network file systems as well as ranging from low-level hardware to high-level software problems. While networks are a subject of intense debates at standards conferences, there are many proprietary schemes, site constraints, financial restrictions and changing technologies. So, approach networking with an open mind. Expect the solutions to require a lot of design work. There are few easy answers in the real world of networking.

Simply getting your UNIX machine on a network requires addressing the low-level hardware and software issues. The network may be a proprietary network such as Appletalk or a standard network such as IEEE 802.3. You will need the hardware such as interfaces to Ethernet, fiber optic or twisted pair, and you will need some software that understands the network protocols.

Once you have your system connected to the network, you need software that understands the other machines on the network. This includes networked file systems but can also mean print spooling, electronic mail, windowing, remote computation and distributed processing.

Two of the most common total solutions are TCP/IP based and OSI based. Many UNIX boxes are sold with TCP/IP support bundled in, making this very popular. TCP/IP was originally designed under a grant by the U.S. government to support the Arpanet, a network used by the Defense Department. Strictly speaking, it is not a product but a design. However, anyone's TCP/IP products are "interoperable" meaning that they allow any machine to communicate with any other machine no matter what operating system is running or how many bits in a byte one uses. For more information on TCP/IP, contact the Arpanet Network Information Center.

Remote Procedure Call (RPC)

Some of the technology used to implement network file systems is based on the concept of a remote procedure call. Code executing on one machine may call subroutines on a different machine. Distributed computing becomes possible with this technique as well.

OSI (Open Systems Interconnect) is a set of international standards that are also interoperable. However, the standards are much newer, and while potentially technically superior, have not been implemented by as many vendors as the TCP/IP protocols have. MAP and TOP are OSI-based standards designed specifically for particular environments. MAP from General Motors is used in manufacturing environments, and TOP from Boeing Computer Services is used in office environments. GOSIP from the U.S. National Bureau of Standards, is an OSI-based standard for government use.

The idea of interoperability is rather nice in theory but requires a substantial amount of computer power. For example, translating every single byte, say from EBCDIC to ASCII, can greatly slow down a file transfer. PCs, Macintoshes and other small computers are not capable of supporting multiple processes or anything requiring heavy computations. Thus, networking UNIX machines to many personal computers requires much more limited solutions. A good article on this topic is "PC DOS/UNIX Networking" by Judi Uttal in *UNIXWORLD*, vol. 4, no. 10, October 1987.

There are several other forms of networking readily available for UNIX systems, although not as popular as TCP/IP and OSI. These include SNA (IBM), XNS (Xerox), DECnet (DEC) and Appletalk (Apple). All of these started out as proprietary systems. And while some of them are technically sound, their strength is more due to their large installed bases and support by their parent company. TCP/IP and OSI, on the other hand, are successful due to their openness and availability. A good article on SNA in the UNIX environment is "SNA Communications Under UNIX" by Jerome Yochelson, *DEC Pro Extra*, May 1986.

12.10   Parallel Processing
"llooggiinn::"

For physical reasons related to gate delays, finite wire length and the propagation of electric signals, it is expected that CPU performance will reach a limit that cannot be broken no matter what technology is used. Our fastest computers use hardware within an order of magnitude of this limit. In order to surpass it, we must use multiple processing units at the same time. This is the basis of parallel processing.

Parallel processing can occur at many levels in a system. The lowest levels in hardware are quite common. For example, busses usually have separate lines for each address and data bit so they can be active concurrently. Going up a level, it is also quite common for CPUs to pipeline instruction fetching, decoding and execution with at least three separate processors working in parallel.

Machines with multiple execution units are capable of even richer parallelism. This level is typically the lowest level that is controllable by software making it the first level of interest to UNIX designers and programmers. And of course, the software that is concerned first with such hardware is the kernel.

The UNIX kernel was not originally written for parallel processing. Although device drivers work in parallel with the CPU, they do not have the same liberties to roam through memory that the CPU does. Modifications that must be made to the kernel to support multiple processors are typically to provide some type of protection to data structures that only the primary CPU accesses. For instance, multiple cooperating processors may share the queue of processes ready for service. When a processor is finished with one task, it takes the next ready process. The idea is that if we have say 100 processes and three processors, we can run in one-third the time required by only one processor. And if we add a processor, we will run in one-fourth the time. In reality there is some overhead for sharing access to common data structures but this can be quite minimal compared to user processing time. Systems using this technique are Encore, Elxsi and Sequent.

Certain types of hardware provide parallelism explicitly under user control. A limited form of this is when code must be generated to access CPU-peripherals such as a dedicated floating-point chip. One possible way of signaling this is by calling the C compiler with a different math library. The math library then accesses the floating-point chip like a peripheral.

A more sophisticated form appears in the VLIW (Very Long Instruction Word) technology of Multiflow Computer, Inc. Instructions generated by the VLIW compiler control a large number of dedicated logic units, allowing many operations to occur in a single cycle. In this case, the compiler effectively provides the parallelism at the user level, but without any assistance from the user. (This might be considered taking horizontal microcode to the extreme.)

Classical pipelining is available on supercomputers such as the Cray-2. Here, parallelism occurs at the user level. Although it is not necessary for the user to control it directly, algorithms designed for parallel execution show great improvements when running in such environments. On the other hand, more flexible communications exhibited by systems such as the BBN Butterfly and the Intel Hypercube demand much attention to algorithm design to show any improvement at all.

Good references on such systems are "Parallel Processing," a series of articles by Omri Serlin that appeared in *UNIXWORLD* starting in January 1986. The series reviews various types of parallel processing on UNIX machines. Other UNIX companies producing parallel computers include Alliant Computer Systems Corp., Arete Systems Corp., Concurrent Computer Corp., Elxsi, Encore Computer Corp., EnMasse Computer Corp., Flexible Computer Corp., Masscomp, Sequent Computer Systems Inc.

12.11   Real-Time Processing, UNIX Executives
"I want it now." – Elizabeth Ressler (at age 4)

Real-time computing refers to a computer system's ability to trigger and respond to external events within a known time period. For example, a computer that is controlling a robot arm might have to provide new joint positions 100 times per second in order to produce smooth motion.

UNIX was developed as a timesharing system with little regard to response time. There are only very crude tools in most UNIX systems for dealing with the problems of response and latency.

For instance, before BSD 4.2 and System III, it was impossible to get the system to suspend a process for intervals of less than a second. And even if you asked to `sleep` for some number of seconds, the system made no guarantees about when the process would resume saying, "*...may be an arbitrary amount longer because of other activity in the system.*"

Workarounds to these problems became common, but unfortunately, differed from site to site. Busy-waiting was the simplest solution for most users, although it provided no guarantees either. Another was to create an I/O device in which, reading n bytes from it, would do nothing but have the side effect of taking n milliseconds to do it. This had the advantage of better response, since the driver (running in the kernel) could reschedule the process as soon as it was done. However, there were still no guarantees since another process could still be executing with higher priority.

Worse, processes could be swapped out to disk while system calls were executing. There was no way to lock a process or particular pages of a process in memory.

Besides timing, there are other longstanding problems with UNIX supporting real-time processing. For example, scheduling is crude. The `nice` system call provides hints to the scheduler, but in a very limited way. Most systems do not support creating files contiguously for optimal disk access, or locking pages of memory, or otherwise communicating with the pager. Many systems have unreliable or overly complex and expensive signaling and synchronization mechanisms for access to shared resources.

Newer versions of UNIX, beginning with System III and 4.2BSD, support finer levels of control with the addition of extra system calls. These systems still do not guarantee response times, but they improve the likelihood dramatically. The resulting systems are sufficiently responsive that real-time tasks can be implemented. Even better are UNIX systems designed for real-time response to begin with. While you may see what resembles a UNIX system, do not be surprised to find that these real-time UNIX systems have completely rewritten kernels. Some of the companies providing real-time UNIX systems are Alcyon, AT&T, Gould, Hewlett-Packard (Spectrum), Honeywell, IBM (AIX/VRM),

Integrated Solutions (UniWorks), MassComp (RTU), Modcomp (REALIX), and Motorola (cXV/RT).

Since UNIX has been so lacking in real-time facilities, many companies have offered UNIX-like systems built around an entirely new kernel. With standardization of real-time UNIX extensions expected after 1989, it is entirely reasonable to look to a non-AT&T based UNIX-workalike. Some companies providing such real-time UNIX-like systems are Action Instruments (IC-DOS), Charles River Data Systems (UNOS), Technical Systems Consultants (UniFLEX).

Yet another alternative for generating fast UNIX systems is a UNIX executive. *Executives* are operating systems without a lot of baggage, like a file system, a shell and all the user-level programs. Again, this is an area that is not standardized, but typically such systems are used for controllers that require a set of cooperating applications under control of a minimal UNIX kernel.

Such systems are often completely ROM'ed (a floppy is a luxury here) and start running at power-on. Good candidates for running under executives are applications that do not change often, but are complex and have real-time requirements, such as network gateways, laser printers and robot controllers.

Companies offering these kinds of executives are Emerge Systems (RTUX), Eyring Research Institute (pDOS), Industrial Programming Inc. (MTOS), JMI Software (C Executive), Ready Systems (VRTX) and Software Components Group (pSOS). Many of these also include cross-development tools such as downloaders, cross-compilers, cross-debuggers and cross-assemblers.

An excellent reference for further information on real-time UNIX is the article "UNIX Overcomes Its Real-Time Limitations" by Wendy B. Rauch-Hindin in *UNIXWORLD*, vol. 4, no. 11, November 1987.

12.12   Security

"If you give someone who knows about computer systems enough time ..., he'll find a way to defeat the existing controls." – David Stryker in *Subversion of a 'Secure' Operating System*

UNIX originally had a nominal security system that followed the classic philosophy of solving 90 percent of the problems with 10 percent of the work. But while spartan, the security system of UNIX was nonetheless superior to that of most other operating systems at the time.

   UNIX was also unique in being up front about its security system. The fascinating papers "On the Security of UNIX" by Dennis Ritchie, and "Password Security" by Robert Morris and Ken Thompson, document the evolution of UNIX security, including several times when it was successfully compromised. The authors note that one of the biggest blemishes in UNIX security is that the concept of a superuser with unlimited privileges means that it is possible to breach an entire system with only one password. This is kind of like putting the trap door right on your front porch, where everyone knows to start looking for it. (Serious security is only achieved by buying your own machine, and not hooking it up to modems or a networks.)

Crypt Breaker's Workbench

UNIX was originally supplied with an encryption function based on the German WWII Enigma cipher. Passwords were encrypted this way, for example. The cipher was known to be breakable, but as Morris and Thompson point out, key searching using dictionaries, mailing lists, valid license plate numbers in the state, and so on, was easier than trying to develop a general method of inverting the encryption algorithm.

In 1984, Reeds and Weinberger published a paper in the BLTJ describing several cryptanalytic techniques that could be used to defeat the UNIX Enigma implementation. In 1986, Bob Baldwin released the "Crypt Breaker's Workbench." CBW incorporated Reeds and Weinberger's suggestions with several enhancements, providing a set of tools that allows you to easily crack most ciphered messages. CBW is available in the `comp.source.unix` archives.

UNIX is now supplied with the U.S. National Bureau of Standards' DES (Data Encryption Standard). DES is much stronger than Enigma, and although also theoretically breakable, would require the resources of a supercomputer for several days even with the CBW approach. DES is slow when implemented in software, but key searching on a hardware implementation of DES is probably still a profitable means of attack.

Export of DES to *nonfriendly* countries is controlled by the U.S. Department of Commerce. They have taken a very conservative stance on DES, and thus a restricted version of System V exists, solely for export. This *International Edition* comes without the crypt command, and various other extensions which use DES.

Of course, this was partly for convenience. After all, the designers were the primary users of the system. And UNIX grew up in research laboratories and schools, where security was not a priority. The default file protection allowed anyone to read anyone else's files.

This was great for learning. For example, when you wanted to see an example of how to use a function you weren't familiar with, and there wasn't enough (or any) documentation in the manuals, you could just search the entire system (usually with a `grep` nested in a `find`).

Now that UNIX lives in a networked environment, this security (or lack of it) extends across networks. While networks often enforce a layer of security of their own, many LANs bend over backwards attempting to extend the ease of using UNIX from one machine, to the entire network. (For example, some local area networks allow a superuser from one machine, root access to all the machines on the network.)

Nonetheless, people insisted on keeping data secure, and UNIX has certainly grown in complexity because of this. Most UNIX systems give you a fair chance at doing a good job of protecting your data, if you use a little common sense and plug all the right holes. (For example, using long passwords and changing them frequently is a must on any computer, and no less so on a UNIX system.)

There are several commercial products that actually prowl through your UNIX system looking for possible security problems. These include SystemAdmin (UniSolutions Associates) and USECURE (Unitech Software Inc.). Another way to learn about security holes is to read the `comp.unix.wizards` newsgroup on Usenet.

The National Computer Security Center of the U.S. Department of Defense has established a grading system (known as the *Orange Book*) for all computer system's security. Actually getting a rating requires a lengthy period (don't bet on under a year) and a lot of work, so it is not surprising that few UNIX vendors are even applying for the lowest, weakest rating. As of July 1987, only Gould's UTX/32S had a C2 (minimal security) rating.

Secure Doesn't Mean Idiot-Proof

After having the NCSC certify UTX/32S at the C2 level of security, Gould offered a color television to anyone who could read a particular protected file, during the 1987 UNIX Expo.

Darryl Wagoner decided the system was indeed secure, but that the operators weren't. He convinced one of them to run `ls` in his directory, which contained a trojan-horse version of `ls`. Normally this would not have been a problem, but the operators had earlier followed a third-party vendor's directions while installing some software. The directions included putting . at the beginning of the path. Once they had committed that mistake, the trojan horse could execute, and Darryl had his way.

Unfortunately, modifying UNIX to be more secure means denying some of the freedom that has made it so attractive in the past. For example, the superuser notion allows unrestricted freedom to bypass any normal security conventions. This concept has no place in a secure system.

The article "How Secure is 'Secure'" by Gary Grossman in *UNIX REVIEW* vol. 4, no. 8, August 1986 is recommended for further reading on UNIX and the Orange Book ratings. Another article on security is "Security for Superusers, Or How to Break the UNIX System" by Rick Farrow in *UNIX-WORLD*, vol. 3, no. 5, May 1986. Two papers on B-level systems appeared in the *Summer 1987 USENIX Conference Proceedings*: "UNIX without the Superuser" by M. S. Hecht et al., and "Partial Model for a B-Level UNIX" by Frank Knowles. The October 1984 AT&T BLTJ has a set of papers on security, including the one discussing how to break `crypt`.

12.13   Workstations

Workstations are difficult to define rigorously. Our definition of a workstation is a single-user multitasking computer system with at least 4Mb of RAM, a 1,000 x 1,000 pixel screen in either black and white or color, a pointing device such as a mouse, disk storage of at least 100Mb, and a 1 to 10MIPS CPU. In practice, this definition may fail to capture certain attributes that are important to people. For example, many workstations have no disks, accessing files over a local area network.

More important than the minutiae of the definition is the spirit of it. Workstations are almost as powerful as mainframes for a fraction of the price. They're personal – they sit on your desk. No one else steals your cycles. If your coworker's workstation crashes, yours continues running.

While UNIX wasn't born or designed to run on a workstation, it has clearly come to dominate it and reshape it. Yes, it did exist before UNIX infested the world, but on expensive hardware with proprietary operating systems that made dedicated applications like CAD/CAM the primary user of such tools.

Besides destroying most other operating systems throughout the workstation world, the primary thing that UNIX did was to bring down their price. While some may argue that this was inevitable given time and the ever decreasing price of hardware, UNIX forced vendors to be price competitive as well as to allow functional comparison of workstations. This was impossible before UNIX arrived.

Indeed, prior workstation vendors have either left the scene (e.g., Three Rivers Corp.), admitted UNIX into their universe (e.g., Apollo), or slashed profit margins to the bare minimum to survive. Whether new workstation vendors provide UNIX or something much superior and innovative, they face stiff competition in the real world.

Don't get us wrong – we would willingly give up our UNIX workstations if only there was something better. We keep careful watch on potential hopefuls including the Amiga, the Atari ST, the Mac II and the many Smalltalk workstations.

After the JAWS wars (covered in the History chapter), the market has settled out somewhat. A few of the original workstations vendors remain such as Apollo, Sun and numerous vendors using Microsoft's and SCO's XENIX. Some markets have specialized vendors such as Silicon Graphics and Pixar for graphics and Masscomp for real-time scientific work. All of the old mainframe vendors (IBM and the seven dwarfs) have deigned to offer UNIX workstations to survive including IBM, Data General, DEC, HP and Unisys (the merger of Sperry, Rand, Univac and countless other companies). Other workstation vendors worthy of note include Intergraph Corp., Prime Computer Inc., and Tektronix Inc.

Appendix A: Addresses

This appendix contains the addresses of vendors, schools, and groups referred to throughout the book. A name in parentheses preceding an address denotes a shorthand name that many refer to the addressee by. For example, the "Association for Computing Machinery" is usually referred to as "ACM." (And who can blame them with a name like that?!)

Electronic mail addresses, when given, are preferred over phone or postal mail.

3B/Journal
(See Owens-Liang Publications, Ltd.)

ABC Development Systems, Inc.
2489 Rice Street, #40
St. Paul, MN 55113
612-482-8584

Abmind Corporation
722 Live Oak Way
San Jose, CA 95129
408-257-7298

Absoft Corp.
4268 N. Woodward Avenue
Royal Oak, MI 48072
313-549-7111

Access Technology, Inc.
6 Pleasant Street
South Natick, MA 01760
617-655-9191

Ace Microsystems Ltd.
Challenger House
125 Gunnersbury Lane, London
England W3 8LH
01-993-5036

Acme Computer Co.
P.O. Box 51193
Seattle, WA 98115
206-522-6655

Acorn Systems, Ltd.
911 South 47th Street
Philadelphia, PA 19143
215-387-6150

Adaptive Optics Associates
54 Cambridgepark Drive
Cambridge, MA 02140
617-864-0201

Addison-Wesley Publishing Co.
Jacob Way
Reading, MA 01867
800-447-2226

Adobe Systems, Inc.
1585 Charleston Road
P.O. Box 7900
Mountain View, CA 94039-7900
415-961-4400

AGS Computers, Inc.
1139 Spruce Drive
Mountainside, NJ 07092
201-654-4321

AIM Technology
3350 West Bayshore Road, Suite 203
Palo Alto, CA 94303
415-856-8649

Alcyon Corp.
5010 Shoreham Place
San Diego, CA 92122
619-587-1155

Alliant Computer Systems Corp.
42 Nagog Park
Acton, MA 01720
617-263-9110

ALMA
Rue du Tour de l'eau
ZAC de Champ Roman
38400 St. Martin d'Heres
France
33-76-51-23-00

ALSYS S.A.
29 Avenue de Versailles
78170 La Celle Saint-Cloud
3-918-12-44

Altos Computer Systems
2641 Orchard Parkway
San Jose, CA 95134
408-946-6700

Amdahl Corp.
1250 East Arques Avenue
P.O. Box 3470
Sunnyvale, CA 94088
408-737-5489

American Management Systems Inc.
1777 N. Kent Street
Arlington, VA 22209
703-841-6289

AMIX, c/o IPA
P.O. Box 919
Ramat-Gan
Israel, 52109
00972-3-715770
amix@bimacs.bitnet
amix@bimacs.biu.ac.il

Ana-systems
697 Saturn Court
Foster City, CA 94404
415-341-1768

ANSI
1430 Broadway
New York, NY 10018
212-354-3300

ANSI X3J11 Committee
c/o Thomas Plum, Vice Chair
Plum Hall Inc.
1 Spruce Avenue
Cardiff, NJ 08232

Apple Computer, Inc.
20525 Mariani Avenue
Cupertino, CA 95014
408-996-1010

Apollo Computer Inc.
330 Billerica Road
Chelmsford, MA 01824
617-256-6600

(ADUS)
Apollo DOMAIN Users' Society
c/o Andrea Woloski, ADUS Coordinator
Apollo Computer Inc.
330 Billerica Road
Chelmsford, MA 01824
617-256-6600, x4448

Ardent Computer Corp.
880 Maude Avenue
Sunnyvale, CA 94086
408-732-0400

Arete Systems Corp.
2040 Hartog Drive
San Jose, CA 95131
408-263-9711

Arpanet Network Information Center
SRI International
Menlo Park, CA 94025
415-859-3695
NIC@SRI-NIC.ARPA

Artelligence, Inc.
14902 Preston Road, Suite 212-252
Dallas, TX 75240
214-437-0361

Asicom, S.A.
Aragon, 264, 264, 6
08007 Barcelona
Spain
3-2159000

ASP
711 Chemeketa Drive
San Jose, CA 95123
408-226-8819

(ACM)
Association for Computing Machinery
11 West 42nd Street
New York, NY 10036
212-869-7440

Association Francaise des Utilisateurs d'UNIX
Supelec, Plateau du Moulon
91190 Gif-Sur-Yvette
France
1-60-19-1013

AT&T Bell Laboratories Technical Journal
Room 1H321
101 J. F. Kennedy Parkway
Short Hills, NJ 07078

AT&T Customer Information Center
2833 North Franklin Road
Indianapolis, IN 46219
800-432-6600

AT&T Information Systems
190 River Road
Summit, NJ 07901
201-658-7690

AT&T UNIX Software Licensing
P.O. Box 25000
Salem Building
Greensboro, NC 27420-5000
800-828-8649

AT&T UNIX System Training
P.O. Box 45038
Jacksonville, FL 32232-9974
800-247-1212

August Mohr Consulting & Publishing
2670 Lode Street
P.O. Box 1757
Santa Cruz, CA 95061
408-475-9711

Autodesk, Inc.
2320 Marinship Way
Sausalito, CA 94965

(AUUG)
Australian UNIX Users' Group
P.O. Box 366
Kensington
N.S.W. 2033
Australia
61-3-344-5225
uunet!munnari!auug
auug@munnari.oz.au

(BRL)
Ballistic Research Lab
ATTN: SLCBR-SE-P
Aberdeen Proving Ground, MD 21005
301-278-6884

Basis Inc.
5700 Harper Drive NE, #290
Albuquerque, NM 87109
505-821-4407

Basmark Corp.
1717 East Ninth Street, #911
Cleveland, OH 44114
216-621-7650

bbj Computers International Inc.
3707 Williams Road
San Jose, CA 95117
408-249-9900

(BellCore)
Bell Communications Research
435 South Street
Morristown, NJ 07960

BIM, S.A.
Kwikstraat 4
B-3078 Everberg
Belgium
2-759-59-25

Boeing Computer Services Company
Software and Education Products Grp.
P.O. Box 24346, Mail Stop 7K-10
Seattle, WA 98124

(BBN)
Bolt Beranek and Newman, Inc.
10 Moulton Street
Cambridge, MA 02238

BOSS Systems
942A Sherwood Avenue
Coquitlam, British Columbia
Canada V3K 1A9
604-522-0661

Britton Lee, Inc.
14600 Winchester
Los Gatos, CA 95030
408-378-7000

(BSTJ)
See AT&T Bell Laboratories Technical Journal

BYTE
70 Main Street
Peterborough, NH 03458
603-924-9281

CAETEC Systems, Inc.
1 Dunwoody Park
Suite 130
Atlanta, GA 30338
404-395-7844

Cambridge Digital
P.O. Box 568
65 Bent Street
Cambridge, MA 02139
800-343-5504

Canadian Information Processing Society
221 Jameson Avenue
Toronto, Ontario
Canada M6K 2Y3

Canadian UNIX Network & Int'l Xchange
62 Simpson Street
St. Catharines, Ontario
Canada

(CMU)
Department of Computer Science
Carnegie-Mellon University
Pittsburgh, PA 15213
412-268-2565

CBM Type
549-A Weddell Drive
Sunnyvale, CA 94089
408-734-4300

Clever Connections Ltd.
Unit 2.10, 75 Whitechapel Road
London
England E1 1DU
01-247-7467

Columbia University
Computer Science Department
New York, NY 10027

Comeau Computing
91-34 120 Street
Richmond Hill, NY 11418
718-849-2355

CommUNIXations
(see /usr/group)

Computer Literacy Bookshop
520 Lawrence Expressway
Sunnyvale, CA 94086
408-730-9955

Computer Systems Resources, Inc.
Annette Hall
1170 South Omni International
Atlanta, GA 30303
404-586-9663

Computer Technology Group
310 South Michigan Avenue
Chicago, Illinois 60604
800-323-8649

Computing Systems
(see USENIX Association)

Concentric Associates, Inc.
Harmon Cove Towers, #8A
Secaucus, NJ 07094
201-866-2880

Concept Omega Corp.
102 Old Camplain Road
P.O. Box 1035
Somerville, NJ 08876
201-722-7790

Concurrent Computer Corp.
197 Hance Avenue
Tinton Falls, NJ 07724
201-758-7000

Conner Scelza Associates, Inc.
4204 East Ewalt Road
Givsonia, PA 15044
412-443-3222

Control-C Software Inc.
6441 SW Canyon Court
Portland, OR 97221
503-292-3508

Convex Computer Corp.
701 Plano Road
Richardson, TX 75081
214-952-0200

Cray Research Inc.
608 Second Avenue
Minneapolis, MN 55402
612-333-5889

CRIL
12 Bis Rue Jean Jaures
92807 Puteaux
France
1-47-76-34-37

Cromemco, Inc.
280 Bernardo Avenue
P.O. Box 7400
Mountain View, CA 94039
415-964-7400

Cucumber Bookshop, Inc.
5611 Kraft Drive
Rockville, MD 20852
301-881-2722

C Users' Group
(see R&D Publications, Inc.)

Custom Software Systems
P.O. Box 678
Natick, MA 01760
617-653-2555

Daniel Farkas and Associates
P.O. Box 74
Katonah, NY 10536
914-232-3875

Data Access Corporation
1400 SW 119 Avenue
Miami, FL 33156
305-238-0012

Databoard Inc.
323 Vintage Park Drive
Foster City, CA 94404
415-571-8811

Data Language Corporation
47 Manning Road
Billerica, MA 01823
617-663-5000

Datix Systems
30 Rustic Road
Yaphank, NY 11980
516-924-7920

Definicon Systems
31324 Via Colinas #108/9
Westlake Village, CA 91362
818-889-1646

(DEC)
Digital Equipment Corporation
Continental Boulevard
Merrimack, NH 03054
603-884-0884

(DEC Educational Services)
Digital Equipment Corporation
Educational Services BUO/58-12
12 Crosby Drive
Bedford, MA 01730
617-276-4949

(DECUS)
DEC Users Society
219 Boston Post Road
BP02
Marlborough, MA 01752
617-480-3418

Digital Information Systems Corp.
11070 White Rock Road, #210
Rancho Cordova, CA 95670
916-635-7300

Digital Sound Corporation
2030 Alameda Padre Serra
Santa Barbara, CA 93013
805-569-0700

Djavaheri Bros.
697 Saturn Court
P.O. Box 4759
Foster City, CA 94404
415-341-1768

(DKUUG)
Dansk UNIX-system Burger Gruppe
Studiestrade 6
DK-1455 Copenhagen K
Denmark
45-1120115

D. L. Buck and Associates, Inc.
6920 Santa Teresa Boulevard
San Jose, CA 95119
408-972-2825

DSD Corporation
10632 N.E. 37th Circle
P.O. Box 2669
Kirkland, WA 98083
206-822-2252

Dyadic Systems, Ltd.
Park House, The High Street
Alton, Hampshire
United Kingdom GU34 1EN
420-87024

Eakins Associates, Inc.
67 East Evelyn Avenue
Mountain View, CA 94041
415-969-5109

Elsevier Science Publishers Co Inc.
P.O. Box 1663
Grand Central Station
New York, NY 10163

Elxsi
2334 Lundy Place
San Jose, CA 95131
408-942-111

Encore Computer Corporation
257 Cedar Hill Street
Marlborough, MA 01752
617-460-0500

ENDOT, Inc.
11001 Cedar Avenue
Cleveland, OH 44106
216-229-8900

EnMasse Computer Corp.
125 Nagog Park
Acton, MA 01720
617-263-8711

Enterprising Ideas, Inc.
2190 West Drake, Suite 325
Fort Collins, CO 80526
303-223-5345

(EUUG)
European UNIX Systems User Group
Owles Hall
Buntingford, Herfordshire
England SG9 9PL
44-763-73039
uunet!mcvax!inset!euug
euug@inset.co.uk

Fenix Software
P.O. Box 15649
Sarasota, FL 34277
813-351-5532

Flexible Computer Corp.
1801 Royal Lane, Bldg. 8
Dallas, TX 75229
214-869-1234

Frame Technology Corporation
2911 Zanker Road
San Jose, CA 95134
408-433-3311

Franz Inc.
1995 University Avenue
Berkeley, CA 94704
415-548-3600

Free Software Foundation
1000 Mass Avenue
Cambridge, MA 02138
617-876-3296

The Gawain Group
47 Potomac Street
San Francisco, CA 94117
415-626-7581

GE Consumer Services
Department 02B
401 North Washington Street
Rockville, MD 20850
800-638-9636

General Motors Corp.
BOC HQ – Facilities Engineering
30009 Van Dyke Avenue
Warren, Michigan 48090

Genus Systems Ltd.
9A St. Colme Street
Edinburgh
United Kingdom
031-225-6934

Global Engineering Documents
2805 McGaw
Irvine, CA 92714
714-261-1455

Glockenspiel, Ltd.
30 Iona Crescent
Dublin 9
Ireland
+353-1-735140

Government Computer News
1620 Elton Road
Silver Spring, MD 20903
301-445-4405

Grand Software, Inc.
8464 Kirkwood Drive
Los Angeles, CA 90046
213-650-1089

Handle Technologies Inc.
5429 LBJ Fwy., Suite 720
Dallas, TX 75240
214-458-1415

HCR Corp.
130 Bloor Street West
10th Floor
Toronto, Ontario
Canada M5S 1N5
416-922-1937

(HP)
Hewlett-Packard, Co.
19447 Pruneridge Avenue
Cupertino, CA 95014
408-447-5126

Holistic Technology
Grona Gatan 59
414 54 Gothenburg
Sweden

Icon International, Inc.
774 S. 400 E.
Orem, UT 84058
800-225-6888

IEEE, Computer Society of the
1730 Massachusetts Avenue, N.W.
Washington, DC 20036
714-821-8380

IEEE/CS P1003
Chairperson, c/o James Isaak
Digital Equipment Corp.
ZK03-2/Y24
110 Spit Brook Road
Nashua, NH 03062
603-881-0480
decvax!isaak
isaak@decvax.dec.com

Impacc Associates
P.O. Box 93
Gwynedd Valley, PA 19437
215-699-7235

IMSL Inc.
2500 ParkWest Tower One
2500 City West Boulevard
Houston, TX 77042
713-782-6060

Inference Corporation
5300 W. Century Boulevard
Los Angeles, CA 90045
213-417-7997

InfoPro Systems
P.O. Box 220
Rescue, CA 95672
916-677-5870
infopro!unique

Information Builders, Inc.
1250 Broadway
New York, NY 10001
212-736-4433

Information Concepts, Inc.
1331 H Street, NW
Washington, DC 20005
202-628-4400

Information Technology Coordinator
Carnegie-Mellon University
Pittsburgh, PA 15213
412-268-6700

Informix Software Inc.
4100 Bohannon Drive
Menlo Park, CA 94025
415-322-4100

The Instruction Set
City House, 190 City Road
London
England EC1V 2QH
44-1-251-2128

Intergraph Corp.
1 Madison Industrial Park
Huntsville, AL 35807
205-772-6318

Integrated Computer Systems
P.O. Box 45405
Los Angeles, CA 90045
213-417-8888

Integrated Micro Products
1140 Ringwood Court
San Jose, CA 95131
408-943-1902

Intel Corp.
2404 W. Beardsley Road
Phoenix, AZ 85027
602-869-3805

Intellicorp
1975 El Camino Real West
Mountain View, CA 94040
415-965-5700

Intel Scientific Computers
15201 N.W. Greenbrier Parkway
Beaverton, OR 97006
503-629-7608

Interactive Development Environments
150 Fourth Street, #210
San Francisco, CA 94103
415-543-0900

Interactive Systems Corp.
2401 Colorado Avenue
Third Floor
Santa Monica, CA 90404
213-453-8649

(IBM)
International Business Machines Corp.
Old Orchard Road
Armonk, NY 10504
814-765-1900

International Computers Ltd.
GSBC, Lovelace Road
Bracknell, Berkshire
England RG12 4T2
01-788-7272

International Data Corp.
5 Speen Street
Framingham, MA 01701
617-872-8200

(ISO)
International Organization for Standardization
1, rue de Varembe
Geneve, Switzerland

Intrinsic OY
Kauppakatu 3 A
33200 Tampere
Finland
c77@intrin.fi

I.P. Sharp Associates, Inc.
1200 First Federal Plaza
Rochester, N.Y. 14614
(716) 546-7270

Irish UNIX Systems User Group
c/o John Carolan
19 Belvedere Place
Dublin 1 Ireland
353-1-735159

Japan UNIX Society
#505 Towa-Hanzomon Corp. Bldg.
2-12 Hayabusa-cho
Chiyoda-ku, Tokyo 102
Japan
81-03-234-2611

Jim Joyce's UNIX Bookstore
47 Potomac Street
San Francisco, CA 94117
415-626-7581

JMI Software Consultants, Inc.
904 Sheble Lane
P.O. Box 481
Spring House, PA 19477
215-628-0846

Korean UNIX User Group
ETRI
P.O. Box 8
Daedug Science Town
Chungnam 300-32
Republic of Korea
82-042-822-4455

Laboratory Microsystems, Inc.
3007 Washington Boulevard #230
P.O. Box 10430
Marina del Rey, CA 90295
213-306-7412

Lachman Associates Inc.
1901 North Naper Boulevard
Naperville, IL 60566
312-505-9100

Lifeboat Associates, Inc.
55 South Broadway
Tarrytown, NY 10591
914-332-1875

Locus Computing Corp.
3330 Ocean Park Boulevard, #101
Santa Monica, CA 90405
213-452-2435

Logic Programming Associates, Ltd.
Royal Victoria Patriotic Building, #4
Trinity Road, London
England SW18 3SX
01-871-2016

Logicware Inc.
1000 Finch Avenue W., Ste. 600
Toronto, Ontario
Canada M3J 2V5
416-665-0022

Lucid, Inc.
707 Laurel Street
Menlo Park, CA 94025
800-843-4204

Lugaru Software Ltd.
5740 Darlington Road
Pittsburgh, PA 15217
412-421-5911

Lurnix
Number Fifty-two
2560 Bancroft Way
Berkeley, CA 94707
415-849-2167

Marc Software International, Inc.
260 Sheridan Avenue
Palo Alto, CA 94306
415-326-1971

Mark Williams Company
1430 W. Wrightwood Avenue
Chicago, IL 60614
312-472-4459

(MIT)
Massachusetts Institute of Technology
545 Technology Square
Cambridge, MA 02139

MASSCOMP
1 Technology Park
Westford, MA 01886
617-692-6200

MetaWare Inc.
903 Pacific Avenue, Suite 201
Santa Cruz, CA 95060
408-429-6382

Micro Applications and Hardware
15 Princess Street
Sausalito, CA 94965
415-331-6459

Micro Focus
2465 East Bayshore Road
Suite 400
Palo Alto, CA 94303
415-856-4161

Microport Systems, Inc.
10 Victor Square
Scotts Valley, CA 95066
408-438-8649

Microsoft Corp.
16011 N.E. 36th Wy.
P.O. Box 97017
Redmond, WA 98073
206-882-8080

Micro/Systems Journal
M&T Publishing, Inc.
501 Galveston Drive
Redwood City, CA 94063
415-366-3600

Microtek Research
3930 Freedom Circle
Suite 101
Santa Clara, CA 95054
408-551-5554

Microware Systems Corp.
1866 NW 114th Street
Des Moines, IA 50322
515-224-1929

Miller Freeman Publications
Circulation Department
500 Howard Street
San Francisco, CA 94105
415-397-1881

MindCraft, Inc.
953 Industrial Avenue, #125
Palo Alto, CA 94303
415-493-7277

MIPS Computer Systems
930 Arques Avenue
Sunnyvale, CA 94086
408-720-1700

Mortice Kern Systems
35 King Street North
Waterloo, Ontario
Canada N2J2W9
519-884-2251

Mosaic Software Inc.
1972 Massachusetts Avenue
Cambridge, MA 02140
617-491-2434

Motorola Computer Systems Inc.
10700 North De Anza Boulevard
Cupertino, CA 95014
408-864-4122

Mt. Xinu
2560 Ninth Street #312
Berkeley, CA 94710
415-644-0146

Multiflow Computer, Inc.
175 North Main Street
Branford, CT 06405
800-777-1428

(NBS)
National Bureau of Standards
Gaithersburg, MD 20899
301-975-2000

(NCSC)
National Computer Security Center
9800 Savage Road
Fort Meade, MD 20755
301-859-4500

National UNIX User Group/Netherlands
p/a Xirion bv Strawinskylaan 1135
1077 XX Amsterdam
The Netherlands

Nayland Associates
Route 2, Box 352
Nebo, NC 28761
704-652-1801

Neal Nelson & Associates
185 N. Wabash Avenue, #1908
Chicago, IL 60601
312-332-3242

(NZUSUGI)
New Zealand UNIX Systems User Group, Inc.
P.O. Box 585
Hamilton
New Zealand
64-9-454000

NKR Research
4040 Moorpark Avenue, Suite 209
San Jose, CA 95117
408-249-2612

Numerical Algorithms Group
1101 31st Street, Suite 100
Downers Grove, IL 60515
312-971-2337

Oasys
60 Aberdeen Avenue
Cambridge, MA 02138
617-491-4180

Oesterreicheische UNIX Benutzergruppe
P.O. Box 119
A-1041 Vienna
Austria
222-58801-4056

Olympus Software Inc.
1733 S. 1100 E.
Salt Lake City, UT 84105
801-487-4534

Omtool Corp.
1445 Main Street #26
P.O. Box 477
Tewksbury, MA 01876
617-851-6245

Oracle Systems Corp.
29 Davis Drive
Belmont, CA 94002
415-854-7350

Oregon Software
6915 S.W. Macadam Avenue
Portland, OR 97219
503-245-2202

Oregon State University
Department of Computer Science
Corvallis, OR 97331

O'Reilly & Associates, Inc.
632 Petaluma Avenue
Sebastopol, CA 95472
(707) 829-0515

Owens-Liang Publications, Ltd.
P.O. Box 2409
Redmond, WA 98073-2409
206-868-0913
attmail!alpha!jou

Palomino Computer Systems, Inc.
2111 E. Baseline F-5
Tempe, AZ 85283
602-838-5993

Parallel Computers Inc.
3004 Mission Street
Santa Cruz, CA 95060
408-429-1338

ParcPlace Systems
2400 Geng Road
Palo Alto, CA 94303
800-822-7880

Patricia Seybold's Office Computing Group
148 State Street
Boston, MA 02109

Parkridge Computer Systems Inc.
710 Dorval Drive, Suite 115
Oakville, Ontario
Canada L6K 3V7
416-842-6873

PD32 Users Group
Dan Efron
8910 Westmoreland Lane
Minneapolis MN 55426

Philon, Inc.
641 Avenue of the Americas
New York, NY 10011
212-807-0303

Pixar
P.O. Box 13719
San Rafael, CA 94913
415-258-8100

Plum Hall, Inc.
1 Spruce Avenue
Cardiff, NJ 08232
609-927-3770

Plus Five Computer Services
765 Westwood Drive, #10A
Clayton, MO 63105
314-725-9492

Portal Communications Co.
19720 Auburn Drive
Cupertino, CA 95014
408-973-9111

Practical Computing, Inc.
1030 West Maude Avenue, #511
Sunnyvale, CA 94086
408-749-8900

Prentice-Hall, Inc.
Route 9W
Englewood Cliffs, NJ 07632
201-592-2223

Prime Computer, Inc.
Prime Park
Natick, MA 01760
617-655-8000

Project Athena
MIT E40
77 Massachusetts Avenue
Cambridge, MA 02139

Quadratron Systems Inc.
15260 Ventura Boulevard, 18th Fl.
Sherman Oaks, CA 91403
818-789-8588

Quality Software Products
348 South Clark Drive
Beverly Hills, CA 90211
213-659-1560

Quantitative Technology Corporation
8700 SW Creekside Pl. Suite D
Beaverton, OR 97005
503-626-3081

Quintus Computer Systems, Inc.
2345 Yale Street
Palo Alto, CA 94306
415-494-3612

Radian Corporation
8501 MoPac Boulevard
P.O. Box 9948
Austin, TX 78766
512-454-4797

Rapitech Systems, Inc.
75 Montebello Rd
Suffern, NY 10901
914-368-3000

R&D Publications Inc.
P.O. Box 97
McPherson, KS 67460
316-241-1065

Relational Technology
1080 Marina Village Parkway
Alameda, CA 94501
800-446-4737

Rhodnius Inc.
250 Bloor Street E.
Toronto, Ontario
Canada M4W 1E6
416-922-1743

The r/l group
7623 Leviston Street
El Cerrito, CA 94530
415-527-1438

Robinson, Schaffer & Wright
711 California Street
Santa Cruz, CA 95060
408-429-6229

Root Computers Ltd.
Saunderson House, Hayne Street
London
England EC1A 9HH
44-1-606-7799

R Systems, Inc.
10310 Markison Road
Dallas, TX 75238
214-343-9188

Ryan-McFarland Corp.
609 Deep Valley Drive
Rolling Hills Est., CA 90274
213-541-4828

Saber Software, Inc.
30 JFK Street
Cambridge, MA 02138
617 876-7636

(SCO)
The Santa Cruz Operation, Inc.
400 Encinal Street
P.O. Box 1900
Santa Cruz, CA 95061
800-626-8649

Scientia Computer Applications Pte Ltd.
10 Anson Road, #24-16A
International Plaza
Singapore 0207
65-2242866

Scientific Placement, Inc.
P.O. Box 19949
Houston, TX 77224
713-496-6100

Sequent Computer Systems Inc.
15450 S.W. Koll Parkway
Beaverton, OR 97006
503-626-5700

SHL Systemhouse, Inc.
99 Bank Street, 3rd Floor
Ottawa, Ontario
Canada K1P 6B9
613-236-9734

Silicon Graphics Inc.
2011 Sterling Road
Mountain View, CA 94043
415-960-1980

Silicon Valley Software, Inc.
10011 North Foothill Boulevard, #111
Cupertino, CA 95014
408-725-8890

Silvar-Lisco
1080 Marsh Road
Menlo Park, CA 94025
415-324-0700

SimuCad
920 Incline Way, Bldg. 2
Box 3400
Incline Village, NV 89450
702-831-1399

Simulation Software Ltd.
760 Headley Drive
London, Ontario
Canada N6H 3V8
519-657-8229

Singapore UNIX Association
c/o Computer Systems Advisors Ltd.
203 Henderson Road, #1207-1214
Singapore 0315
273-0681

Smart Systems Technology
7700 Leesburg Pike
Falls Church, VA 22043
708-893-0429

Sobell Associates
333 Cobalt Way, #106
Sunnyvale, CA 94086
415-856-3460

Software A & E
1500 Wilson Boulevard
Suite 800
Arlington, VA 22209
703-276-7910

Software Alliance, Inc.
385 Elliot Street
Newton, MA 02164
617-965-5815

Software Development Systems
3110 Woodcreek Drive
Downers Grove, IL 60515
312-971-8170

Software Innovations Inc.
410 Amherst Street, Ste. 325
Nashua, NH 03063
603-883-9300

Software Ireland Ltd.
26 Linehall Street
Belfast
Northern Ireland
44-232-247433

Software Research, Inc.
625 Third Street
San Francisco, CA 94107
415-957-1441

(STUG)
Software Tools User Group
140 Center Street
El Segundo, CA 90245
213-322-2574

Sorites Group, Inc.
8136 Old Keene Mill Road
P.O. Box 2939
Springfield, VA 22152
703-569-1400

Southwest Technical Products Corp.
219 W. Rhapsody
P.O. Box 32040
San Antonio, TX 78216
512-344-0241

Southwind Software Inc.
4250 E. 47th Street S.
Wichita, KS 67210
316-524-9100

Specialized Systems Consultants, Inc.
P.O. Box 55549
Seattle, WA 98155
206-367-8649

Spectrum Technology Group, Inc.
1110 Douglas Avenue, Suite 2040
Altamonte Springs, FL 32714
305-682-1300

Specialized Systems Consultants, Inc.
P.O. Box 7
Northgate Station
Seattle, WA 98125
206-367-8649

Springer-Verlag
175 5th Avenue
New York, NY 10010
212-460-1500

SPSS Inc.
Suite 3000
444 North Michigan Avenue
Chicago, IL 60611
312-329-3680

Sritek
6615 W. Snowville Road
Cleveland, OH 44141
216-526-9433

SST Data, Inc.
4701 W. Schroeder Drive, #100
Milwaukee, WI 53223
414-355-6990

Stanford University
Computer Science Department
Stanford, CA 94305

Stellar Computer Inc.
85 Wells Avenue
Newton, MA 02159
617-964-1000

Sun Microsystems, Inc.
2550 Garcia Avenue
Mountain View, CA 94043
415-960-1300

(SUG)
Sun Microsystems User Group, Inc.
2550 Garcia Avenue M/S 10-16
Mountain View, CA 94043
415-691-4343
users@sun.com
sun!users

(EUUG-S)
Svenska Unixanvandares forening
ENEA DATA Svenska AB
Box 232, S-183 23 Taby
Sweden
46-8-756-7220

Symbolics Inc.
11 Cambridge Center
Cambridge, MA 02142
617-577-7500

Systems & Software, Inc.
3303 Harbor Boulevard
C-11
Costa Mesa, CA 92626
714-241-8650

Systems Designers Software, Inc.
444 Washington Street, Suite 407
Woburn, MA 01801
617-935-8009

Systems Union Ltd.
34 Delancey Street
London NW17NH
England
1-354-3131

Tandy Corporation
1700 One Tandy Center
Fort Worth, TX 76102
817-390-2728

(TC22 WG15)
James Isaak
Chairperson, IEEE/CS P1003
Digital Equipment Corp.
ZK03-2/Y24
110 Spit Brook Road
Nashua, NH 03062
603-881-0480
decvax!isaak
isaak@decvax.dec.com

Technical Solutions, Inc.
P.O. Box 1148
Mesilla Park, NM 88047
505-524-2154

Technology Research Group Inc.
750 Hammond Drive
Bldg 4, Suite 100
Atlanta, GA 30328
404-257-9000

Tech Valley Publishing
444 Castro Street
Mountain View, CA 94041
415-940-1500

Teknowledge, Inc.
525 University Avenue
Suite 200
Palo Alto, CA 94301
415-327-6600

Tektronix, Inc.
26600 S.W. Parkway Avenue
P.O. Box 1000, M/S 60-770
Wilsonville, OR 97070
503-685-2231

TeleSoft
10639 Roselle Street
San Diego, CA 92121
619-457-2700

TeleVideo Systems, Inc.
1170 Morse Avenue
Sunnyvale, CA 94088
800-835-3228

Template Graphics Software Inc.
9685 Scranton Road
San Diego, CA 92121
619-457-5359

Terotech
1 Nottingham Road
Melton Mowbray, Leics. LE13 0NP
England
0664-500423

Texas Internet Consulting
701 Brazos Suite 500
Austin, TX 78701
512-320-9031

Textset, Inc.
416 Fourth Street
P.O. Box 7993
Ann Arbor, MI 48107
313-996-3566

Textware International
P.O. Box 14, Harvard Square
Cambridge, MA 02238
617-864-8398

TITN, Inc.
1601 N. Kent Street, #904
Arlington, VA 22209
703-528-2662

Toshiba America Inc.
9470 Irvine Boulevard
Irvine, CA 92718
800-537-5450

Transmediair Utrecht BV
Melkweg 3
3721 RG Bilthoven
Holland
30-78-18-20

T&W Systems
7372 Prince Drive
Huntington Beach, CA 92647
714-847-9960

Ubiquitous Systems
1333 Bel-Red Road NE
Bellevue, WA 98005
206-641-8030

UNICAD
1695 38th Street
Boulder, CO 80301
303-443-6961

Unicomp
307 Big Horn Ridge Road, N.E.
Albuquerque, NM 87122
505-275-0800

UNICORN
Robert Borochoff
Federal Judicial Center
1520 H Street NW
Washington, D.C. 20005
202-786-6270

Unidot, Inc.
602 Park Point Drive, #225
Golden, CO 80401
303-526-9263

UniForum
2400 East Devon Avenue
Suite 205
Des Plaines, Illinois 60018

Unify Corp.
3870 Rosin Ct.
Sacramento, CA 95834
916-920-9092

Uni-Ops Books
19995 Mt. View Road
Boonville, CA 95415
707-895-2050

UniPress Software, Inc.
2025 Lincoln Highway
Edison, NJ 08817
201-985-8000

Uniq Digital Technologies
28 S. Water Street
Batavia, IL 60510
312-879-1008

Unique
(see InfoPro Systems)

Unisoft Corp.
6121 Hollis Street
Emeryville, CA 94608
415-420-6400

Unisolutions Associates
6520 Green Valley Circle, #13203
Culver City, CA 90230
213-641-6739

Unitech Software, Inc.
1800 Alexander Bell Drive, Suite 101
Reston, VA 22091
703-264-3301

(UCB or Berkeley)
University of California at Berkeley
Pauline Schwartz
Computer Systems Research Group
University of California
Berkeley, CA 94720
415-642-4948
ucbvax!pauline

University of California Press
2120 Berkeley Way
Berkeley, CA 94720

University of Leeds
Dr. A.P. McCann
Dept. of Computer Studies
University of Leeds
Leeds LS2 9JT
England
+44-532-43

University of New South Wales
Department of Computer Science
P.O. Box 1
Kensington, N.S.W. 2033
Australia

University of Utah
Dept. of Computer Science
3160 Merrill Engineering Bldg.
Salt Lake City, UT 84112
801-581-5017

UNIXEXPO
National Expositions Co., Inc.
49 West 38th Street, Suite 12A
New York, NY 10018
212-391-9111

UNIX Interessengemeinschaft Schweiz
Universitat Zurich-Irchel
c/o Institut fur Informatik
CH-8057 Zurich Switzerland
01-2565250

UNIX Magazine
Jouji Ohkubo
c/o ASCII Corp.
jou-o@ascii.junet
81-3-486-4523

UNIX REVIEW
500 Howard Street
San Francisco, CA 94105
415-397-1881

UNIX Systems
Eaglehead Publishing Ltd.
Maybury Road
Woking, Surrey GU21 5HX
England
44-48-622-7661

UNIXuser
210 S. Helberta Avenue
Redondo Beach, CA 90277
213-372-9917

UNIXWORLD
(see Tech Valley Publishing)

USENIX Association
P.O. Box 2299
Berkeley, CA 94710
415-528-8649
{uunet,ucbvax,decvax}!usenix!office
office@usenix.org

USPDI
UNIX and C Seminars
1620 Elton Road
Silver Spring, MD 20903
301-445-4400

/usr/group
4655 Old Ironsides Drive, Suite 200
Santa Clara, CA 95054
408-986-8840

/usr/group/cdn
241 Gamma Street
Etobicoke, Ontario
Canada M8W 4G7
416-259-8122

/usr/group/UK Ltd.
5 Holywell Hill
St. Albans, Hertfordshire
England AL1 1ET
0727-36003

/usr/group Working Group on Databases
Val Skalabrin
Unify Corp.
1111 Howe Avenue
Sacramento, CA 95825
916-920-9092

/usr/group Working Group on Graphics
Heinz Lycklama
Interactive Systems Corp.
2401 Colorado Avenue, 3rd Fl.
Santa Monica, CA 90404
213-453-8649

/usr/group Working Group on Internationalization
Brian Boyle
Novon Research Group
537 Panorama Drive
San Francisco, CA 94131
415-641-9800

/usr/group Working Group on Networking
c/o Dave Buck
D. L. Buck and Associates, Inc.
6920 Santa Teresa Bldg, #108
San Jose, CA 95119
408-972-2825

/usr/group Working Group on Performance Measurements
Ram Celluri
AT&T Computer Systems
Room E15B
453 Western Avenue
Lisle, IL 60532
312-810-6223

/usr/group Working Group on Realtime
Bill Corwin
Intel Corp.
5200 Elam Young Pkwy
Hillsboro, OR 97123
503-640-7588

/usr/group Working Group on Security
Steve Sutton
Computer Systems Division
Gould Inc.
1101 East University
Urbana, IL 61801
217-384-8500

UUNET/Usenix
P.O. Box 2299
Berkeley, CA 94710
Attn: Madeline McCall
415-528-8649

UX Software, Inc.
10 St. Mary Street, Suite 300
Toronto, Ontario
Canada M4Y 1P9
416-964-6909

VenturCom
215 First Street
Cambridge, MA 02142
617-661-1230

Verdix Corp.
Sullyfield Business Park
14130-A Sullyfield Circle
Chantilly, CA 22021
703-378-7600

Vermont Creative Software
21 Elm Avenue
Richford, VT 05476
802-848-7731

Vrije Universiteit
Postbus 7161
1007 MC Amsterdam
The Netherlands

V-Systems, Inc.
1700 E. Garry Avenue, #102
Santa Ana, CA 92705
714-261-9333

Whitesmiths, Ltd.
1500 North Beauregard Street, #110
Alexandria, VA 22311
703-379-9700

Wollongong Group, The
1129 San Antonio Road
P.O. Box 51860
Palo Alto, CA 94303
415-962-7200

(Xerox Parc)
Xerox Palo Alto Research Center
3333 Coyote Hill Road
Palo Alto, CA 94304

Zaiaz International, Corp.
2225 Drake Avenue, #17
Huntsville, AL 35805
205-881-2200

Zortec, Inc.
1717 Elm Hill Pike, Suite B-3
Nashville, TN 37210
615-360-6217

Zortech, Inc.
366 Massachusetts Avenue, Suite 303
Arlington, MA 02174
617-646-6703

Index

Symbols

® *See* registered trademark
† *See* dagger footnote
© *See* copyright
™ *See* trademark
! editor escape   140
shell comment   152
     #! shell selector   152, 170
#define   **179**
#include   98, 165
$ arguments, shell   138
% prompt   134, 139
& background   140, 171
* any string   144–145
-me macros   29
-mm macros   31
-ms macros   33
. current directory   144
.. parent directory   144
.cshrc   139, 207
.h suffix   179
.login   139, 207, 244
.profile   139, 207, 244
/ root file system   143, 196
:-) smiley   233
;login: 31, 111, 125
     name   204
< > include file   98
< redirect stdin   135
<< redirect stdin   135, 154
> redirect stdout   135, 138
>> redirect stdout   135
? single character   145
[ ] character class   145

^ beginning of line   145
| pipe   136–137, 163, 201
' backquote   135

Numerics

10%/90% rule   38, 42, 202, 213, 264, 298
1040 form   157
1BSD   6, 53
2.10BSD   6
2.8BSD   6
2.9BSD   6
2BSD   6, 53
32-bit supermini, first   17
32V   6, 12, 17, 33–34
3B Journal   110, 303
3BSD   6, 17
4.0BSD   6
4.1aBSD   6
4.1BSD   6, 25
4.1cBSD   6
4.2BSD   6, 18, 33, 44, 297
     source directories   96, 98
4.3BSD   6, 34, 77
     manuals   109
4.4BSD   6
4.X BSD   18–19
4BSD   17, 53
4GLs   266
5.0BSD   18
5620 DMD   277
68000   6, 25, 48
68020   83
80386   83
8086   24, 58
8088   6